Kansas Paper Money

Kansas Paper Money

An Illustrated History, 1854–1935

STEVE WHITFIELD
Edited by Fred Reed

McFarland & Company, Inc., Publishers
Jefferson, North Carolina, and London

The present work is a reprint of the illustrated case bound edition of Kansas Paper Money: An Illustrated History, 1854–1935, *first published in 2009 by McFarland.*

Fred Reed is the author of *Show Me the Money! The Standard Catalog of Motion Picture, Television, Stage and Advertising Prop Money* (McFarland, 2005), and the editor of Ronald J. Benice's *Florida Paper Money: An Illustrated History, 1817–1934* (McFarland, 2008) and Neil Shafer and Tom Sheehan's *Panic Scrip of 1893, 1907 and 1914: An Illustrated Catalog of Emergency Monetary Issues* (McFarland, 2013).

LIBRARY OF CONGRESS CATALOGUING-IN-PUBLICATION DATA

Whitfield, Steve, 1940–
Kansas paper money : an illustrated history, 1854–1935 /
Steve Whitfield ; edited by Fred Reed.
p.   cm.
Includes bibliographical references and index.

ISBN 978-0-7864-7738-8
softcover : acid free paper ∞

1. Paper money — Kansas — History —19th century.
2. Paper money — Kansas — History — 20th century.
 I. Reed, Fred, 1948–   II. Title.
HG627.K3W45   2014   769.5'59781—dc22   2008054523

BRITISH LIBRARY CATALOGUING DATA ARE AVAILABLE

© 2009 Steve Whitfield. All rights reserved

No part of this book may be reproduced or transmitted in any form or by any means, electronic or mechanical, including photocopying or recording, or by any information storage and retrieval system, without permission in writing from the publisher.

On the cover: $50 Kansas Valley Bank, Atchison;
$50 Kansas Valley Bank, Atchison; $1, 10¢, and 50¢
Larson Brothers' Paper Merchandise Coins; background © 2014 Shutterstock

Manufactured in the United States of America

*McFarland & Company, Inc., Publishers
Box 611, Jefferson, North Carolina 28640
www.mcfarlandpub.com*

To Diana

Table of Contents

Photographic Credits	ix
Preface	1
How to Use This Book	3
Introduction: Kansas Banking History	7
I — Territorial Period, May 30, 1854–January 29, 1861	13
II — Statehood Period, January 29, 1861–June 1, 1861	65
III — Civil War Crisis, 1861–1863	69
IV — Post–Civil War Period, 1866–1879	131
V — Miscellaneous Scrip Period, 1870–1930s	153
VI — National Bank Note Period, 1864–1935	207
Appendices:	
A. Modern Reproductions	231
B. Altered Notes	235
C. Known Written Denomination Scrip	239
D. Pre-1863 Banks That May Have Issued Scrip	242
E. Printers and Engravers on Pre-1880 Notes	243
F. Round Cardboard Tokens	245
G. Reported Serial Numbers on Rare Notes	247
H. Notices of Scrip Issues in Newspapers	251
Bibliography	253
Index	255

Photographic Credits

Douglas County Historical Society, Lawrence, Kansas: 59 bottom, 115 top, 116 middle
Eric Newman Museum, St. Louis: 97 all, 99 middle and bottom, 100 top and middle, 115 bottom, 125 top
Ernst Ulmer, Kansas: 18 bottom
Fort Scott Museum, Kansas: 76 top
Heritage Auctions, Dallas: 122 middle
Kansas State Historical Society, Topeka, Kansas: 15 all, 17 top, 18 top, 20 middle, 21 middle, 22 middle, 23 bottom, 24 top and bottom, 25 all, 27 top, 33 middle, 34 top, 39 bottom, 41 top and middle, 43 top and middle, 45 top, 50 top, 56 middle, 57 top, 58 top, 66 top, 67 top, 73 top, 81 top and bottom, 84 top, 85 bottom, 86 top, 95 top and bottom, 96 bottom, 110 top, 111 top, 129 middle, 130 middle, 133 bottom, 143 top, 168 bottom, 185 top and bottom, 195 top and middle, 200 middle, 203 top, 205 middle, 218 bottom, 241 middle, 246 top
Smithsonian Institution, D.C.: 55 top and middle, 93 top and middle, 105 middle
R.M. Smythe, N.Y.: 122 top
Stacks Auctions, N.Y.: 121 bottom

Illustrations are from the collection of the author and several unpublished sources, unless otherwise credited.

Preface

The purpose of this revision to the original 1980 Society of Paper Money Collectors catalog of Kansas obsolete notes is to provide as complete a volume about the paper money associated with my adopted state of Kansas as the past 30-plus years of study and research can produce. I also wanted to illustrate as many of these beautiful notes as possible for the enjoyment of fellow collectors, who are unlikely to have the opportunity to see the actual notes.

The obsolete currency of Kansas, with a few exceptions, is extremely rare. Kansas was only in existence for a small part of the obsolete note-issuing period, which lasted from the early 1800s until about 1866. Kansas became a Territory in 1854, a state in 1861, and the federal government took over the paper money issuing function soon thereafter. Thus, Kansas only had about 10 years in which bankers and merchants issued the obsolete notes that are such popular collector items today. In addition, Kansas was on the western frontier, where money was used long and hard, so many of these notes were undoubtedly lost or destroyed.

After years of thinking about the layout of these catalogs and serving as the SPMC Wismer Coordinator, I have come to the conclusion that they should be organized by economic period, such as the small note crisis period of the Civil War, which lasted from the summer of 1861 until the spring of 1863. The war caused the issue of these notes so they are grouped together under that era. Territorial notes are fascinating to paper money collectors. Therefore if a state had note issues during its territorial period, it is more convenient if all those notes are grouped under that period. I have also concluded that miscellaneous scrip issues with their own specialized catalogs, or that should have their own catalog, belong in a separate "miscellaneous scrip" section. Thus depression scrip and college currency are listed under miscellaneous scrip issues rather than under the period when they were actually issued. I did make an exception for sutler scrip, simply because there are so few issues known from Kansas and these issues were caused by the Civil War crisis. (Thus, the exception that proves the rule.)

This effort is a true labor of love as I have spent many hundreds and probably thousands of hours and dollars taking photographs, making copies, traveling to remote data and note sources, doing numerous proofreadings and producing countless retypes of drafts. I have been obsessed for a long time at seeing this thing in print. I have always recognized that the market for such a book includes a few dedicated souls who get the same thrill out of finding an answer to an outstanding question about the fate of a long dead merchant scrip issuer or discovering a previously unlisted note as I do. The true collector will always want more than just to own the note. He wants to know how many were issued, what the issuer looked like, what his store or bank looked like in the 1860s, whether the building is standing today, and what it looks like now, how many of the notes still survive, where he can see one, etc., etc. And these individuals will get as big a kick out of finding a check or draft of that issuer to go along with, or replace, the note they'll never find or get the opportunity to buy.

I must also dedicate this book to all those who have been so supportive or just tolerant of my hobby excesses. First of these is my beloved wife, Diana. When I think of all the outfits she could have bought with what I have spent on this hobby, it boggles the mind. She always pretended to believe me when I said it was really an investment and some day we would get it back. She hopefully knew that I meant in enjoyment and not in dollars. And lots of paper money friends and dealers, also friends, have been helpful in sharing information and reporting things they knew I would be interested in about Kansas. A few even found some great notes for me. So thanks also to Hugh Shull, Lyn Knight, Tom Denly, Don Fisher, Austin Sheheen, and many others. It's been great fun.

And finally, if you know of a Kansas note that is not listed in this catalog, please share it with the hobby and report it in care of SPMC's great magazine, *Paper Money*, at www.spmc.org/. The more we know about these elusive bits of paper, the better off the hobby will be.

How to Use This Book

Organization

This book is an effort to describe as many of the notes issued by and for Kansans, from the 1850s when Kansas first became a Territory, to the 1930s era of the Great Depression. Although much of the book is similar to other Society of Paper Money Collectors state catalogs, i.e., history, listings, rarity of notes, etc., this catalog is separated into economic periods. The notes and the issuers are grouped alphabetically under the period that caused the issue. For example, all notes issued during the territorial period will be found in that section. Because there were also different types of issuers, the notes are further separated into three major categories and listed as such within each section. These include banks, merchants, and municipal governments. Banks are further categorized as fraudulent and intended banks ("wildcats"), of the territorial period; legally chartered banks; and private banks that issued notes. The intent is to list the notes by type of issuer, in the historical period that saw their issue.

Listings are grouped alphabetically by city or town of issue. The issuers are then alphabetically listed under their location. Small denominations precede larger denominations and earlier dates come before later dates. A simple two or three digit catalog number is assigned for shorthand purposes to assist in auction listings or sales advertisements. Only unique design types are given a number. Numbers from the 1980 SPMC book and the 1990 catalog update are used wherever possible. All varieties, such as proofs, minor design changes, etc., get a subscript added to the type number. Subscripts are used as follows: "p" indicates proof; "r" indicates a modern reproduction, "e" is an essay or trial, "s" indicates specimen, "c" would indicate counterfeit (no counterfeit Kansas notes are known), and "?" designates a spurious note. As many notes as possible are fully illustrated.

Over time paper money hobbyists have grouped many obsolete notes into specialized collecting areas, such as Confederate Currency, large size United States notes, and College Currency. Each of these specialized areas has, or should have, its own separate catalog. Such issues from Kansas are listed here under "Miscellaneous Scrip" according to the type of note. Thus, there is a section that lists all known Kansas depression scrip issues of 1907/1914 and another lists all known Kansas advertising pieces through about

1880. One appendix lists the known write-in denomination scrip from Kansas' territorial period. Generally, write-in scrip is not included in this catalog because such scrip was issued by so many Kansas cities and towns well into the 1880s. Emphasis is on notes with a printed denomination that were intended to pass unendorsed among the public as currency, or demands on whatever was acceptable as money.

The index includes issuers and their locations for quick reference to locate notes from a specific location.

Rarity

There are nearly 150 different Kansas obsolete notes known to collectors. This includes proofs and distinct types or varieties of notes issued by banks, merchants, and municipalities prior to 1864. Nearly 60 of these notes are reported as unique examples. Therefore nearly 40 percent of known Kansas notes are unique. Ten more have no surviving examples confirmed (SENC), although they are listed in contemporary newspaper articles. Thus nearly half of the known notes can be considered to be uncollectable. The scarcity of material and the high value placed on the rarer notes make it very difficult to start a Kansas collection and expect much success at building a diversified holding. However, it is still possible to put together a good representative collection. This is especially true if one expands into the category of miscellaneous scrip, including Depression Scrip, Advertising Notes and items such as College Currency.

If one has a bottomless checkbook, it is still possible to build a great collection of Kansas material. This has been proven time and again. Not many of us find ourselves in those circumstances, however, so what is achievable? Several attractive Kansas notes are available in sufficient quantity to appear fairly frequently at auctions or in dealer stocks. These include Union Military Scrip, the city notes of Leavenworth, Wyandott and Chetopa, Certificates of Deposit on the Kansas State Savings Bank at Wyandott, and several of the intended banks or wildcat bank notes of the territorial period. Once in a great while notes for the State Bank of Lecompton, the Redwing Bank of Lawrence, Scott, Kerr & Co. of Leavenworth and the chartered Lawrence Bank at Lawrence appear on the market, but these opportunities are rare.

Most commonly the collector will find advertising or depression notes from Kansas. Many of these are also reported as unique. However, it is expected that more of these will surface over the years as previously unreported denominations, or issuers, appear from hiding. With the exception of a few known private bankers in operation during the Civil War, who were likely to have issued scrip that is presently unknown, it is firmly believed that we will not see many new Kansas discoveries for the period before 1865. However, it is expected that additional proofs of the known notes may surface.

Rarity ratings that are assigned to the notes reflect in most cases actual census data of 30+ years on note sightings and collection inventories. For the more common notes, estimates were based on the frequency that such notes turn up. Many more of the Delaware City and Easton frauds (or altered notes) should turn up in the future from Delaware and Pennsylvania collections where they are occasionally found mislocated.

Rarity ratings follow the standard SPMC numbers used in past catalogs as follows:

R-1	201 or more known	No Kansas notes this common are known to exist.
R-2	101 to 200 known	No Kansas notes this common are known to exist.
R-3	51 to 100 known	
R-4	26 to 50 known	
R-5	11 to 25 known	
R-6	6 to 10 known	
R-7	2 to 5 known	
Unique (U)	A single example is reported.	
SENC	No surviving example has been confirmed of a reported note.	

Value

Value remains a function of supply and demand. Common Kansas notes are still available for less than $100. Rare notes have brought more than $10,000 and the proof sheet of four notes on The Kansas Valley Bank at Atchison brought more than $30,000 in 1990. If I were rich, it would have brought whatever it took to own it, but alas...

Introduction:
Kansas Banking History

Most people are unaware that the Federal Government did not always regulate banking and the issue the paper money that we use. The first circulating federal paper currency of the United States (outside of a small issue during the War of 1812) commenced in 1861 to meet the rising costs of the Civil War. Prior to that time, and until about 1865, banking and the issue of paper money were left to the discretion of the individual states and territories. Some legislatures granted exclusive charters to banks, while others allowed anyone who desired to become a banker, providing certain widely varying requirements were met. In some states and territories, unchartered or "private" banks were allowed to operate. In many areas various combinations of chartered and private banks existed.

Many of the early banks were "banks of issue," i.e., they issued their own paper money. These paper issues were backed with various securities, such as public stocks, bonds, or land mortgages. Some issues were backed with silver and gold coin, or specie, but many had no backing at all. Without security and with little or no regulation many banks failed, thereby making their notes worthless almost overnight. In addition, counterfeiting of the thousands of differently designed notes in circulation was widespread, as was the deliberate printing and circulation of notes for non-existent banks. It has been estimated that at the start of the Civil War, as much as one third of the paper money in circulation was counterfeit or otherwise worthless. The conduct of ordinary business was in a state of near chaos.

Political Considerations

When Kansas became a territory, the Democratic Party of Andrew Jackson was in power in Washington. Jackson had waged a personal campaign against the Second Bank of the United States that resulted in extinguishing the bank's charter in 1836. The ensuing flood of unsecured banknotes throughout the country, in combination with other factors, resulted in a nationwide financial panic and the Depression of 1837. In 1838, the state of New York passed a free banking law, which set up a system of banking regulation that would be copied by many states.

The Democrats of the period are generally considered as anti-banks of issue, i.e., against the issue of any paper money, although some historians have questioned this generalization. Conversely the Whigs, the opposition party at the time, are thought of as pro-paper money. The country stumbled along through the 1840s assisted by numerous public borrowings by the Treasury to pay its debts. When gold was discovered in California in 1848, large amounts of sound money were created upon which the nation's economy could expand. For the first time in its history, the United States was not solely dependent on foreign capital in order to develop industry and transportation systems. Hard money or specie in the form of silver and gold was, for a time, adequate to supply the money needs of the country.

Development of a Banking System

In territorial areas, where settlers were initially importers and consumers rather than producers and exporters, money was always a scarce commodity. Friends and relatives from the east supplied some funds and relief societies donated money to these areas in times of emergency. Most real money left the territory rapidly as it was used to purchase farm tools, building materials, livestock, seed, and other necessities. This was the situation in Kansas soon after the territory was opened for settlement in 1854.

Economic conditions in Kansas from 1854 to 1857, with the slavery issue, very little agriculture, and virtually no manufacturing, did not create an immediate need for banks. This did not deter speculators and crooks, who attempted to start banks or simply had notes printed that purported to be from banks in Kansas. Most of these were hoaxes and many of these notes were sold at discount in the east to unsuspecting immigrants. The notes of the so-called Merchants Bank of Fort Leavenworth are typical examples of this swindling practice.

The first real banks were established in Kansas as early as 1856. Eastern financiers and bankers financed them with outside capital. These banks also turned out to be premature and most failed during the nationwide banking crisis in the fall of 1857. As commerce continued to develop without banks, many merchants were gradually forced to provide basic banking services to their customers in order to conduct business. These services included collection of drafts, taking money on deposit, and the extension of credit. There were also many land speculators in the area who loaned money and dealt in exchange. Between 1856 and 1859, a number of these merchants and speculators became full-time bankers. By 1860 all of the significant territorial banks, or their predecessors that would issue paper money, had been established in Kansas.

Early Practices

The early bankers engaged in almost any legitimate activity that might turn a profit. They sold real estate and steamship tickets, acted as notary publics and rent collectors, were lawyers and shopkeepers, and dealt in gold, exchange and foreign money. Some of these early bankers performed many banking activities without ever opening a bank as such. They frequently operated from an office that accepted deposits and perhaps dealt in exchange. For this reason it is sometimes difficult to distinguish between an actual bank and a merchant banker.

Several "bankers," apparently by paying the new federal tax of $100 based on their commercial activities, thought they had taken out some sort of a federal license during the war that authorized them to perform banking services. R.H. Farnham at Topeka, Lewis Kurtz at Manhattan and John S. Miller at Fort Scott are examples of the merchant banker category. The description of their operations and the notes they issued will be found in the Merchant Scrip portion of the Civil War chapter.

Where Banks Were Established

Atchison and Leavenworth were logical choices for establishment of early banks in Kansas because of their locations on the river and their development. The Missouri River, at that time, was the major transportation artery in the area. In addition, large overland freighting firms were established at these towns to supply the military and assist western migration of settlers. Both towns were centrally located to large agricultural areas by 1859, and Leavenworth also had the military post with its government payrolls. The military and overland trade were bringing millions of dollars to the area annually by that time. Lawrence was the third early banking town because it was the population center for many "free state" settlers, and also due to agricultural development in Douglas County.

Thus, the gradual development of commerce in the early Kansas towns eventually created the need for a system of banking. Banks were required to facilitate orderly transmission of funds between consumers and producers, as well as to accumulate and inject capital into the business enterprises of the developing state.

Early Legislation

There had been some support for establishment of banks of issue from the earliest beginnings of Kansas Territory. The subject was introduced before the various territorial legislatures on a number of occasions, only to be tabled. The legislature did, however, pass several laws designed to restrict or prevent establishment of banks in Kansas.

In 1855, the legislature passed an act which prohibited non-banking corporations from engaging in any kind of banking activity. This act prevented firms chartered to do business in Kansas from performing any banking services unless they were chartered as a bank. Since no banks had been chartered up to that time, it meant that no chartered firms could operate as banks. Presumably unchartered banks were not prohibited from doing business at that time. In January 1857, the legislature closed the loophole allowing unchartered banks to operate when a law was passed making it illegal for anyone to operate an unchartered banking association. This law also nullified all notes, drafts, bills of exchange, and checks of any such illegal banks then in existence. In fact, there were some unchartered banks operating in Kansas at the time as well as several others in the planning stage. It is unknown whether passage of this law had any effect on the proposed

Drovers Bank at Leavenworth or the State Bank at Lecompton, although it may help to explain why they never opened.

On February 19, 1857, another law concerned with banking was passed. This act made it illegal for any Kansas bank to issue notes in denominations smaller than $3.00 and at the same time outlawed all notes, checks and drafts drawn for less than $3.00 then in existence. The purpose of such an act was to keep silver and gold coin in circulation. If paper notes existed in denominations that could replace coins in circulation, it stood to reason that people would spend the notes and hoard the coins. This would have resulted in depreciation of the paper with an increase in the general price level for all goods and services.

The three legislative acts concerned with banking between 1855 and 1857 reserved to the Kansas Legislature the exclusive right to charter corporations as banks of issue and made any other banking associations illegal. In addition an effort was made to prevent paper money from replacing all specie in circulation. Enforcement of these laws was lax or non-existent.

The legislative act of February 19, 1857, had also granted a banking charter to the Kansas Valley Bank of Leavenworth. This was apparently an attempt to create a state controlled banking system similar to that used by a number of other states. The Kansas Valley Bank was to have branches at Atchison, Doniphan, Fort Scott, Lecompton and Shawnee. The branches were not to be sub-offices of the main bank, as we think of branch banking today, but rather would be separate banks whose notes would be redeemable at any of the other branches. Thus, a widely acceptable currency would be established in the territory.

The following legislature had a change of heart about the bank when, on February 3, 1858, it passed an act repealing the charter. The Atchison Branch was nearly ready to do business and therefore Samuel Pomeroy, associated with the bank and having some influence with the legislative body, intervened on behalf of the bank. He was successful and a special act was passed which excluded the Atchison Branch from the charter repeal. Thus only the Kansas Valley Bank at Atchison ever organized and conducted business under the charter.

Since the "free state" party had gained control of the territorial government, in 1858 they passed an act chartering their own bank of issue. This was the Lawrence Bank, chartered on February 11, 1858. The same act that chartered the Lawrence Bank may have granted a retroactive charter to a defunct bank at Leavenworth. This was the City Bank, organized in November 1856, which had conducted business and issued paper money before it failed in the fall of 1857.

Other Considerations

Beginning around 1858, when Kansas had been secured for freedom (by adopting a constitution outlawing slavery), eastern Kansas began to lose population. Gold discoveries near Pikes Peak, then part of Kansas Territory, lured many people away from the eastern towns. A terrible drought in 1860 that dried up wells and rivers and destroyed most crops caused thousands of settlers to leave Kansas. The Civil War did not create an increased need for banks as much of the male population departed for service in the

Union Army. Such a need did not surface again until near the end of the war, when the railroads reached Kansas. By 1864, however, the federal government was well along in developing a national banking system with federal controls and restricted issue of currency. This new system, along with a hefty tax burden enacted in 1865 to go into effect in 1866, virtually ended the era of local bank issues of paper money. National Bank notes replaced the private and state chartered banks of issue. Following the war, agriculture, cattle driving, and railroads would provide the major impetus for modern Kansas banking development. It would also replace the pioneer banking centers of Atchison, Lawrence, and Leavenworth with Topeka, Wichita, and Kansas City.

Types of Bank Note Issues

There were three types of state and private banks that issued paper money in Kansas. The first of these was the chartered bank of issue, a commercial bank of issue incorporated under state or territorial law. These banks were authorized to discount commercial paper, accept money for deposit, and issue paper money in the form of bank notes. There were two such banks chartered in Kansas that actually organized and conducted business. They were the Kansas Valley Bank at Atchison and The Lawrence Bank. It is possible that the City Bank of Leavenworth received a charter after it had failed.

The second type of bank was the unchartered or private commercial bank. These banks performed the same functions as chartered banks except that they could not legally issue paper money. In fact the law of January 1857 made these banks illegal. During the small denomination money crisis of 1861–1863, many of these banks did issue notes and no action was taken against them for doing so. There were also a number of private banks operating in Kansas during this period that made no currently known issues of such notes. Several of them are likely candidates for having done so, and it will be no surprise if one or two discoveries surface in the future.

The third type of bank to issue notes was the chartered savings bank. Savings banks, first chartered in Kansas in 1859, were organized to provide for the investment of bank capital into land mortgages and property, a function prohibited to commercial banks at the time. In fact savings banks in Kansas also performed all of the services of commercial banks, and such practices were eventually upheld in the state courts. Savings banks were, however, prohibited from issuing any type of paper money. In the 1860s and 1870s they found a way around the restrictions by issuing "Certificates of Deposit" that looked like money and were produced in common denominations of federal currency. By issuing such certificates without demanding a corresponding deposit, the banks were able to create money. This was exactly what the restrictions were designed to prevent.

One Kansas savings bank is known to have engaged in this practice. This was the Kansas State Savings Bank at Wyandott, now part of Kansas City, Kansas. The bank issued certificates in denominations of $1, $2, and $3 between 1868 and 1872.

In addition to bank issues of paper money, during times of coin shortages or other economic hardship, local merchants frequently issued scrip to give out as change for purchases at their place of business. Such scrip also served a useful advertising purpose for the merchant as well as returning a profit on notes lost or never redeemed. The majority of this type of scrip was issued during the Civil War. Merchant scrip was most often issued in denominations of less that $1, but occasionally included higher values. These additions to the money supply usually only circulated locally, but occasionally were redeemable in other towns. Very little Kansas merchant scrip has survived.

And finally, municipal governments, to include cities and towns, frequently issued notes to pay off debts to legislators, jurors, employees and others when they were short of cash. Cities also issued small denomination notes during periods of financial crises to provide local businessmen with a circulating medium. Scrip issued as a public borrowing often bore interest and was only redeemable for certain obligations or at some future date. Although designed to look like money and to circulate as such, such issues usually depreciated quickly and were frequently not redeemed. Speculators bought these issues at discount and hoped to profit if the notes were redeemed. The known issues from Kansas occurred in the 1870s, with few genuinely signed notes known. The federal government put a stop to this practice after 1875, but some of these notes continued to turn up well into the 1920s.

Relating the Past to the Present

It is interesting to note that all of the Kansas banks known to have issued their own notes prior to 1864 can be related to a national bank that existed in Atchison, Lawrence and Leavenworth into recent times. The thread was occasionally only through an individual who served as a bank officer of one bank and then closed up another of the banks through liquidation or receivership. Many of the early bankers remained associated with local town banks all their lives. The surviving notes and other artifacts of these banks tell a fascinating story of the economic development of the state and the perseverance of the pioneers who developed it. In recent years more and more historic banks have been swallowed up in acquisitions and consolidations. That is what has happened to the pioneer banks of Kansas.

I

Territorial Period, May 30, 1854–January 29, 1861

Kansas officially became a Territory of the United States on May 30, 1854. Prior to that time the area was set aside for Indian tribes, although trappers, traders, merchants and missionaries had moved into and through the area for many years. Soon settlers hungry for land, or eager to ensure that the area would become a free or a slave state, began to establish settlements. As in any newly settled area, immigrants initially brought their own money and goods with them. But soon the new towns developed a need for financial services to deal in land warrants and exchange, to transmit funds, and to loan money to farmers and merchants. With little or no regulation and no laws to establish rules for banks, the populace was open to manipulation of unscrupulous dealers and money lenders, who established fraudulent banking operations. Every new territory experienced this phenomenon. Kansas would be no exception.

In addition to intended banks, outright frauds, and enterprises that went broke, there were some legitimate issuers of scrip during this period. These included town companies, municipal governments and merchants with established businesses. Several issues of territorial scrip were made in Kansas by these organizations.

As the territorial legislature gained power, and controls were exerted over the institution of banking, legitimate banking enterprises were established by charter. Controls and limitations on the issue of currency were attempts to ensure that the population could trust the banknotes issued by banks, and that such notes would be redeemable in coin. Two banks were chartered in Kansas by the territorial legislature and both lasted into the early years of statehood. One of them may be considered an ancestor of a bank still doing business at Atchison.

The following locations, including a couple of Kansas ghost towns, issued notes, or notes were designated as having been issued from them during the territorial period: Delaware City, Easton, Fort Leavenworth, Lawrence, Leavenworth, Lecompton, Sumner and Tecumseh.

Note: Only printed denomination notes that were intended to be used as circulating money are included in the listings and descriptions. There were also numerous examples of handwritten scrip widely used throughout Kansas.

THE ELDRIDGE BROTHERS
(Merchant Scrip)

The four Eldridge Brothers, Shalor W., Edwin S., Thomas B., and James M., came west in 1855 to make their fortune. They would manage the hotels of the New England Emigrant Aid Society at the Cities of Kansas, Missouri and Lawrence, Kansas, operate a stagecoach line in eastern Kansas, and become involved in a number of banking ventures.* Eastern Kansas, especially the area around Lawrence, was the scene of a bitter struggle over the slavery question at the time. Hatred and revenge were the order of the day and prior to 1857/1858, the pro-slavery faction had the "law" on its side.

The Free State Hotel at Lawrence was an imposing stone structure in an otherwise drab village. It was completed and furnished for opening by May, 1856, but the scheduled grand opening was in jeopardy. The pro-slavery grand jury at Lecompton had recently "indicted" the new hotel, along with the two newspapers at Lawrence as "dangerous nuisances." On May 21, 1856, without waiting for the formality of a trial, the Kansas Militia, mostly men from Missouri led by the "Douglas County Sheriff" Samuel J. Jones, a Missouri Postmaster, rode into Lawrence and destroyed the hotel. They fired a cannon at its stone walls, tried to blow it up with gunpowder, and finally settled for burning it down. One account relates that David Atchison, former United States Senator from Missouri, personally aimed the first cannon shot. However, free use made of the hotel's liquor cellar had apparently dimmed his vision, since the ball completely missed the three story building from a distance of only 75 feet.† The newspapers were destroyed and the town was sacked.

The town's population had offered no resistance to the militia, which initially was under command of a "Federal Marshal." The "militia" had come to Lawrence to arrest several of the Free State leaders, who had also been indicted. Once the arrests were made, the Marshal, instead of dispersing the militia as promised, turned them over to "Sheriff" Jones. Jones had a personal grudge against the town since he had been bested on several previous occasions by the local citizens, and once had been wounded in an unsuccessful assassination attempt at Lawrence. "Sheriff" Jones now had his opportunity for revenge and he took full advantage of it.

It was to be a short-lived victory for the pro-slavery forces, however, as widespread publicity of the sack of the defenseless town did much to revive the then declining support for the "Free State" cause. Money and new settlers from the north soon poured into the territory.

Shalor Eldridge was determined to rebuild and set about raising the necessary capital. It took awhile, but finally a new hotel, bigger and more luxurious than the former, was erected at the same location on Massachusetts Street. The new Eldridge House was opened to the public in January, 1859. The town held a fund raising ball on January 29, specifically to help furnish the building. Meanwhile Edwin had purchased an interest in Robert Morrow's boarding house at Lawrence, and Shalor had started a stagecoach line in eastern Kansas.

Shalor Eldridge was later associated with organization of the Lawrence Bank. Thomas would establish a bank at Fort Scott.

†*The writer recalls that this cannon ball was discovered during the 1920s during a street-grading project. The source, thought to be a newspaper article, could not be relocated.*

I. Territorial Period, May 30, 1854–January 29, 1861

Left to right: Shalor W. Eldridge, Thomas B. Eldridge, Edwin S. Eldridge, James M. Eldridge

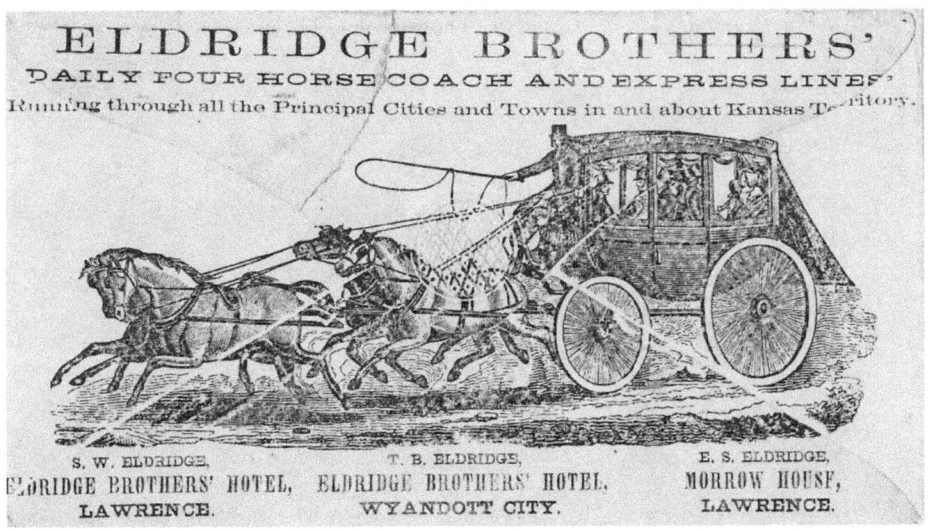

Middle and above: Kansas territorial advertising cover for Eldridge Brothers' Lines.

FREE STATE HOTEL BALL

"TRUTH CRUSHED TO EARTH SHALL RISE AGAIN."

Yourself and Ladies are respectfully invited to attend the Ball to be given in the **NEW FREE STATE HOTEL**, **FRIDAY EVENING, JANUARY 29.** The proceeds of Tickets sold are to be appropriated towards furnishing said Hotel, and in some degree retrieving the loss sustained by Col. Eldridge in the destruction of the ELDRIDGE HOUSE, on the 21st day of May, 1856.

Tickets admitting one gentlemen, with ladies, may be had at the different Hotels, at Woodward & Finley's, at O. Wilmarth's, and at the door, for Five Dollars each, supper included.

Charles Robinson,	J. H. Lane,	G. W. Smith,
W. Y. Roberts,	C. W. Babcock,	G. W. Deitzler,
Gaius Jenkins,	Robt. Morrow,	J. H. Robinson,
H. J. Adams,	C. K. Holliday,	A. J. Mead,
O. E. Learnard,	Lyman Allen,	E. D. Nash,
J. G. Crocker,	S. N. Wood,	James Blood,
H. Miles Moore,	H. Stratton,	Abraham Barry,
S. C. Harrington,	L. C. Tolles,	Wm. Hutchinson,
B. W. Woodward,	A. D. Searl,	M. F. Conway,
J. S. Emery,	John Hutchinson,	L. Bullene,
J. F. Hill,	O. B. Holman,	P. B. Plumb,
Geo. F. Earle,	G. W. Collamore,	Wm. M'Clure,
J. M. Winchell,	J. G. Haskell,	C. H. Branscomb.

Music by the Lawrence Cornet Band.

Invitation to a fund-raising ball to furnish the rebuilt hotel after destruction by pro-slavery forces. Ball was held at the hotel on the evening of January 29, 1858.

HO! FOR KANSAS!

ELDRIDGE BROTHERS'
Express & Daily
POST COACH LINE

Fare to Lawrence $3.50

THROUGH FROM KANSAS CITY TO LECOMPTON IN ONE DAY.

One Daily Line from **LAWRENCE** to **OSAWATOMIE**, and Two Daily Lines from **LAWRENCE** to **LEAVENWORTH CITY**.

Passengers by this Line have an opportunity of traveling over the most attractive and cultivated portion of the Territory in Splendid Four Horse Concord-built Coaches, and will save at least TEN MILES of tedious travel, making it the Shortest, as well as the Cheapest and most agreeable Route to the

INTERIOR OF KANSAS.

Passengers leaving Kansas City by the Morning Line, breakfast at Wyandott, dine at Wolf Creek, and arrive at Lecompton in time for supper, making five changes of horses between Kansas City and Lecompton.

Express Freights taken at the Lowest Rates & delivered with Promptness & Despatch.

OFFICE, 109 LEVEE, Opposite the Steamboat Landing, **KANSAS CITY.**

AGENTS.---Kansas City, M. F. Caswell; Wyandott & Lawrence, Eldridge Bros.; Leavenworth, Buckley.

S. W. ELDRIDGE, J. M. ELDRIDGE,
T. B. ELDRIDGE, E. S. ELDRIDGE, Prop's.

Rate broadside for Eldridge Brothers' Express & Daily Post Coach Line.

Eldridge House before Quantrill's raid.

I. Territorial Period, May 30, 1854–January 29, 1861

Eldridge House in ruins after Quantrill's raid (Harper's Weekly).

The Eldridge Stage line was in operation by February, 1858. The line originally ran between Lawrence and Leavenworth in competition with another line operated by a Mr. Southerland. Soon thereafter a line was added to Osawatomie. A new competitor then entered the fray by opening a line connecting Kansas City and Lawrence, so Eldridge added an operation from Lawrence, through Wyandott, to Kansas City. The competition lasted for about nine months, when they all sold out to a fellow named Hanks and a Captain Terry from Ohio, who formed the Kansas Stage Company. The new company was headquartered at Leavenworth with connections that ran from Topeka to Kansas City via Lawrence, Topeka to Leavenworth, and reverse. In the summer of 1859, lines were added from Topeka to Junction City, Leavenworth to Kansas City and Leavenworth to Atchison. An early broadside advertising the Eldridge stage line from Kansas City to Lawrence exists in the collections of the Kansas State Historical Society. The fare to Lawrence was $3.50.

Sometime during 1858, the Eldridge Brothers issued scrip printed by the Herald of Freedom Print, a newspaper at Lawrence. The notes are unusual in that they are the only known obsolete currency issued in Kansas that specifically states "redeemable in gold." It is also one of two known issues of merchant scrip during the territorial period in Kansas. The $1 note has a slightly different design than the other denominations, which are all identical. The notes are very rare with a total of seven known surviving specimens, including a complete set of all five denominations held by the Kansas State Historical Society. There are no known signed, issued examples of the notes.

The Eldridge Hotel was completely destroyed for the second time, on August 21, 1863, when 450 guerrilla raiders, under William Clarke Quantrill burned the town and murdered more than 150 men and boys. The Eldridges, in spite of their heavy losses,

Opposite, bottom: Quantrill's raid on Lawrence in 1863.

decided to rebuild again. The third Eldridge House, erected at the same location as the former, was completed and opened for business in December, 1865. The new hotel was not as lavish as its predecessor because of the large financial loss. The state would eventually pay Shalor Eldridge only $1,500 against his $60,000 war claim.

The Eldridges built and managed other hotels at Atchison, Coffeyville, and Kansas City, Kansas. Shalor lost his money in the depression of the 1870s, did some gold prospecting in Arkansas and finally lived out his remaining years in Lawrence. He died in 1899.

The 1865 Eldridge House was torn down and replaced in 1924 by the building standing as of 1999 at the site. It still operates under the name of "Eldridge House." It is an important and historic name, and structure, to the pioneer history of the state.

The "Herald of Freedom Print" at Lawrence printed the notes, although the $1.00 note has no maker's imprint.

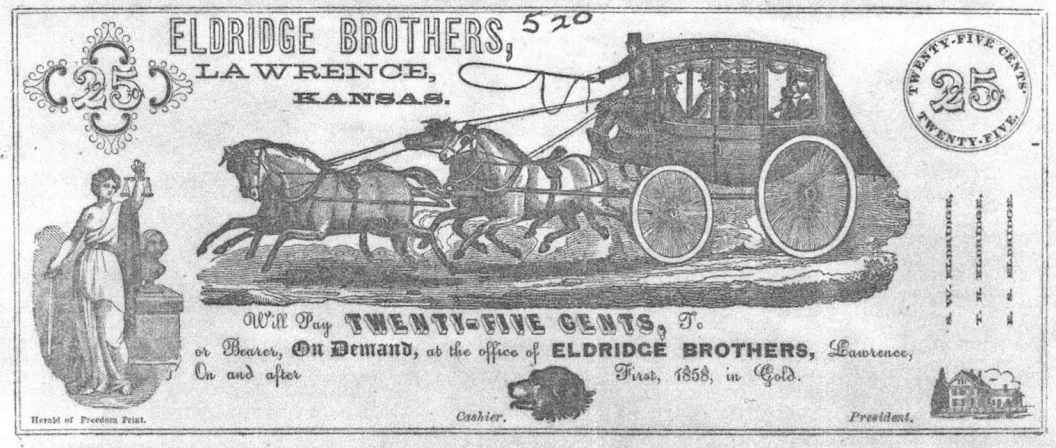

199. 25¢, First, 1858 printed, balance of date to be written in . . . . Unique

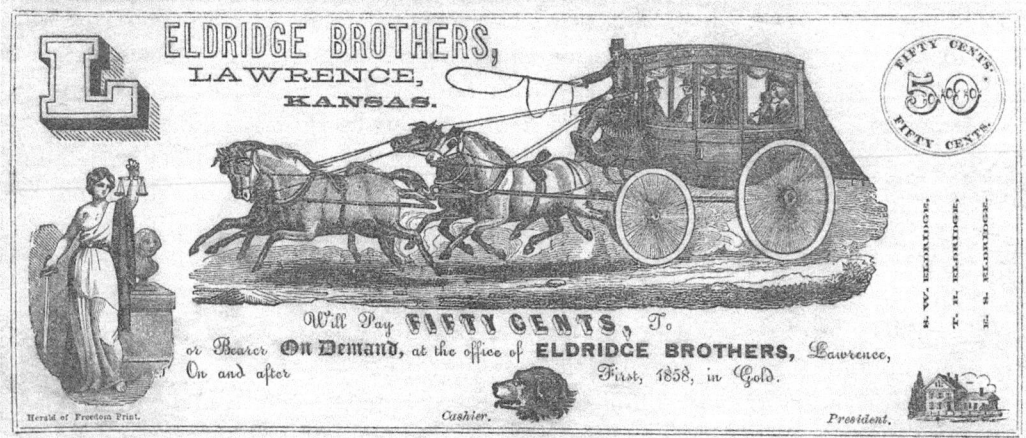

200. 50¢, First, 1858 printed as above R-7

I. *Territorial Period, May 30, 1854–January 29, 1861* 21

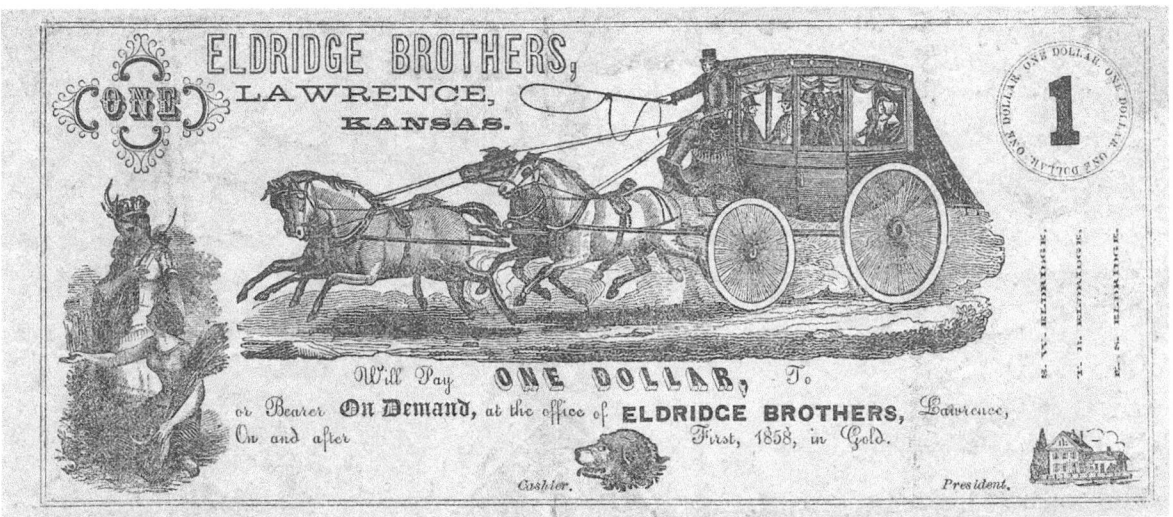

201. $1, First, 1858 printed as above R-7

202. $2, First, 1858 printed as above .... Unique

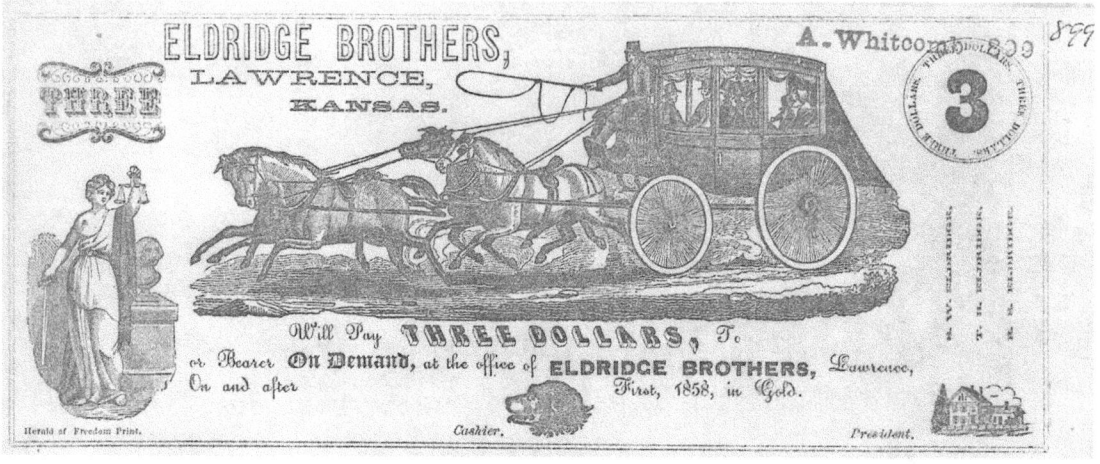

203. $3, First, 1858 printed as above . . . . Unique

THE KANSAS MINING COMPANY
(Corporation Revenue Bonds)

The Kansas Mining Company was incorporated in 1855 for the purpose of mining coal and other minerals in the Territory. Among the incorporators were A.G. Woodward, H. Miles Moore, S.E. Frazer, and Peter T. Abel, all prominent Kansas pioneers. Section 14 of the Incorporation Act allowed the company to raise capital by issuing "bonds" in denominations of $10 or more, redeemable two years or more after the date of issue, and bearing interest not to exceed 15 percent per year. The $10 plate was prepared by Rawdon, Wright, Hatch & Edson of Cincinnati. The American Bank Note Company reproduced this piece in 1978, from an original plate in its archives, as part of a "Time-Life series on the Old West." A Copy certificate is on back. No issued copies of the note have surfaced, and it remains unknown whether other denominations were prepared. At least one modern proof was created, without the copy certificate on the back.

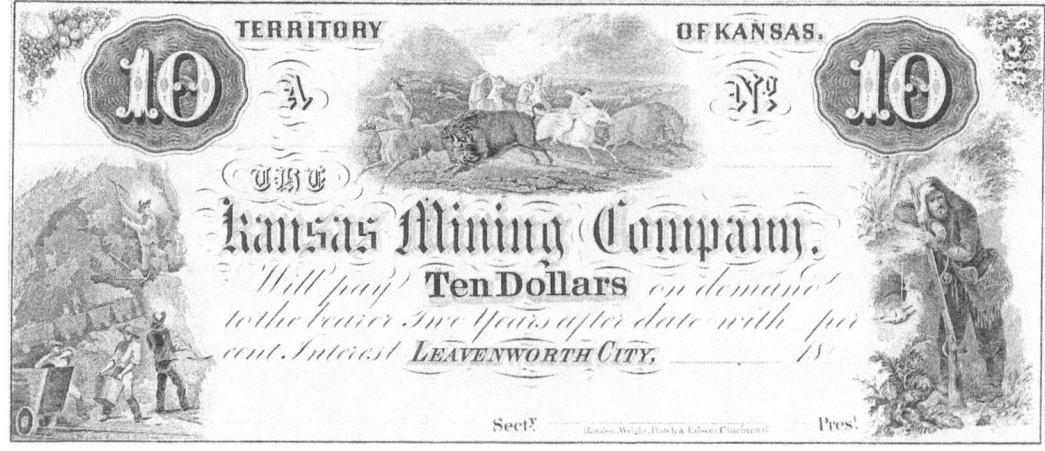

307r. $10, Plate Letter A. Modern reproduction . . . . Actual note SENC

The Sumner Company
(Municipal Scrip)

The Sumner Company was a township development organization that existed to promote the settlement and sale of lots at Sumner. This was an "abolitionist" town site that was established to rival the pro-slavery town of Atchison. The town was named after George Sumner, brother of Senator Charles Sumner of Massachusetts, and a stockholder in the company. Sumner was incorporated in 1858 on the West Bank of the Missouri River approximately 10 miles above Atchison. The corporation consisted of C.F. Currier, Samuel Harsh, I.G. Losse, John P. Wheeler, and Jenkin W. Morris. Morris would later establish a private bank at Leavenworth in 1862. Mr. Wheeler was the actual town founder. He also founded the town of Hiawatha, Kansas. An early promoter of the town, who wrote extensively of its development and prospects was John J. Ingalls, who went on to become United States Senator from Kansas in 1876. In 1888 he donated the notes that have survived to the Kansas State Historical Society. They were printed by T.R. Hiland, Lith., Boston.

Sumner, Kansas, bird's-eye promotional view

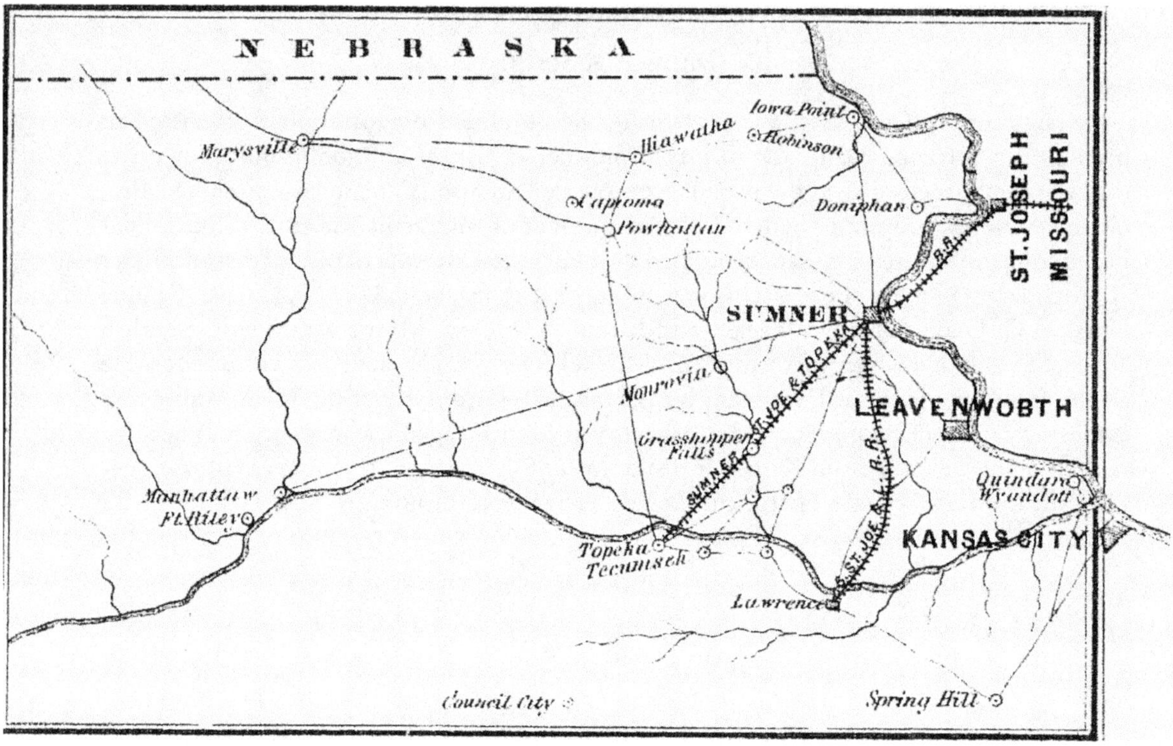

Sumner, Kansas, promotional map.

The population of Sumner had grown to nearly 2,000 persons by June, 1858, when an election to choose the county seat was held. Becoming a county seat of government was practically a guarantee of the town's future. After considerable argument it was decided that Atchison was the winner. This doomed the hopes of the Sumner Company. Many of the buildings were moved to Atchison as the town declined. In June, 1860, a tornado administered the *coup de grâce* to what was left of Sumner.

382. $1, 185_ printed, balance of date to be entered. Uniface, no plate letter ... R-7

I. *Territorial Period, May 30, 1854–January 29, 1861* 25

383. $2, Date as above. Uniface no plate letter R-7

384. $3, Date as above. Uniface, no plate letter R-7

385. $5, Date as above. Uniface, no plate letter R-7

THE CITY OF TECUMSEH
(Municipal Scrip)

Tecumseh was a small village east of Topeka when the "pro-slavery" legislature named it as the county seat of Shawnee County in July, 1855. Almost immediately bonds were issued for erection of a courthouse there. However, all attempts to collect taxes were so strenuously resisted by the "free state" settlers that by 1858 the county was indebted for nearly $11,000. In October, 1858, after the "free state" party had gained control of the legislature, an election was held for designation as county seat. Topeka won the election. After some difficulties in getting the records from Tecumseh, they were transferred in January, 1859. The legislature then repudiated the debts contracted by Tecumseh. That debt included nearly $2,500 in scrip issued to court jurors.

The only scrip known to have survived is dated January 1, 1859. This scrip was actually in the form of 90 day, non-interest-bearing promissory notes. This issue, which was receivable for city taxes, was made right after Tecumseh had lost the county seat election and just before the debt repudiation. It may have been a final effort to pay city employees or to prepare more juror scrip.

The loss of the designation as county seat doomed the hopes of the city planners and the town faded into obscurity. All that remains today is the name associated with a residential area. The $1 note that has survived has genuine signatures of the appropriate officials of the period.

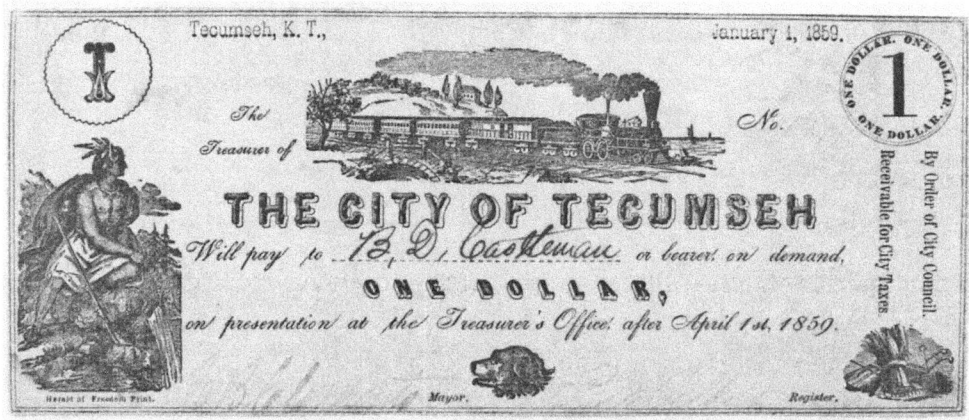

395. $1, January 1, 1859 printed date. Uniface, no plate letter. .... Unique
  Imprint: Herald of Freedom Print

I. Territorial Period, May 30, 1854–January 29, 1861

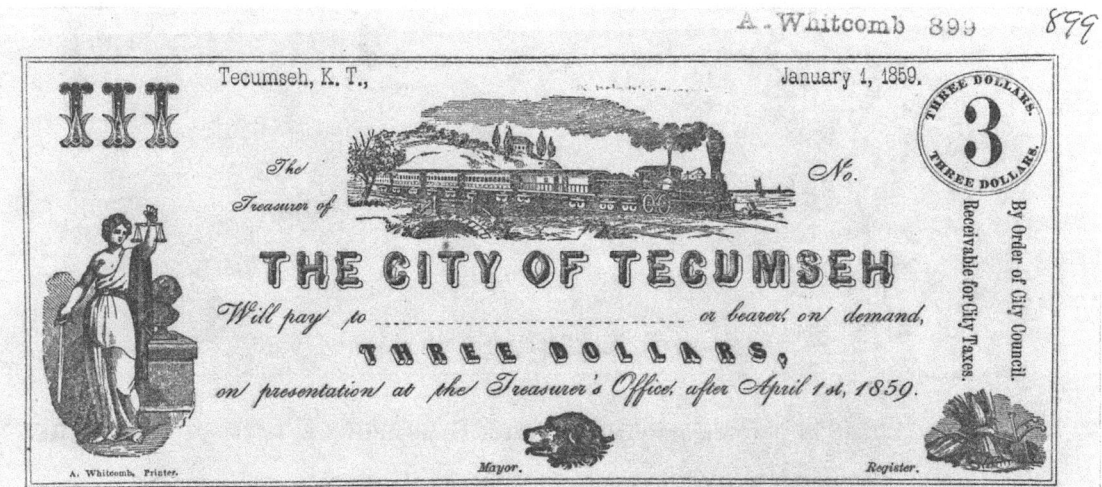

396. $3, Printed date as above. Uniface no plate letter. . . . . Unique
Imprint: A. Whitcomb, Printer

The Delaware City Bank
(Frauds)

Delaware City was located on the Missouri River, a few miles southeast of Leavenworth. The town never progressed enough to have a bank, and the town site was abandoned by 1880. Two different dated issues are known for this alleged bank. Most of these notes are found altered to pass on a genuine bank in the state of Delaware. In fact, one of the notes appears to have been designed to mimic the vignettes and counters of its genuine counterpart. The notes are listed in contemporary bank note reporters as worthless. A tiny "KAN" is found in the foliage below the upper right counter on the 1854 notes. The 1858 notes have "KANSAS" printed vertically on upper right border.

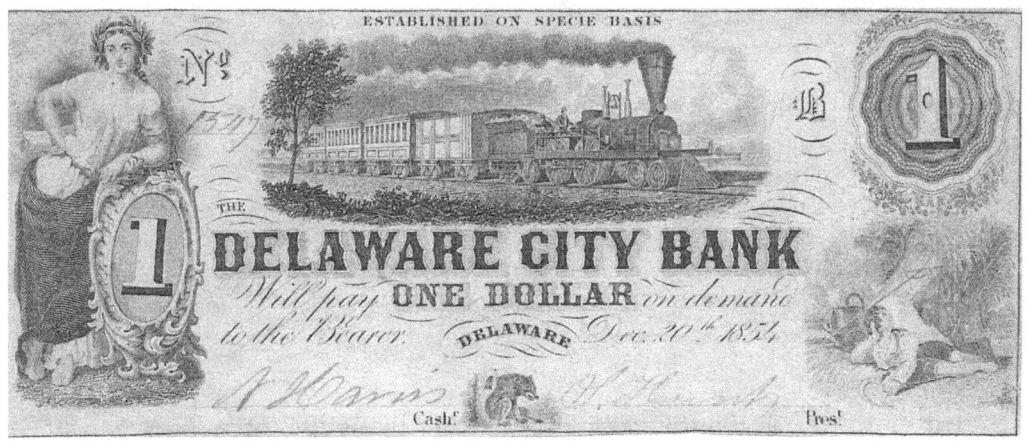

81. $1, Dec 20, 1854 printed date. Plate letter B. Uniface, ... R-5
no maker's imprint

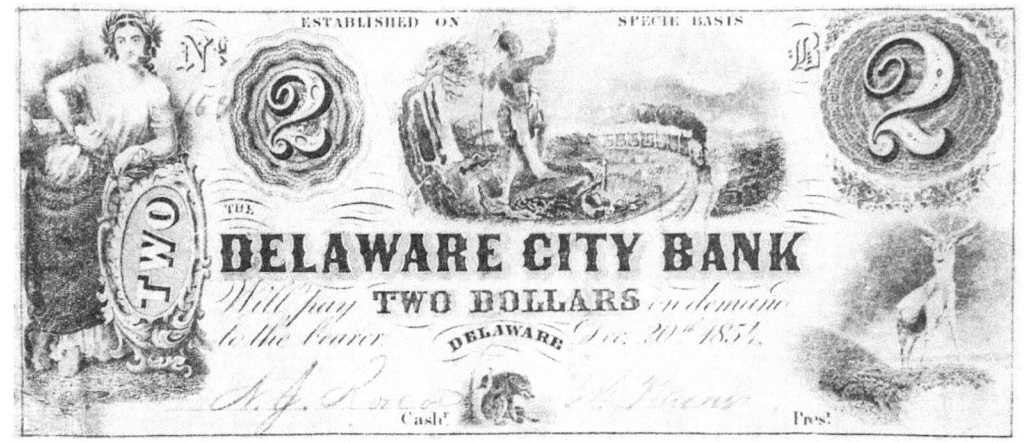

82. $2, Dec 20, 1854 printed date. Plate letter B, as above R-7

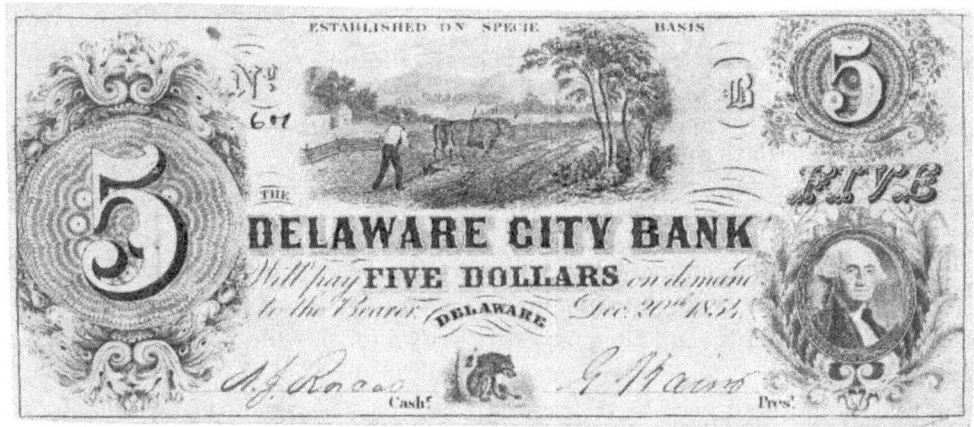

83. $5, Dec 20, 1854 printed date. Plate letter B, as above R-7

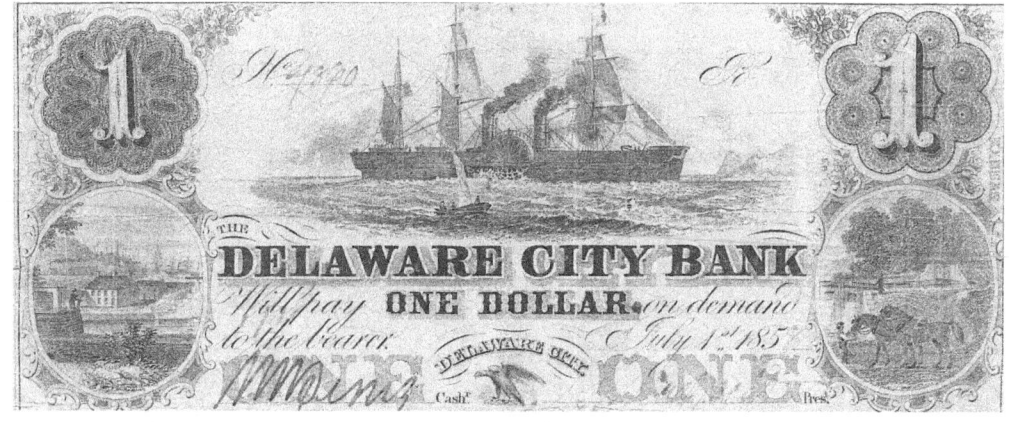

85. $1, July 1, 185_ printed, remainder of date to be written in. R-5
    (All known copies dated 1858) Plate letter B, no maker's imprint

I. Territorial Period, May 30, 1854–January 29, 1861

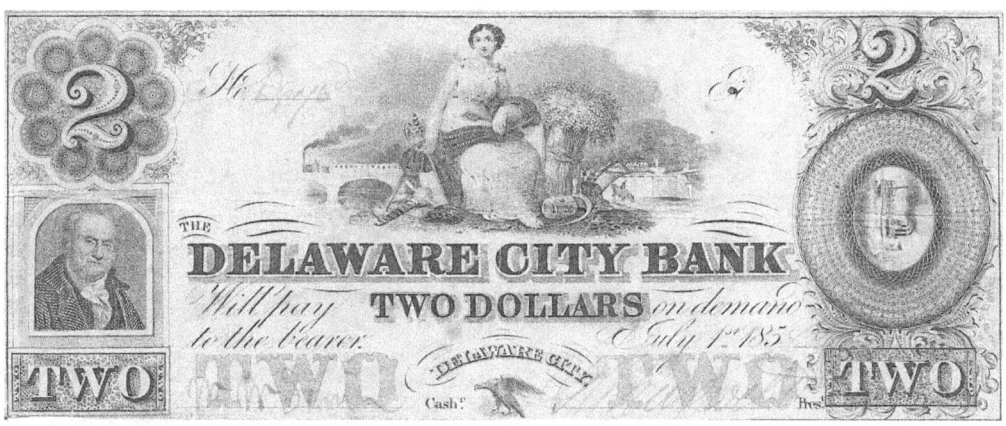

86. $2, July 1, 185_ printed as above. Plate letter B, no maker's imprint. R-5
 (All known dated 1858) (L) Portrait of Elias Boudinot.
 Although the vignettes differed somewhat, this note would
 have been described exactly the same in bank note reporters
 of the period as the genuine Delaware City, Delaware $2 note

THE EASTON BANK
(Frauds)

Easton was, and still is, a small village located about ten miles southwest of Leavenworth at the crossing of "Big Stranger Creek" on the old Fort Riley Road. The town was originally named "EASTIN" after General L.T. Eastin, one of the early organizers of the place. The name was changed to "EASTON" because Governor Andrew Reeder favored the spelling of his birthplace at Easton, Pennsylvania. A post office was established there in 1855. These notes are similar in design to the Delaware City notes and may all be alterations of those notes as reported by Haxby. By 1882, the town could boast of several churches, a blacksmith shop, two general stores and a grocery. The population had grown to about 85 people.

93. $1, Sept. 20, 1855 printed date. The note is nearly identical to the 1854 .. R-7 Delaware City Bank note, except for the small bear vignette at the bottom of that note and omission of the claim "ESTABLISHED ON SPECIE BASIS." Uniface, no maker's imprint. This note reported in Haxby as altered from the Delaware City Bank note.

94. $2, Sept. 20, 1855 printed date. Nearly identical to the 1854 $2 .... R-7 Delaware City Bank note and an obvious alteration. Same exceptions as noted for the $1 above. Uniface, no maker's imprint.

I. Territorial Period, May 30, 1854–January 29, 1861   31

95. **$5, Sept. 20, 1855 printed date. Plate letter B, uniface, no** R-7
    maker's imprint.
    (L) "5" on fancy rosette. (C) Farmer plowing field with oxen.
    (R) Bust of Washington in oval. Similar to Delaware City Bank
    $5 note.

THE DROVERS BANK OF KANSAS
(Intended Bank)

Notes of the Drovers Bank exist in several varieties. Often found with signatures and serial numbers added in red ink, the Kansas notes come in two location varieties. The $1, $2, and $3 denominations, apparently ordered first with the location shown as "Ft Leavenworth," are usually found with the "Ft" designation scratched through in ink. The same $1, $2 and $3, along with a $5 and $10 note, also appear with the location shown as "Leavenworth City." The $1, $2 and $3 were also produced with the location shown as Salt Lake City, Utah. (An early listing for Utah notes stated that the $5 note was also printed for Salt Lake City, but this note has not been seen.) All three varieties are frequently found overprinted with advertising for a fish and game dealer located at St. Joseph, Missouri.

There was an obvious connection among all three of the varieties. Leavenworth, as a city, was fairly well established by the time this bank tried to organize, so the changeover from "Ft Leavenworth" to Leavenworth City" is easy to understand. There was also a connection between Leavenworth and Salt Lake City through the trade route to Utah. The U.S. Army, in mounting an expedition against the Mormons, during the 1857 Mormon War, departed from Fort Leavenworth. Apparently the Drovers Bank organizers had in mind common banks at both ends of the route, which could have circulated each other's notes fairly easily. In any event the bank or banks never got organized, although notes, stock certificates, drafts and promissory notes were prepared and delivered by W.L. Ormsby of New York.

The printed bank notes soon became useless for much other than use as vehicles for printed advertising. An enterprising St. Joseph merchant appears to have acquired most of them, including the Utah varieties, for his fish and game business. Different colored fish overprints are known along with notes advertising other businesses. (One example seen advertises apple cider from a firm at Wathena, Kansas.) A book of blank stock certificates for this bank, along with drafts, and certificates of deposit was donated to the Kansas State Historical Society in the 1880s by a former state legislator. These notes are fairly common for Kansas notes. Most obsolete note dealers usually have a note or two in stock. A number of sheets and partial sheets have also survived.

115. $1, July 1, 1856 printed. Plate letters A and B. Imprint: W.L. Ormsby, .. R-5 New York. Ft Leavenworth location.

Ornate back design in orange

116. $2, July 1, 1856. As above. Plate letter A R-5

117. $3 July 1, 1856. As above. Plate letter A R-5

Drover's Bank of Kansas, Fort Leavenworth, stock certificate.

MERCHANTS BANK
(Fraudulent Bank)

These notes are true wildcat notes. The story of their origin is found in the *Kansas Weekly Herald* newspaper issues of November 10, 1854, and January 19, 1855. A Mr. Lucien Ayer traveled to Fort Leavenworth in the fall of 1854 and announced his intentions to establish a local bank.

The bank was never opened, but a large quantity of the notes of this bank were printed and apparently sold in the northeast before the fraud was discovered. These uniface notes are often found altered to banks in other states. All Kansas examples are hand dated Aug. 21, 1854. The notes were printed in four note sheets by W.L. Ormsby of New York. A large number of these notes surfaced in the 1990s. Sheets are known.

Lucien Ayer eventually went to prison in New Hampshire after being convicted on an unrelated arson charge.

I. Territorial Period, May 30, 1854–January 29, 1861 35

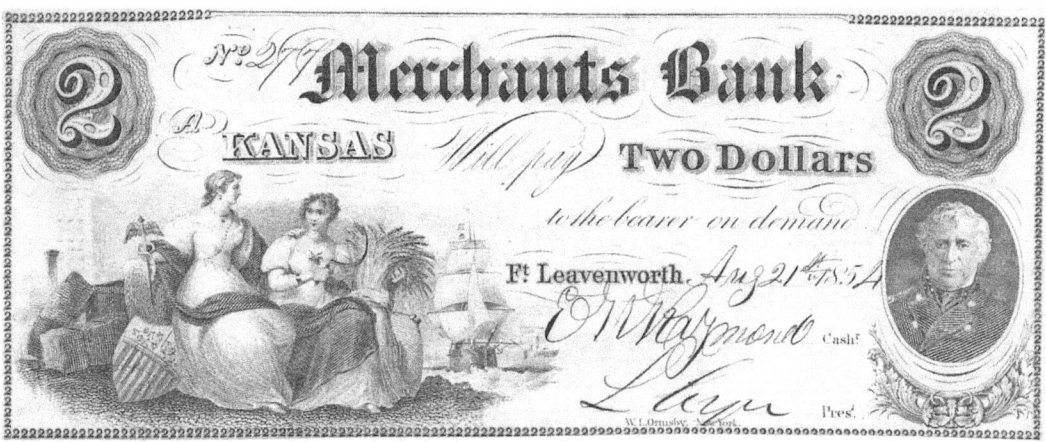

Q 130. $2, 185_ printed. Plate letter A; (R) Zachary Taylor portrait R-3

Q 131. $3, 185_ printed. Plate letter A; (R) William Henry Harrison R-3
portrait

Q 132. $5, 185_ printed. No plate letter; (R) Zachary Taylor portrait R-4

Q 133. $10, 185_ printed. Plate letter A. R-4

THE REDWING BANK
(Unknown)

These notes, inscribed Lawrence, Kansas, were payable at 25 Market Street, Boston, Massachusetts. They could almost be considered as "foreign exchange" drafts, meant to circulate in a remote area. No evidence of such a bank at Lawrence has surfaced. There was a "West Indies Trading Company," owned by one George W. Torre, located at 25 South Market Street in Boston during the period.

Legislation passed in Kansas at about this time prohibited circulation of anything other than notes of chartered banks. These notes may have been an attempt to provide a circulating medium for the abolitionist colony at Lawrence. Support for settlement of the place came largely from New England and the Boston area. The few notes that have turned up surfaced in the northeast. Wellstood, Hay & Whiting, New York & Boston printed the notes. The four-note plate was auctioned in 2007.

239. $1, April 18, 1857 printed. Plate letter A. Back, ornate panel in red .... Unique

I. Territorial Period, May 30, 1854–January 29, 1861

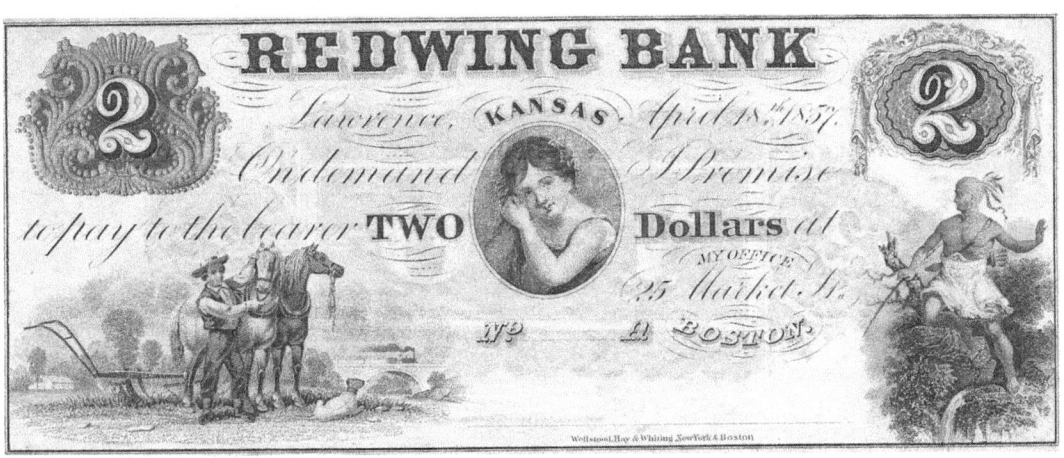

240. $2, April 18, 1857 printed. Plate letter A. Back, ornate panel in red R-7

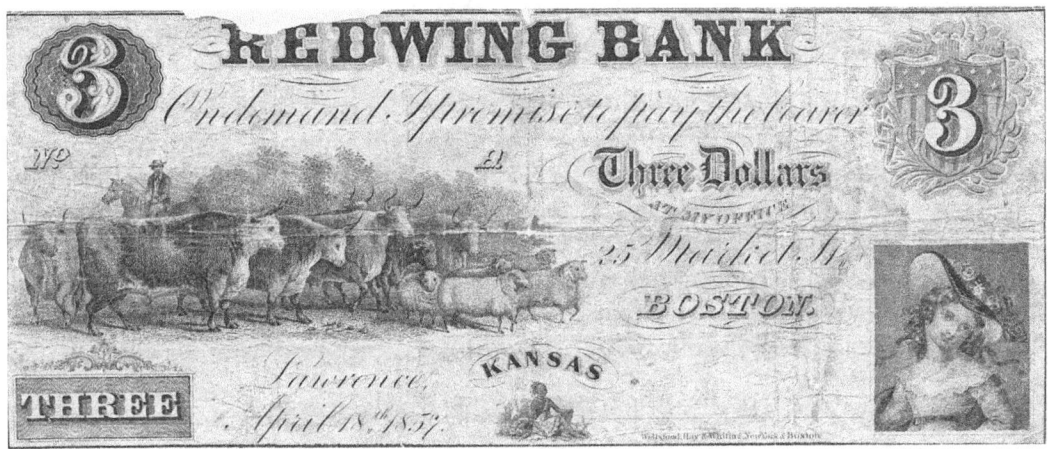

241. $3, April 18, 1857 printed. Plate letter A. Back, ornate panel in red R-7

242. $5, April 18, 1857 printed. Plate letter A. Back, ornate panel in red R-7

Ornate back design in red

THE CITY BANK
(Broken Bank)

The City Bank of Leavenworth was organized in November, 1856, as indicated by the printed date that appears on the existing bank notes. The bank may not have opened for business until the spring or summer of 1857. Advertisements for the bank began to appear in local newspapers about that time. The bank was located on the south side of Delaware Street, between Second and Third Streets, where #213 stands today. Henry J. Adams, who served as the first "free state" mayor of Leavenworth in 1857, was president and A.C. Swift served as cashier. Swift would later become cashier of the Kansas Valley Bank at Atchison in 1858 thereby linking the short lived City Bank with the banking history of Atchison.

The City Bank organized and originally issued paper money without authority of the territorial legislature. Ironically, the legislature may have authorized this bank and its issue of currency by the Act of February 11, 1858, after the bank had failed. The act to charter a bank at Leavenworth listed as incorporators, Henry J. Adams, William H. Russell, I.[sic] W. Morris (undoubtedly J.W. Morris) and several others. Because Adams' name was included, it is possible that the intent was to charter the City Bank.

The City Bank issued large amounts of unsecured paper money just prior to the nationwide banking crisis of October, 1857. The crisis was particularly hard on western banks and brought down the City Bank along with many others. As people demanded coin, the bank was unable to redeem its notes and consequently failed with heavy losses. It is reported that the bank owed $15,000 when it closed for good. This bank is probably the only note-issuing bank in early Kansas that met the traditional definition of a "broken [i.e. failed] bank." W.L. Ormsby of New York printed the notes. Several sheets have been seen: $1A, $1B, $2A, $3A.

Henry J. Adams

I. Territorial Period, May 30, 1854–January 29, 1861

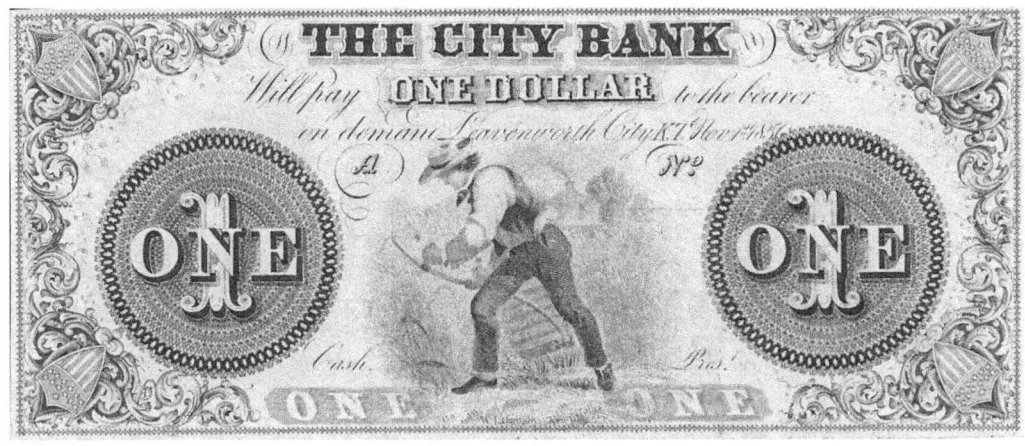

289. $1, Nov. 1, 1856 printed date. Plate letters A and B. Back in red R-5

Ornate back design in red

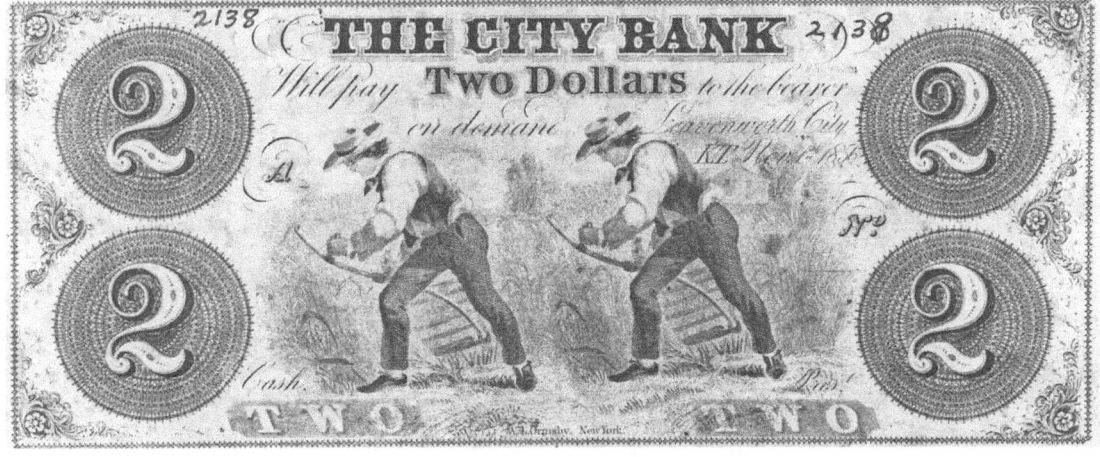

290. $2, Nov. 1, 1856 printed date. Plate letter A. Back design in red R-5

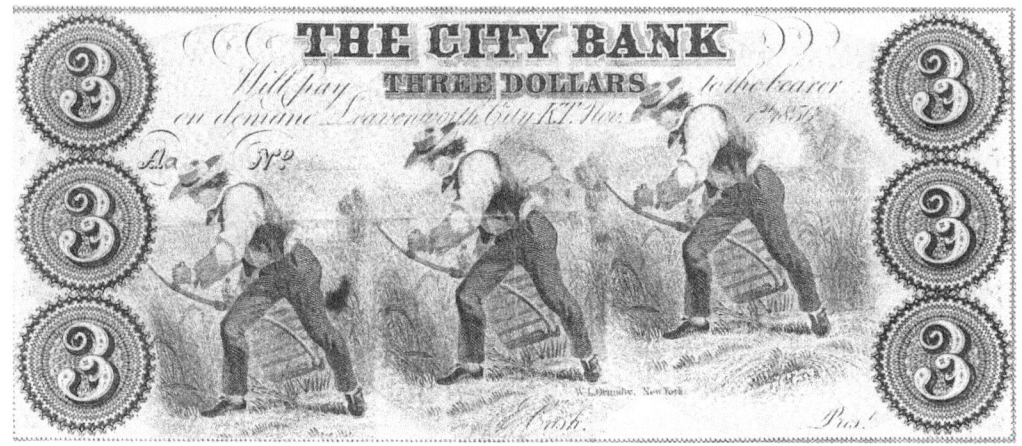

291. $3, Nov. 1, 1856 printed date. Plate letter A. Back design in red (below) ... R-5

DROVERS BANK
(Broken Bank)

Notes with this title and location of "Leavenworth City" are varieties of the "Fort Leavenworth" location. Around 1857 Leavenworth could stand on its own as a city. Refer to the listing for the Drovers Bank of Kansas at Fort Leavenworth for available information. Sheets are known.

118. $1, Same as #115 under Fort Leavenworth except location is now R-4
Leavenworth City. Plate letters A and B

119. $2, Same as #116 under Fort Leavenworth except location R-4

120. $3, Same as #117 under Fort Leavenworth except location R-4

121. $5, Nov. 1, 1856, printed date. Plate letters A, B and C. R-5
Ornate back design in orange. Imprint W.L. Ormsby, New York

Ornate back design in orange

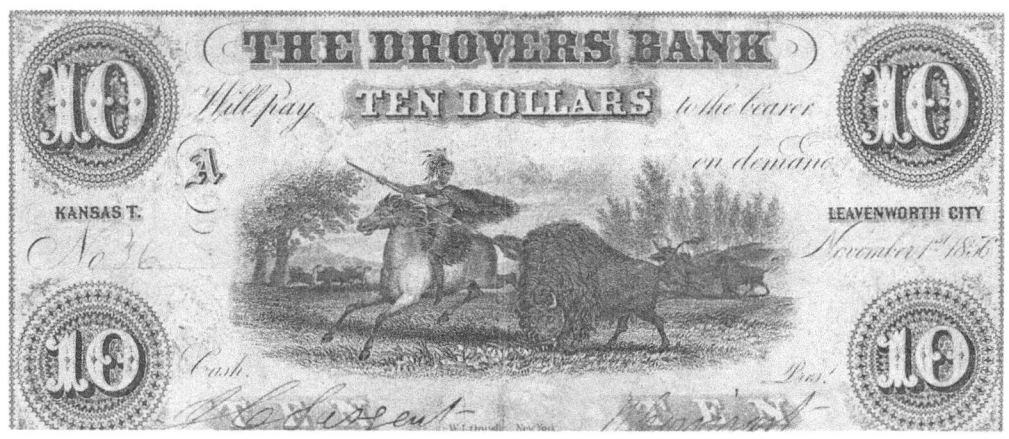

122. $10, Nov. 1, 1856 printed date. Plate letter A. Back is ornamental R-5
design in orange. Imprint Ormsby.

I. Territorial Period, May 30, 1854–January 29, 1861 43

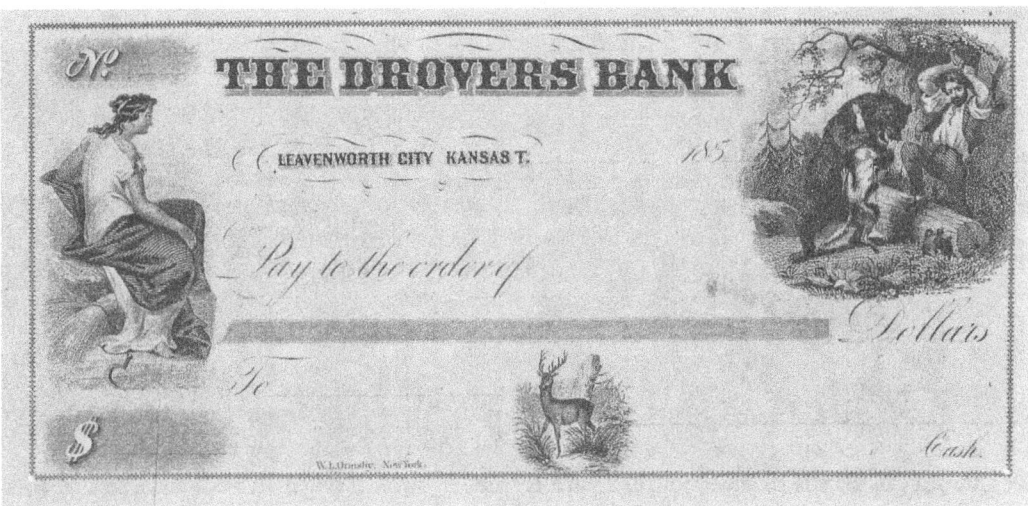

Drovers Bank, Leavenworth City, draft.

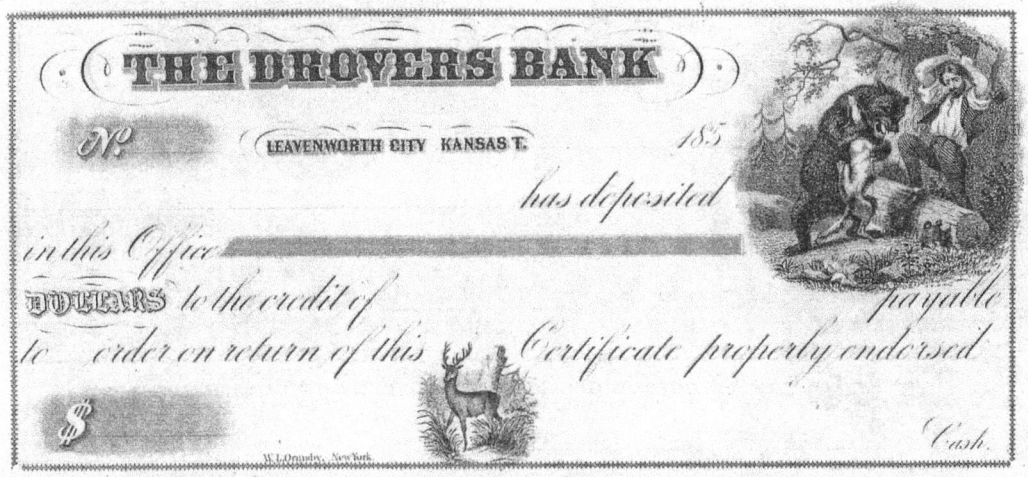

Drovers Bank, Leavenworth City, certificate of deposit.

THE DROVERS BANK
(Intended Bank)

Notes with the designation of Salt Lake City, Utah, are known in denominations of $1, $2, and $3. They are otherwise identical to the Leavenworth, Kansas, varieties. These notes are often found overprinted as advertising notes for merchants in the Kansas-Missouri area. See listing of "Fort Leavenworth" for additional details. It is possible that the Utah varieties were alterations of the Leavenworth notes.

$2.00, July 1, 1856, printed date. Plate letter A, back design in red R-4

Back of $2 note imprinted with advertising message

THE STATE BANK
(Intended Bank)

Lecompton is located on the South Bank of the Kansas River, approximately midway between Lawrence and Topeka on the Oregon Trail. During the 1850s it was headquarters for the pro-slavery party in Kansas Territory, and was intended to become the state capitol. Lecompton was known throughout the country before the Civil War, as the "bloody warfare" in Kansas was widely reported in the national press. The United States territorial land office was located there, and the city seemed destined for prosperity. After the free-state party gained control of the legislature in the 1857 election, Lecompton was doomed and the town rapidly declined. In 1861, the land office was relocated to Topeka.

The State Bank was an intended bank that never got organized. Its incorporators were James G. Bailey and Edward W. Wynkoop. Bailey was later prominent in an effort to charter a branch of the Kansas Valley Bank of Leavenworth at Fort Scott. Edward Wynkoop was a free-state sympathizer who later became one of the founders of Denver,

Colorado (actually in Kansas Territory at the time). The State Bank never opened for business.

Edward W. Wynkoop and "Captain Jack" Crawford.

333. $1, Nov. 1, 1856 printed date. Plate letter A, back design in red R-7

334. $2, As above except for denomination R-7

335. $3, As above except for denomination R-7

336. $5, As above except for denomination R-7

I. Territorial Period, May 30, 1854–January 29, 1861

$3 Postcard of Chase Money Museum with design of $3 note of The State Bank of Lecompton

THE KANSAS VALLEY BANK
(Chartered Bank)

The Kansas Valley Bank of Leavenworth was chartered by the Territorial Legislature on January 29, 1857. The act incorporating the bank became law on February 19 of that same year. This bank was probably intended as a state bank. Branches were chartered at Atchison, Doniphan, Fort Scott, Lecompton and Shawnee. The "branches" were to be separate banks, in no way accountable to the parent bank at Leavenworth. Provisions of the charter reflected many of the then current concerns about banks of issue, i.e. those authorized to issue currency. The maximum allowable loan interest was 10 per cent and loan periods were limited to one year. This resulted in limited availability of loanable funds, which worked to the disadvantage of local merchants and farmers.

The bank was authorized to issue paper money. Special provisions in the charter ensured that the notes would be redeemable in coin. The smallest allowable denomination was $3.

Samuel C. Pomeroy

Efforts to establish the Atchison branch and the Fort Scott branch included opening subscription books at those locations. At Doniphan a building to house the proposed bank was erected. In Atchison initial attempts under the direction of Peter T. Abell were unsuccessful. James C. Walker and associates mounted a second attempt from Weston, Missouri. These men were able to organize the bank by July, 1857, but for various reasons were unable to open for business. They did order and receive currency printed by the engraving firm of Danforth, Wright & Company, in denominations of $3, $5 and $10.

The notes were printed in four-note sheets as $5A, $3, $5B and $10. (A proof sheet of these notes surfaced in the ABNCo sale by Christie's in 1990.) Apparently there was also a separate sheet arrangement of $3s. The notes were printed with an orange undertint using stock vignettes. The title printed on the notes was "Kansas Valley Bank, Branch at Atchison." When these notes were printed, the other branches were still authorized to organize. Had any of them been successful it is surmised that their notes would have been of the same design, but with different branch names.

In the meanwhile there were continuing political efforts to repeal the bank's charter. On August 28, 1857, an editorial appeared in the *Kansas Weekly Herald* of Leavenworth expressing delight that the Kansas Valley Bank charter had been "saved." The editor offered to take the bank bills as payment for subscriptions, and made the argument that the territory needed local Kansas banks.

On January 7, 1858, an association headed by Samuel C. Pomeroy bought control of the Atchison branch from the Walker group. Pomeroy had been an agent for the New England Emigrant Aid Society working to establish Kansas as a free state. He was to become one of the first two United States Senators from Kansas in 1861. He would also serve as president of the Santa Fe Railroad.

Pomeroy's group had the bank organized and about ready to open when the legislature repealed the bank charter. This nearly ended the enterprise until Pomeroy was able to "influence" enough of the legislators to exempt the Atchison branch from the charter repeal. This was accomplished on February 12, 1858, in the last minutes of the session. The charter repeal effectively ended efforts to establish the branch at Fort Scott, and also eliminated the remaining branches of the intended system.

Therefore the Atchison branch was the only bank of the chartered Kansas Valley Bank system to actually organize and conduct business. On February 26, 1858, after satisfying the necessary territorial officials as to its financial condition, the bank opened for business in Atchison. The bank was located in a building at the southwest corner of Fifth and Commercial Streets. Samuel C. Pomeroy was president and A.C, Swift, of the recently failed City Bank of Leavenworth, was cashier. The initial opening was to be short-lived, however, as the bank was forced to close its doors sometime in April, 1858, after only two months of sporadic operation.

I. Territorial Period, May 30, 1854–January 29, 1861 49

Left to right: George Fairchild, Wm. Russell, Wm. Waddell

The bank may have circulated some of its currency during those two months. No notes have been seen from this period. However, by July 3, 1858, the Atchison banking firm of Holbert, Davis & Co. was advertising in the local papers to "buy Kansas Valley Bank notes." In addition, some of the earliest bank ledgers survive and contain a notation including the number of notes signed by Walker and Swift.

During the summer of 1858, powerful banking and transportation firms from Leavenworth became interested in the bank. William Russell, Luther Smoot, and William B. Waddell, representing the freighting firm of Russell, Majors and Waddell, and the Smoot, Russell Bank, each invested $10,000. Mr. George Fairchild, Atchison pioneer and former banker from New York, committed another $11,700, and Samuel Pomeroy also pledged $10,000. In July, 1858, the Kansas Valley Bank reopened at Fifth and Commercial Street. Samuel Pomeroy was president and George Fairchild was cashier. Fairchild also owned the bank property.

A ledger entry made on July 20, 1858, lists the bank's currency as follows: "4,000 impressions of the $5, 3, 5, 10 plate at $23, making in all $92,000, plus 7,000 impressions of $3, for another $21,000, totaling in all $113,000." It also indicates the number of sheets signed as: "1,100 sheets (@$23 each) signed by Walker and 770 sheets (@$23 each) signed by Swift, for a total of $43,010." The dollar amount of the signed sheets is approximately equal to the total allowable circulation of the bank. Of the $43,010 included in the signed sheets, $2,369 (103 sheets @ $23 each) may already have been placed in circulation, leaving a balance of $40,641. Another notation lists the circulation account at $40,641, as of May 14, 1858. The circulation account was obviously made up of signed sheets, ready to issue, and the dollar amount of the circulation account was limited by the charter.

Samuel Pomeroy apparently never paid in his $10,000 capital. This may have been the reason that William Russell replaced him as president on November 12, 1858. Pomeroy became vice-president of the bank at that time. The bank eventually was to sue him for non-payment of his note for capital and win a judgement against him for more than $20,000 in 1864.

Atchison, Kansas, in 1859

Mr. William Russell would later be the driving force behind establishment of the Overland Pony Express and the California Pikes Peak Stage Company. Both ventures were financial disasters and contributed heavily to bankruptcy of the Russell, Majors and Waddell firm in 1862. The stage line was taken over by Ben Holladay and finally sold to Wells Fargo. The Pony Express became obsolete in 1861 upon completion of the telegraph system.

The new bank owners ordered new bank notes to be prepared. The old $5, $3, $5, $10 plate was altered. The phrase "branch at Atchison" was removed and the stock vignette of a farmer, which had appeared at the right side of the $5 note, was replaced with an engraved portrait of George Fairchild, cashier. Since the American Bank Note Company had been recently formed from several engraving firms, including Danforth, Wright & Company, the logo "ABCo" was added to the plate. Two issued notes from this plate have been seen. They are a $3 and $5 note dated November 15, 1858, and signed by Russell as president and Fairchild as cashier.

At the same time a new three-note plate was prepared by American Bank Note Company for the larger denominations of $20, $50 and $100. William Russell was depicted on the $20, William Waddell appeared on the $50 and portraits of Samuel Pomeroy and Luther Smoot appeared on the $100 note. As stated previously, Russell was president, Pomeroy was vice president and Waddell and Smoot were directors. William B. Waddell was the business director of Russell, Majors and Waddell, a huge government contractor and freight hauler. Luther Smoot was partnered with Russell in the Smoot Russell Bank at Leavenworth.

From published statements it is known that by December 11, 1858, the bank had placed nearly $18,000 of its currency into circulation. This amount increased to almost $40,000, the maximum allowed to the bank, by March 26, 1859. From that date forward the circulation amount declined.

The bank was fairly profitable for several years. In 1859 an unsuccessful effort was

KANSAS VALLEY BANK

CAPITAL, - - - $300,000

WM. H. RUSSELL, President.   **G. H. FAIRCHILD**, Cashier.

DIRECTORS.

| W. B. WADDELL, | P. T. ABELL, | SAMUEL DICKSON, | G. H. FAIRCHILD. |
| ALEX. MAJORS, | L. C. CHALLISS, | S. C. POMEROY, | |

COLLECTIONS AND REMITTANCES

Made at Current Rates of Exchange.

New York City Correspondents, Thompson Bros.   St. Louis, W. H. Barksdale & Co.

Advertisement from 1860/1861 Atchison City Directory

made to relax restrictive clauses in the charter, including limits on interest rates. The restrictions coupled with existing economic conditions and increasing competition would eventually cause the bank to close. As the war approached people redeemed their paper money for coin and by January 11, 1860, the Kansas Valley Bank's circulation had declined to about $9,000. By December 1 of that year it was reduced to $2,264. Things got so bad that the Kansas legislature passed a law in June, 1861, which allowed chartered Kansas banks to forgo redemption of their circulation in coin and authorized redemption by other means. Such a small amount of note circulation for a bank of issue, which depended on its power to create money, forecast the eventual demise of the bank. With little or no circulation the bank was forced to operate on its paid in capital without any reserve for bad debts.

On January 25, 1861, just four days before Kansas was admitted to the Union as the 34th state, the legislature changed the name of the bank to the Bank of the State of Kansas. They may have still envisioned a statewide banking system. Most likely the name change merely reflected attainment of statehood. The bank soon ordered notes to be printed with the new title. The old $5, $3, $5, $10 plate was altered once again by changing the bank title. New notes were printed and apparently some were circulated, probably to redeem worn out notes as they were turned in. The new notes had a green undertint. No issued notes of this type have been seen, however, several unissued remainders have survived.

On March 22, 1861, Mr. Eugene B. Allen replaced Russell as president. Russell went off to Washington to serve as a transportation advisor to the government during the war and was busy elsewhere. He probably had never taken an active role in management of the bank. About the same time Mr. Robert Levi Pease became cashier and George Fairchild

Steamboat vignette

moved to vice president. Samuel Pomeroy went off to Washington as one of the first United States Senators from Kansas.

Kansas suspended specie redemption on June 3, 1861, and by the following December the entire nation was authorized to redeem by other means than specie. The first circulating United States currency was issued in 1861 to finance the war. The smallest denomination created was the $5 bill. Anything smaller than a $5 quickly disappeared from circulation. It would be the spring of 1863 before the federal government would fill the void with fractional denomination notes. Therefore the public came up with substitutes in the form of paper "good fors," or "promises to redeem," small notes for various goods and services. With such a demand for small change the Kansas legislature passed an act on March 2, 1862, that specifically authorized the Bank of the State of Kansas to issue $1 and $2 notes. The original charter had established the $3 denomination as the smallest that could be issued by the bank. This new authorization brought about the last note issue from the bank. American Bank Note Company prepared a plate for $1 notes, which were printed, and delivered to the bank. Several genuinely issued notes signed by Mr. Pease as cashier with Allen as president and another with Fairchild as vice president have been seen. Plates A and B are known but the sheet arrangement has not been determined. A single proof has survived; the $2 denomination was apparently never prepared.

The war years proved unprofitable for the bank. Merchants and other borrowers became delinquent, or did not pay their debts at all, forcing the bank to foreclose on depreciated land and other worthless assets. Sometime in 1863, R.L. Pease left the bank to become agent for the Central Overland and Pikes Peak Express Company at Denver. John D. New replaced him as cashier. By May of 1864, the bank had relocated to the north side of Commercial Street, between 2nd and 3rd Streets. In 1865 the bank sold the property at 5th and Commercial, which the bank had purchased from George Fairchild in December 1861.

Robert Pease returned to Atchison in 1865 and re-associated with the bank. By then it was clear that a national charter would be necessary for profitable survival of the bank.

I. Territorial Period, May 30, 1854–January 29, 1861

At that time, a Mr. David Auld and associates were attempting to obtain a national charter for a separate bank at Atchison and they had the support of Senator Pomeroy. Pease attempted to get a charter for the Bank of the State of Kansas, but the senator turned his back on his former associates and the charter went to the Auld group. Auld then converted the private Stebbins and Porter Bank into the First National Bank of Atchison in 1867.

In March 1865 the United States Congress passed a 10 per cent tax on the circulating notes of all state banks in an effort to force conversion to the new national banking system. The tax was scheduled to go into effect on July 1, 1866. Faced with the impending tax, increasing competition from the Stebbins & Porter/First National Bank, and failure to obtain a national charter, the stockholders decided to close the bank. The small amount of outstanding circulation was redeemed. The remaining capital stock and assets of the bank were sold at auction on March 19, 1866. William Hetherington was the successful bidder at the sale. With these assets he reorganized and reopened his old Exchange Bank in the former Bank of the State of Kansas' offices. Hetherington's bank obtained a national charter in 1882, and is still going strong at Atchison.

Officers of the Kansas Valley Bank/Bank of the State of Kansas

Date	President	Cashier	Vice President
4/24/57	Peter T. Abell		
7/8/57	J.C. Walker	J.C. Walker?	
1/7/58	S.C. Pomeroy		
2/26/58	S.C. Pomeroy	A.C. Swift	
7/17/58	S.C. Pomeroy	Geo H. Fairchild	
11/12/58	Wm H. Russell	Geo H. Fairchild	S.C. Pomeroy
3/22/61	E.B. Allen	R.L. Pease	Geo H. Fairchild
by 10/1/63	E.B. Allen	John D. New	

Note: After 1862 no subsequent elections of officers were held until December, 1864.

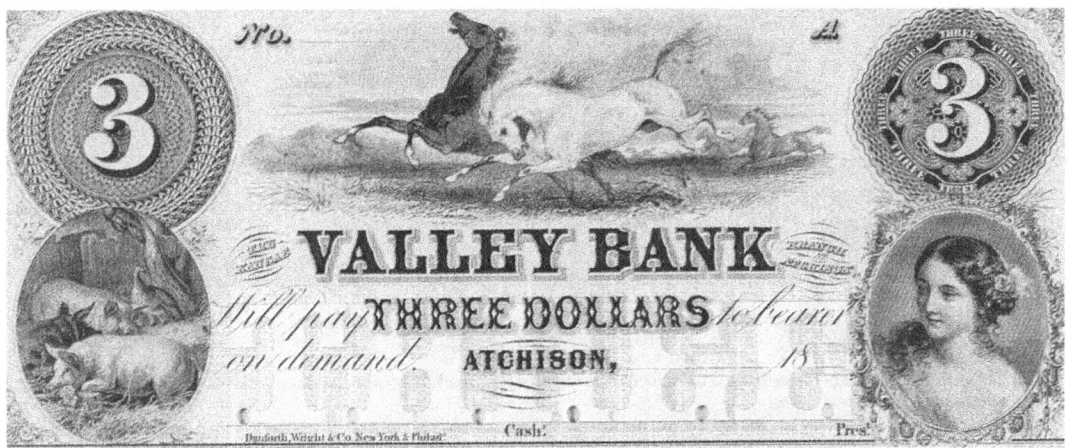

41. $3, 18__ printed, balance of date written in. "Branch" designation. .... Unique
    Imprint Danforth, Wright & Co. Uniface, plate letter A.
    Orange undertint

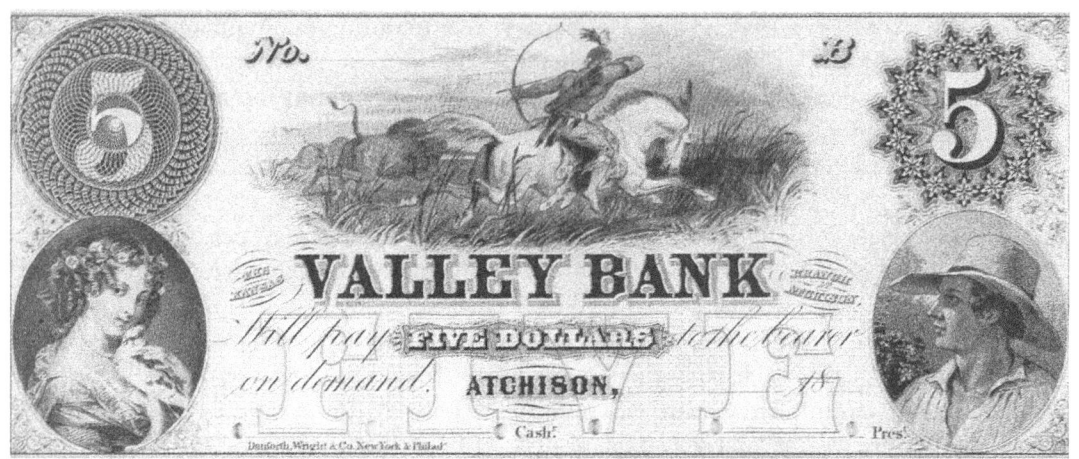

42. $5, 18__ printed, as above. Plate A and B R-7

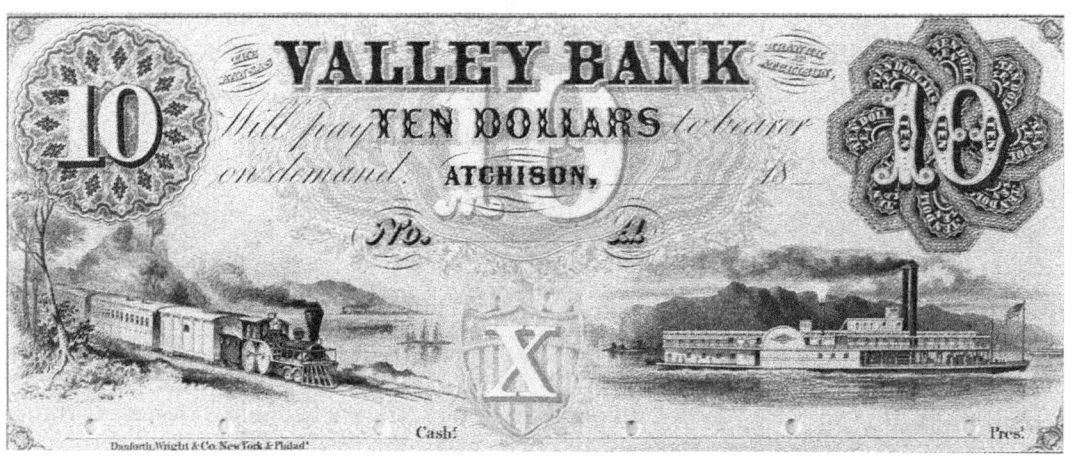

43. $10, 18__ printed, as above. Plate letter A .... Unique

Note: Numbers 41–43 are part of the unique proof sheet that surfaced in the Christie's sale of 1990.

I. Territorial Period, May 30, 1854–January 29, 1861 55

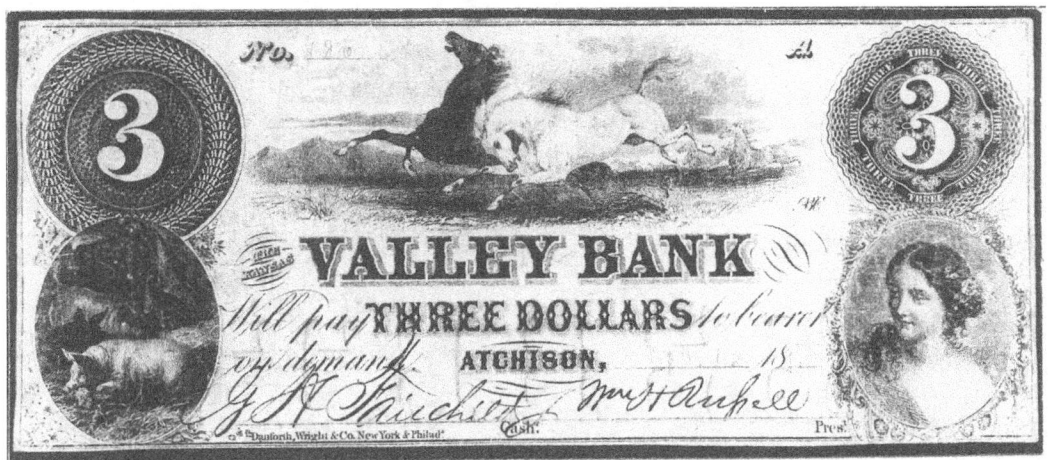

41a. $3, 18__ printed, as above. Same as #41 except no branch .... Unique designation and ABCo logo added

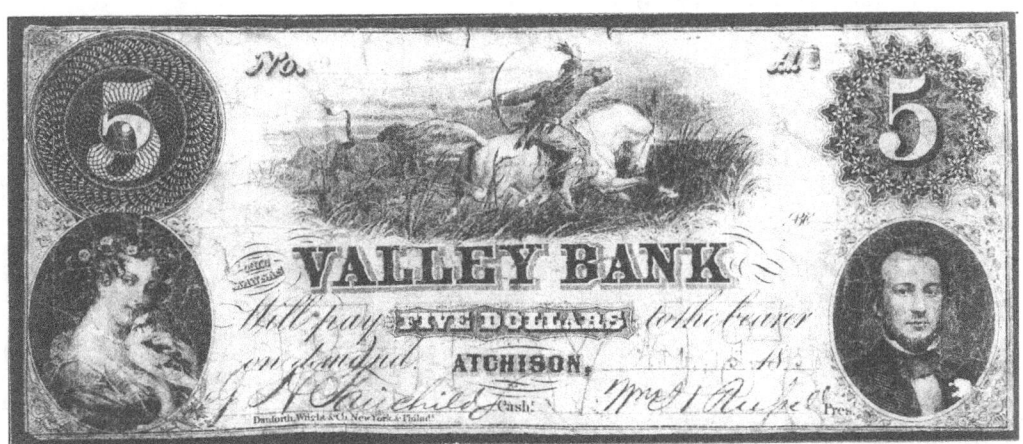

42a. $5, 18_- printed, as above. Same as 42 above except for branch .... Unique and logo, and portrait of George Fairchild, cashier, replaces farmer vignette at right

43a. $10, 18__ printed, as above. Same as 43 above except branch and logo .. SENC

44. $20, 18__ printed. Imprint: American Bank Note Co., New York. R-7
Uniface, orange tint plate. (R) Portrait of William H. Russell
(an unissued remainder of this note disappeared from a State
House exhibit in 1956)

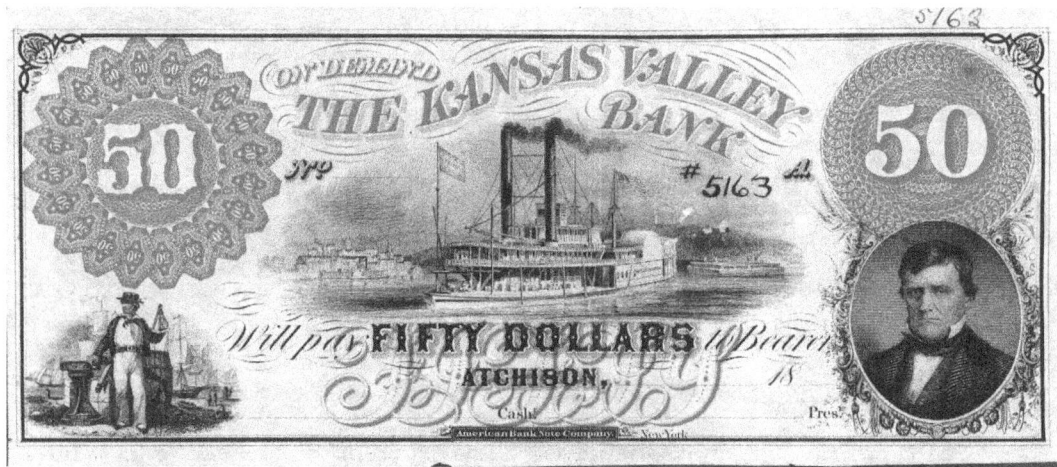

45. $50, 18__ printed, as above. (R) Portrait of William B. Waddell R-7

I. Territorial Period, May 30, 1854–January 29, 1861 57

46. $100, 18__ printed, as above. (L) Portrait of Samuel Pomeroy. . . . . . . Unique
(R) Portrait of Luther Smoot

THE LAWRENCE BANK
(Chartered Bank)

By 1857 the Free State party was in control of the Territorial Legislature. On February 8, 1858, they repealed the charter of the Kansas Valley Bank of Leavenworth, the planned state banking system previously chartered by the pro-slavery party. (The legislature would later exempt the Atchison Branch from the repeal.) On February 11, 1858, the legislature chartered its own bank of issue, to be called the Lawrence Bank at Lawrence. The enabling act actually granted one-year charters to three banks of issue to be located at Lawrence, Leavenworth and Wyandott. The proposed Leavenworth Bank was to be organized by the men associated with the recently failed, private City Bank. It is possible that the charter was intended to resuscitate that bank. The Wyandott bank also failed to materialize. Later that same year another act was introduced to extend the banking privilege to three additional banks, at Highland, Topeka and the "Osage River Bank at Osawattomie." This act was not passed.

The Lawrence Bank was the only one that organized and opened for business in May 1860. This was more than a year after the charter had technically expired, but no one seemed to notice, nor care, at the time. The bank quarters were located on the East Side of Massachusetts Street, across from the Eldridge House. Shalor Eldridge was one of the original incorporators of the bank, along with James Blood and several other prominent pioneers. When the bank opened, Robert Morrow, Charles Robinson, and Robert S. Stevens were principal stockholders.

Robert Morrow had arrived at Lawrence in August, 1855, where he became prominent in the free-state cause. In 1856 he built and operated the Morrow Boarding House, at the northwest corner of Massachusetts and Winthrop (Seventh) Street. When the bank opened for business, he was its president.

Charles Robinson was an agent for the New England Emigrant Aid Society. He later claimed to have selected the original townsite of Lawrence. He had guided one of the first parties of settlers to Lawrence in 1854. In 1861 he was elected governor of the new state.

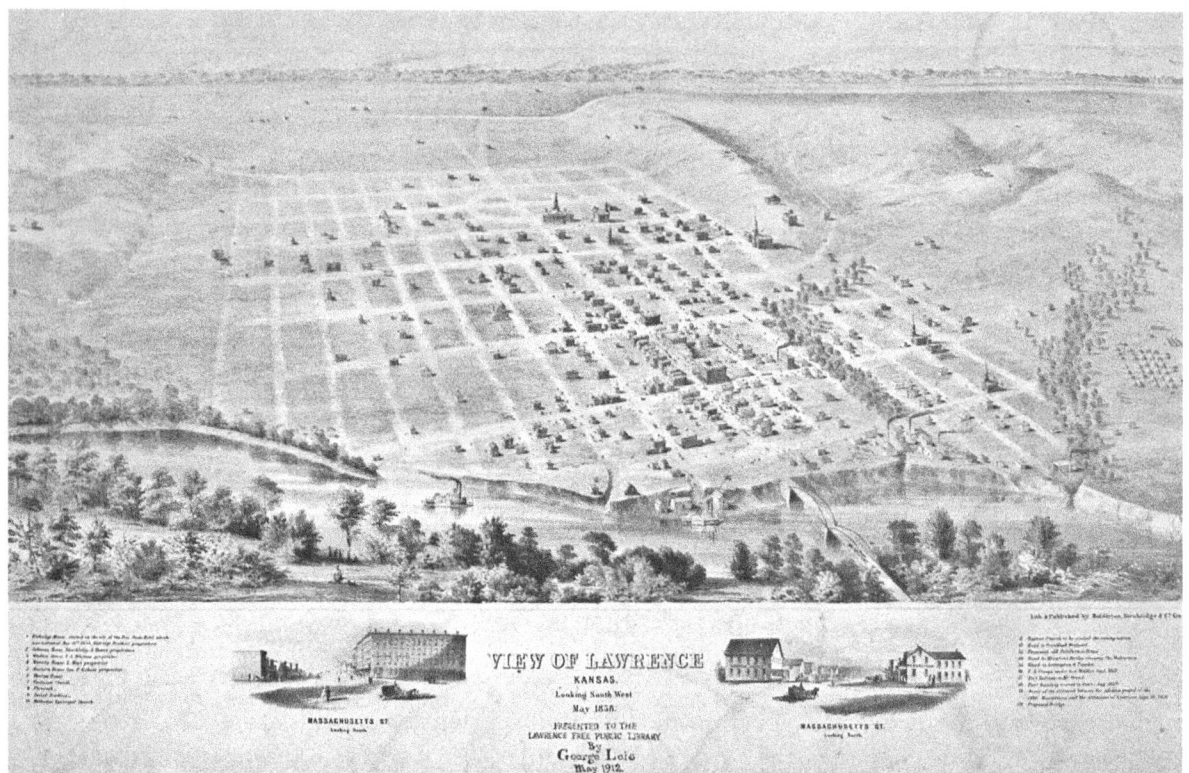

Robert Stevens was a speculator and politician who had relocated to Lawrence from Lecompton. He later served in the Kansas Legislature and would become a principal figure in the Kansas State bond scandal during Governor Robinson's administration. In later years he was a major influence for development of the Missouri, Kansas and Texas Railroad, the "KATY."

Ethan Allen Smith served as first cashier of the bank. Smith had come to Kansas from Wisconsin. During the Civil War he would hold a position in the Indian Bureau of the Department of the Interior at Washington, D.C. After the war he returned to Lawrence, dabbled in the hotel business for awhile, and then settled down as proprietor of a prominent stock farm near the city.

The Lawrence Bank was authorized to issue circulating currency. The first issues were made during the territorial period dated October 14, 1859, and April 14, 1860. A total of $14,812 in notes were prepared for issue. The notes were apparently difficult to place into circulation for various reasons. There was a good deal of public resistance to the issues of local banks. On June 14, 1860, the following editorial appeared in the *Leavenworth Daily Times* titled "Wild Cat — Look Out." The article read: "If there be any evil which a young territory should guard against, it is a spurious currency... For some days past, bills of the 'Lawrence Bank' have been in circulation among us. — The [*sic*] are not taken in this city by our solid men, nor are they issued, as we believe, upon any sound basis. Good men have charge of the bank: but money greed will blind the best, and hence we caution the people against receiving or circulating these bills. Let us have no wild cat banks in Kansas." This editorial shows that the bank issued notes as early as June of 1860, during the territorial period. No notes dated during the territorial period have been seen.

I. Territorial Period, May 30, 1854–January 29, 1861

Left: Robert Morrow, first president; *right:* Ethan Smith, first cashier.

Kansas became the 34th state on January 29, 1861. The new state constitution had differing requirements from those in the original bank charter regarding the issue of notes. The Lawrence Bank quickly reorganized under terms of the constitution. This required the bank to deposit interest bearing bonds with the state to secure its circulating notes. In addition the bank would be required to maintain at least 10 percent of its circulation in cash for redemption of notes. When these requirements were met, the State Auditor would countersign notes and turn them over to the bank for use. The surviving bank register indicates that the bank's first issue under the new provisions totaled $8,800 on

East side Massachusetts Street looking north, c. 1859

July 1, 1861. The territorial period dated notes, which were based on the original charter provisions, had been turned in at Topeka for destruction prior to the new issue.

Notes, before and after statehood, were issued in denominations of $1, $2, $3 and $5. A number of unissued remainders have survived along with a few very rare, genuinely signed and issued examples. Notes have been seen from the July 1 issue and a later issue, made on November 1, 1862, which probably only included $1s and $2s, during the war related to the small denomination shortage. The later issue replaced $3,273 of the 1861 issue, mostly unissued $5s that were turned in at Topeka for destruction. The state constitution actually made $5 the smallest denomination that was supposed to be issued by chartered banks, but on November 4, 1861, the legislature passed an act reducing that to $1. Several half sheets and a single full sheet of unissued remainders have been seen.

Between July, 1861, and November, 1862, Ethan Smith relocated to Washington, D.C. He was replaced at the bank by Samuel C. Smith (no relation), as acting or assistant cashier. S.C. Smith came to Kansas as a correspondent for an eastern newspaper. He was present at the rescue of Jacob Branson from the pro-slavery forces, which event brought on the so-called "Wakarusa War." He also served as secretary of the Leavenworth Constitutional Convention. At about the same time, Robert Stevens bought out the interests of Robert Morrow and Charles Robinson, although Morrow remained nominally as president.

The Lawrence Bank was used as a repository for the state funds, which angered the banking interests at Leavenworth. Therefore a plot was allegedly hatched whereby the notes of the Lawrence Bank were to be refused at Topeka in exchange for support by Leavenworth to establish the state capitol at Topeka. The alleged plot was apparently unsuccessful at ruining the bank, but Topeka did become the state capitol. The event that doomed the Lawrence Bank may have been the infamous bond scandal of Governor Robinson's administration. In March, 1861, the state legislature authorized the issue of interest-paying state and war bonds to raise funds. Austin Clark and James C. Stone, Leavenworth bankers, were appointed to market the bonds for a minimum of 70 cents on the dollar. They were unsuccessful because the state had no credit at the time.

Somehow, soon after the first attempt had failed, U.S. Senator Samuel Pomeroy convinced the legislature to authorize Robert Stevens to sell the bonds. Stevens then bought from the state, large quantities of the bonds for 40 to 60 cents on the dollar. Unknown to the legislature was the fact that Stevens had previously arranged to sell the bonds for 85 to 95 cents on the dollar to the U.S. Department of the Interior, thereby assuring a fine profit for himself and anyone else who had assisted him in the matter. Although there were denials, evidence indicates that both U.S. Senators, Pomeroy and James Lane, had influenced President Abraham Lincoln to authorize the purchase using Indian trust fund money. On December 19, 1861, more than $100,000 in Kansas bonds were purchased from Stevens. Governor Robinson, the Kansas Secretary of State and the State Auditor had allegedly approved the transaction. It would later be determined that Governor Robinson's name had been forged by one of the other parties.

Robert Stevens then attempted to purchase more of the state bonds, some of which had been used to buy up state scrip at 60 cents on the dollar. He may have been successful as some of these bonds were later used as security for the Lawrence Bank circulation.

When the facts of the bond sale were revealed, Governor Robinson's political enemies, including U.S. Senator James Lane, had the ammunition they needed to impeach the Governor. The impeachment trial began on June 2, 1862, before the state senate. The defendants were Governor Charles Robinson, Secretary of State John Robinson (no relation), and State Auditor George Hillyer. Incredibly, Robert Stevens, a state senator at the time, sat in on the trial although he was excused from voting. Both Hillyer and John Robinson were rapidly convicted of fraud and removed from office. This set the stage for the governor's trial. Against all odds and in the face of a jury packed with his political enemies, the governor was acquitted on June 29, 1862. Although exonerated from guilt in the matter, Robinson was ruined politically by the trial.

Part of the price for the acquittal may have been liquidation of the Lawrence Bank. Shortly after the trial Stevens deposited sufficient United States money with the state to redeem the outstanding bank circulation and withdrew the bonds. The bank continued

Top: "The Mill Door"; ***bottom:*** "St. Louis Waterfront."

to do an exchange business only, redeeming notes for coin or other lawful money, and periodically taking redeemed notes to Topeka to be cancelled and destroyed. This was the situation on August 21, 1863, when Quantrill's guerillas raided the town and robbed and burned the bank. The Lawrence Bank was robbed of a quantity of coin belonging to Robert Morrow, along with whatever notes were on hand. Legend has it that the few genuinely signed notes that survive today were stolen from the bank on that terrible day. After the raid the bank never reopened, but did continue to redeem any notes presented for payment until January, 1864, when it closed for good. All of the outstanding currency had been redeemed or was provided for by the deposit of funds with the state. (The state probably still has a few dollars that were intended to redeem Lawrence Bank notes still outstanding.)

Note: For more details on the Lawrence Bank and its issues, see article in *Paper Money*, Whole Number 155, Sept./Oct. 1991; pgs 144–153.

213. $1, 18__ printed, balance of date to be written in. Uniface, black .... SENC
and orange. Imprint American Bank Note Co., New York.
Possible dates Oct. 14, 1859 (1003 sheets) and April 14, 1860
(289 sheets)

Note: Genuinely signed and dated notes from the territorial period are unknown, SENC. Unissued remainders are illustrated herein.

I. *Territorial Period, May 30, 1854–January 29, 1861* 63

214. $2, 18__ printed, as above; same dates .... SENC

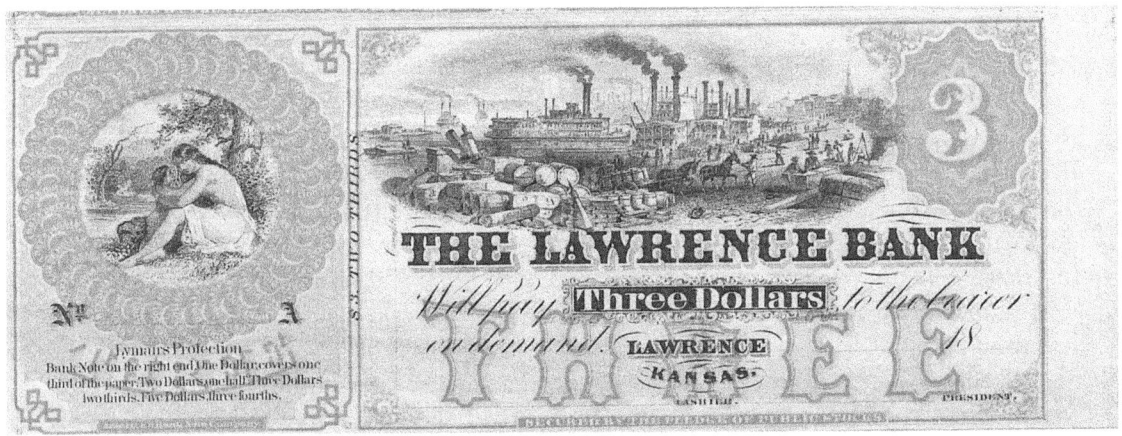

215. $3, 18__ printed, as above; same dates .... SENC

216. $5, 18__ printed, as above; same dates .... SENC

Epilogue

We find this interesting exchange in *Transactions of the Kansas State Historical Society, 1889–1896*, Vol. V. Topeka: Press of the Kansas State Printing Co., page 621, "Governor Medary's Administration":

Executive Office, Kansas Territory, Lecompton, May 26, 1860

To Mr. R.B. Mitchell, Territorial Treasurer;

Sir, I have before me what purports to be a bank note issued by the Lawrence Bank of Lawrence, Kas., signed by E.A. Smith, cashier and R. Morrow, president, and on the margin is engrossed, "secured by the pledge of public stock," and it is countersigned by Rob't Mitchell, and dated April 14, 1860.

I desire to know whether you have countersigned any such bills; or bank notes; and, if so, to what amount in value, and what kind of public stocks you have received for them as security, and by what authority you receive public stocks of any kind as security for the issue of bank bills or notes?

I am, sir, very respectfully, your obedient servant,

HUGH S. WALSH,
Secretary and Acting Governor of Kansas Territory.

Mitchell promptly wrote back, questioning Walsh's authority to ask such questions.

Walsh then turned the issue over to A.C. Davis, U.S. District Attorney for Kansas Territory, as a violation of an 1836 Act of Congress; spurious paper currency, etc., etc.

After several more exchanges, Walsh wrote to Sec'y of State Lewis Cass complaining that Governor Medary was conspiring to have him, Walsh, removed from office for misfeasance/malfeasance. The alleged "conspiracy" was apparently successful as Walsh was soon replaced.

Whatever happened to the note that Walsh had, dated April 14, 1860, and wrote about to Treasurer Mitchell? Could it be in the papers of the Medary Administration at the Kansas State Historical Society? If so, it would be the first recorded, signed survivor of the second Territorial issue of the Lawrence Bank. Anyway, we have further documented proof of the date of this bank issue.

II

Statehood Period, January 29, 1861–June 1, 1861

After several unsuccessful attempts, a constitution was adopted at Wyandott in 1859. This would be the state constitution when Kansas became the 34th state on January 29, 1861. The constitution included an article on banks and currency. A law addressing banking was enacted by the legislature on June 4, 1861, and confirmed by the public in the election of Nov. 4, 1861. No new banks would be chartered under the state law, however the two existing chartered banks did continue to operate after statehood.

The Kansas Valley Bank became the Bank of the State of Kansas on January 25, 1861, and was granted the same banking privileges it had enjoyed under its territorial charter. Plates with the new name were prepared in denominations of $3, $5 and $10, although these notes were probably not issued. On June 3, 1861, another act was passed, which authorized the bank to issue $1 and $2 notes. The American Banknote Company prepared a plate, and $1 notes were produced and issued to the public in 1862. The bank continued to operate until 1866, when it was liquidated.

The Lawrence Bank immediately reorganized under the new state law. It made an issue of $1, $2, $3, and $5 notes dated July 1, 1861, although it appears that few if any of the $5 notes got into circulation. This was probably because the federal government was issuing $5 bills at the time. On November 1, 1862, the Lawrence Bank made another issue of apparently only $1 and $2 bills to help with the small note shortage problem. In order to secure the amount issued, many of the 1861 $5 bills were turned in at Topeka for destruction. There are existing at least three, known, unissued half sheets, containing only the $3 and $5 denomination. The bank was in the process of liquidation when Quantrill's raiders robbed and burned the bank. The Lawrence Bank continued to liquidate until January, 1864, when it closed for good.

For detailed information on these "state banks" and their note issues refer to the territorial section of the book.

BANK OF THE STATE OF KANSAS
(Chartered Bank)

This bank was a continuation of the Kansas Valley Bank. When Kansas became the 34th state in January, 1861, the legislature passed an act changing the name of the bank. Notes were prepared by altering the $5, 3, 5, 10 plate, that had originally been prepared by Danforth, Wright & Co. for the Kansas Valley Bank. The tint plate color was changed to green. Possibly none of these notes were circulated, perhaps because federal notes became available. Modern proofs of the note plate were made by ABNCo in the 1980s or 1990s. The small denomination crisis of 1862, caused the state legislature to amend the charter for this bank permitting the issue of $1 and $2 bills. The $1s were the only notes prepared, and exist with plate letter A and B.

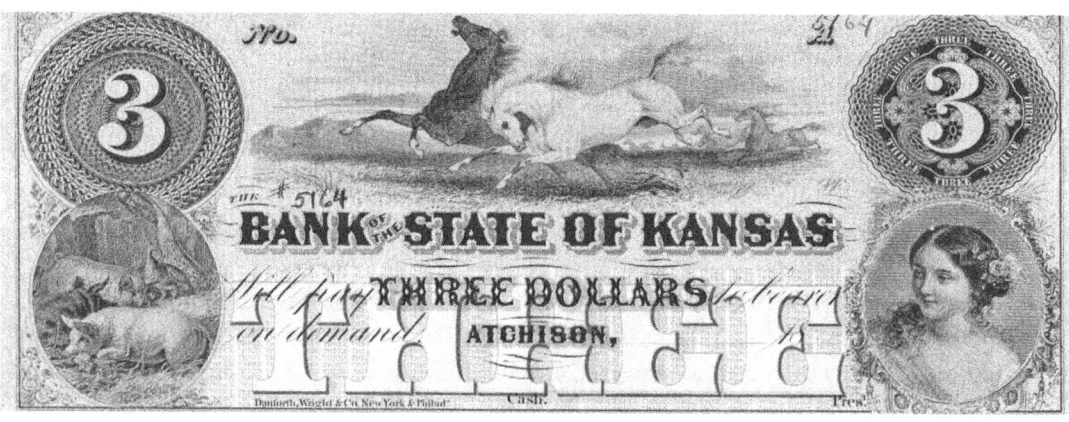

56. $3, Identical to #41a, except for title and green undertint R-7

57. $5, Identical to # 42a, except for title and green undertint R-7
    (an unissued remainder of this note disappeared
    from a State House exhibit in 1956)

II. Statehood Period, January 29, 1861–June 1, 1861

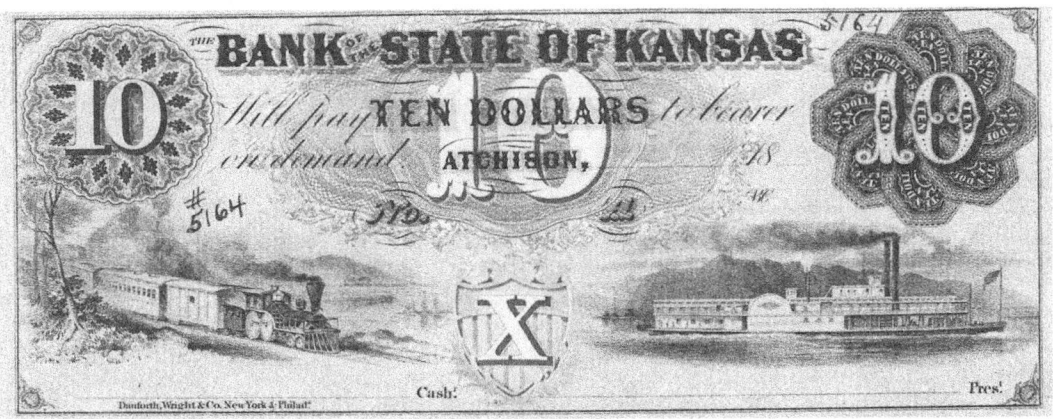

58. $10, Identical to # 43a, except for title and green undertint R-7

Vignette: "Buffalo Hunt"

THE LAWRENCE BANK
(Chartered Bank)

When Kansas became a state in January, 1861, the Lawrence Bank reorganized under provisions of the new state constitution. Notes were issued to replace the territorial period issues as early as July 1, 1861. The earlier dated notes were taken to Topeka for destruction, and bonds were deposited to secure a new note issue. The notes were of the same design as the previous territorial period notes. Notes were countersigned by the state Auditor for circulation. The $5 denomination notes were not easily circulated, but the $1s, $2s and $3s apparently saw good use in the area tributary to Lawrence. Genuinely

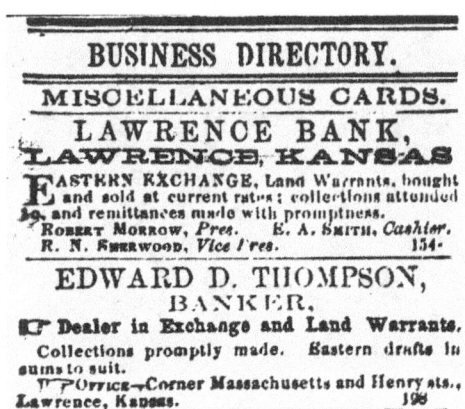

signed and dated notes are very rare. For more information about the bank and its issues, refer to the chartered bank section under the territorial and Civil War crisis periods.

1861 newspaper ad for Lawrence Bank

213a. $1, Same as #213, except hand dated July 1, 1861 . . . . SENC

214a. $2, Same as #214, except hand dated July 1, 1861 . . . . R-7

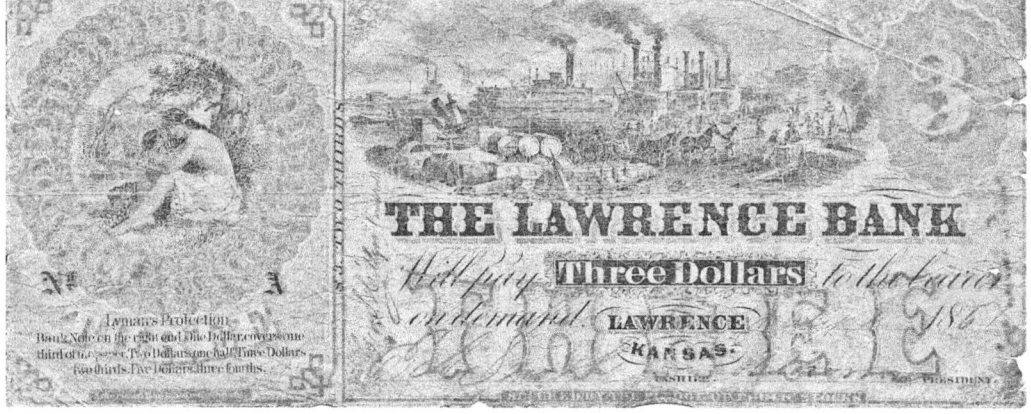

215a. $3, Same as #215, except hand dated July 1, 1861 . . . . R-7
216a. $5, Same as #216, except hand dated July 1, 1861 . . . . SENC

III

Civil War Crisis, 1861–1863

The Civil War created a great financial crisis for the nation. Prior to 1861 the governing and business of, America, with minor exceptions, was carried out on a hard money, or specie basis. Although paper money issued by private and state chartered banks was widely used, it was generally backed with a percentage of silver or gold coin and/or various state bond issues. The war overwhelmed the financing ability of the federal government and the nation's banks. Enormous sums were required to conduct the war, and the only way to get it was for the government to issue circulating paper notes that were not redeemable in coin. The first federal Greenback issues in 1861 were of $5 bills and larger denominations. The population soon hoarded or exported every coin they could get their hands on as the new federal paper money began to depreciate. Without small change with which to conduct business, the populace turned to various substitutes, such as postage stamps, metal tokens and the infamous "good fors."

A "good for" was a small paper note, usually printed by the local newspaper or stationery firm, that typically stated the said piece of paper was "good for" one shave, one drink, one haircut, or 10 cents, 25 cents, etc., and would be redeemed at the place of issue, or elsewhere, when presented in sums of even dollars, such as $1 or $5. Such notes not only served as change for their issuers, but also advertised the type and location of the business. Even better for the issuers, many of these notes were never redeemed as people lost them, gave up trying to accumulate enough to redeem, or even used them to light their smoking pipes. In 1862, the federal government began to issue notes in denominations of $1 and $2, which alleviated part of the small money shortage. The issue and availability of true fractional notes by the United States government, such as 10-cent and 25-cent notes, etc., did not eliminate the need for locally issued small scrip until the spring of 1863. Thus, during the period from June, 1861, until about March, 1863, many banks, merchants and local city governments issued unique local currency all over America. These pieces are relatively common from the larger eastern states, but are extremely rare from Kansas. There were undoubtedly many more varieties of these notes issued than are known today, and it is hoped that this publication will generate reports of some presently unknown "Kansas money."

By the time the war began in April, 1861, Kansas had only two legitimate banks. Both had been chartered by the territorial legislature, and continued in operation when

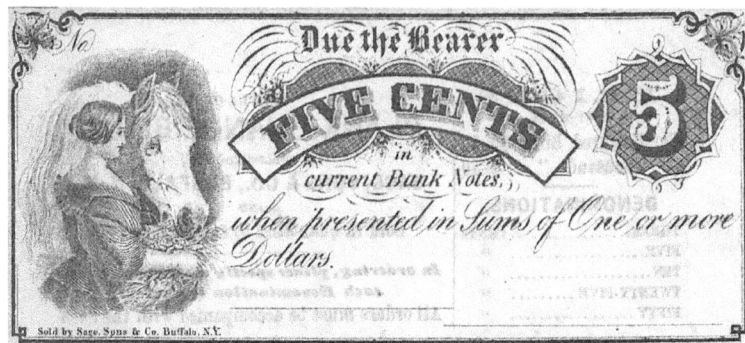

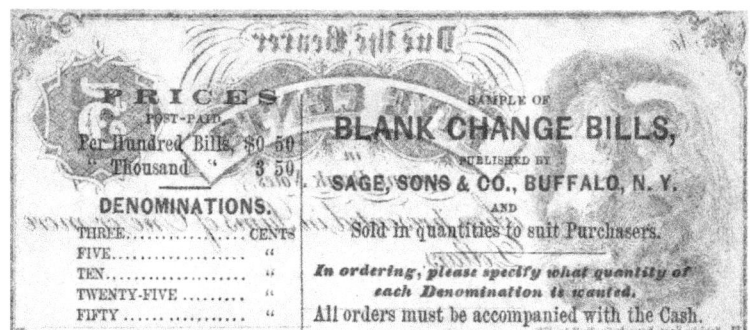

A typical "good for" of the period, which advertises the prices for printing blank change bills

Kansas achieved statehood. They were the Kansas Valley Bank at Atchison, which changed its name to the Bank of the State of Kansas in January, 1861, and the Lawrence Bank at Lawrence. Both were authorized to issue paper money and had done so prior to the war.

On June 3, 1861, the Kansas Legislature passed an act allowing banks based on state bonds to redeem their notes by means other than coin. Immediately thereafter several of the private banks in the state began to issue $1 and $2 bills. In Atchison, notes are known from the Exchange Bank and the later retitled "Exchange Bank of William Hetherington" (predecessor to the Exchange National Bank). In Lawrence, the Simpson Brothers Bank and the Bank of William H.R. Lykins issued notes for as little as five cents. Three private banks in Leavenworth issued mostly $1 bills. They were the Banking House of Clark, Gruber & Co.; Scott, Kerr & Co. (predecessor to the First National Bank of Leavenworth), and the Banking House of J.W. Morris (which became the Second National Bank of Leavenworth). Most of the known issues, including the fractional denominations, occurred during the fall of 1862.

The state legislature passed an act on March 2, 1862, which allowed the Bank of the State of Kansas to issue notes of $1 and $2 denomination, although the $2 was never used. Both chartered banks issued small denomination notes during 1862, in response to the crisis. As would be expected, most of the known Kansas issues are from the more developed cities or towns of the period.

These notes represent a unique part of Kansas' history. They filled an urgent financial need at a desperate time. They saw heavy use in the daily transactions of commerce and industry that would eventually develop the state. By the spring of 1863 enough of the new federal fractional notes had reached circulation to drive out the local "good fors." Prohibition of such issues, along with confiscatory taxes helped to eliminate them.

Small denomination Civil War scrip notes are known from the Kansas cities and towns of Atchison, Fort Scott, Hiawatha, Junction City, Lawrence, Leavenworth, Manhattan, Paola, Richardson, Seneca, and Topeka; and were also reported from Emporia and the Post Sutler at Fort Riley. A single Civil War unit, sutler issue is known for the 1st Regiment of Kansas Colored Volunteer Infantry.

The largest collection of Kansas scrip and obsolete notes was assembled over the past twenty five years and privately held in the Midwest until recently. The Kansas State Historical Society Museum has a fine collection, although it could always be improved. Several important collections have been broken up and sold over the past thirty years, including the James Lindsay collection, the Gary Sturtridge collection, the Western Reserve Historical Museum collection in Cleveland, Ohio, the Boys Town Numismatic Museum collection at Omaha, Nebraska, the Chase Manhattan Money Museum collection in New York City, the American Bank Note Company collection of proof note impressions, and currently the Herb and Martha Schingoethe collection. A collection in St. Louis has an excellent representation of Kansas notes, and the author has a small collection. Numerous other collectors of this type of material have one or more Kansas pieces. Many of these notes are unique and most are in poor condition.

Unfortunately, we will never see much of the Civil War scrip that was issued in Kansas. Most of it was destroyed or has been lost forever. However, we can hope that some of the great rarities, which have disappeared over the past forty years, will resurface for the enjoyment of future collectors and historians.

The following note issues and their issuers are listed alphabetically, by location.

Atchison

THE CITY OF ATCHISON
(Municipal Civil War Scrip)

In November, 1862, the City Council of Atchison authorized the issue of two to three thousand dollars in small denomination scrip. The notes were in denominations of five cents, ten cents, twenty-five cents and fifty cents. The illustrated note is the only denomination that has surfaced to date. An article in the local paper indicated that this scrip was issued specifically because the federal issue of fractional currency was not yet available. The note is signed by Milton R. Benton, Mayor of Atchison from May, 1862, until May, 1863. William Bowman signed as City Treasurer.

10. .05, Presumed of the same design as the .10 note. No imprint .... SENC

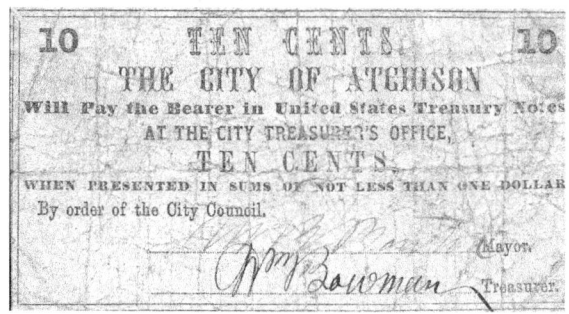

11. .10, See illustration .... UNIQUE

12. .25, Presumed same as above .... SENC
13. .50, Presumed same as above .... SENC

Richardson

RICHARDSON
(Municipal Civil War Scrip)

The town of Richardson was located at a crossing of 110 Mile Creek in Osage County, south of Topeka. The creek was so named because the crossing was 110 miles west of Lexington, Missouri, starting point of the Santa Fe Trail. A U.S. post office was established at Richardson in 1855, and finally abolished by the Post Office Department on September 26, 1874. After 1856, there was a toll bridge at the crossing that cost 20- or 25-cents. The county eventually purchased the bridge for $700 and eliminated the toll. It is possible that the reason for this scrip issue was to facilitate making change for toll crossings.

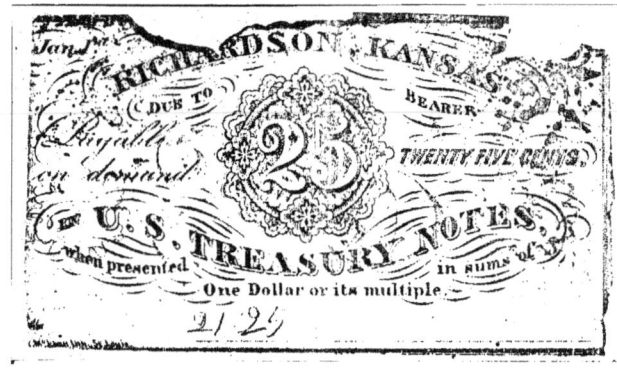

.25, Jan. 1, c. 1863; imprint McLean Lith., St. Louis (?) .... Unique

Emporia

During the Civil War there were no banks located at Emporia. However, there were apparently at least two issues made of local merchant scrip. No notes have turned up to date.

On February 8, 1862, the *Emporia News* advertised to "take county scrip" for subscriptions at .75 cents to the $1. Persons without scrip were advised to bring corn. Like many of the pioneer counties in Kansas, Lyon County obviously also issued scrip. This was more than likely of the "write-in denomination" type. None of this scrip has been seen.

Emporia, Kansas, c. 1862

On June 28, 1862, a small article appeared in the news as follows: "Everything is five dollar bills. You have to go up street on one side and down on the other, to get them 'broke,' and most of the time do not succeed. Change was never so scarce. To meet this emergency, some of our business men have issued shinplasters, in denominations of one dollar and of 50 cents. J.R. Swallow & Co. and Fisk & Eskridge have them out. The former redeems in quantities of $5, when presented. It will undoubtedly be used as a currency as long as change is so scarce."

On July 26, 1862, an article appeared about the new Postage Currency. "Postage Stamps are made legal tender.... They are to be made on thick paper without gum." On August 16, the paper announced that the new Postage Stamp (fractional) currency would be ready in a week or two. On September 9, 1862, an article from the *Washington Republican*, describing the new Postage Currency, was reprinted in the *Emporia News*.

FISK & ESKRIDGE DRY GOODS
(Merchant Scrip)

Fisk & Eskridge ran a dry goods business at Emporia. In June of 1862 they were advertising an extensive stock of goods including, hats, caps, shoes, groceries, tin ware, nails and window frames. They dealt exclusively in cash. They also were offering to purchase both green and dried hides and furs and to pay taxes for non-local property owner/investors. Mr. C.V. Eskridge was a notary public.

By August the firm was also advertising as local agents for the Emporia and Lawrence Express Line. This line apparently ran daily connecting with Leavenworth and the Kansas City area. One could order and receive goods from Leavenworth in only four days!

Charles Vernon Eskridge was born in Virginia in 1833. He went from there to Ohio, Illinois, and Lawrence, Kansas, by 1855. He was initially employed as a printer and writer for the Free State newspaper *Herald of Freedom*. Soon thereafter he moved to Lyon County, where he helped to establish the town of Emporia. He went on to serve the town and the state through his own newspaper, *The Emporia Republican*, and in local and state politics. He served several terms in the State Legislature and profited handsomely from land development and railroad promotion. During the 1890s, Eskridge allied himself with officials of the First National Bank of Emporia. After the bank failed disastrously in 1898, Eskridge never recovered financially and took his own life in 1900.

101. .50 or $1.00, June, 1862; No other information .... SENC

J.R. Swallow & Co.
(Merchant Scrip)

J.R. Swallow was County Treasurer of Lyon County in 1862. In July of that year he advertised in the *Emporia News* to "buy and sell real estate, locate land warrants and pay taxes." He had town lots for sale in Emporia, Americus, Fremont and Neosho Rapids. In 1867, he opened the Bank of J.R. Swallow & Co., which became The Emporia Bank in 1869.

102. .50 or $1.00, June, 1862; Redeemable in sums of $5, ... SENC
no other information

Robert Wilson, Sutler
(Sutler Scrip)

Robert Wilson was the first sutler and post trader at Fort Riley. He served from 1853, when the post was originally established, until June 27, 1863. He built the first house there, and operated a large dry goods establishment, which supplied soldiers and civilians at the fort. Wilson had been a military storekeeper and sutler at other military posts, including Fort Leavenworth and Council Bluffs, Iowa.

In the March, 1862, issue of the *Smoky Hill and Republican Union* newspaper of Junction City a small notice appeared stating: "Shinplasters, Colonel Wilson, Sutler at Fort Riley, has in circulation one dollar notes, redeemable in current funds when presented in sums of five dollars. The scarcity of change makes them quite a convenience." None of these notes have surfaced to date.

Robert Wilson house, Fort Riley

140. $1.00, 1862; Redeemable in sums of $5, ... SENC
no further information

Fort Scott

Fort Scott, the military post, was established in 1842 on the then western border of the United States. Within ten years the frontier had moved further westward as freighters and pioneers moved over the Santa Fe and Oregon Trails, so Fort Scott was deactivated and replaced with new forts further westward in Kansas. The original Fort buildings were sold to the public and became the first homes and commercial buildings of the town of Fort Scott.

During the Civil War, the Union Army took over most of Fort Scott and turned it into a supply depot. All the buildings in town and the old fort were used to store government goods. By 1862, the local population was estimated at about 500 persons and new construction was booming. Volunteer military units were mustered into federal service there, including the First Kansas Colored Volunteer Infantry Regiment. The sutler for this unit, Harvey Spaulding, issued the only known example of sutler scrip yet discovered for the entire state of Kansas.

The *Fort Scott Bulletin* dated January 16, 1863, ran an article stating "The issue of shinplasters is getting to be a nuisance in this section, as well as in other portions of the state. Nearly every peddler, banker and rum shop has his pasteboard in circulation, with the inscription, good for one shave, good for one drink, good for 10 cents, and then signed by Tom, Dick and Harry. If the advance in paper keeps up, as it has during the past month, the blanks will be worth the most in reality. Since the visit of the U.S. Tax Assessor, this currency has very much depreciated. The hundred dollar tax being an item for some of these institutions, they are fast fizzling out." In the same issue there was an article about the glut of U.S. silver coinage in Canada. The local citizens were trying to get rid of it by using it for payment of taxes, etc. Banks were refusing to take silver. At Toronto, U.S.

Street scene at Fort Scott c. 1860

silver was being discounted 5 percent to Canadian paper. They "had it by the bushel," while it was non-existent in the states.

In 1862/1863, three local Fort Scott merchants are known to have issued small denomination notes to alleviate the small change shortage. They were R.D. Lender, who ran an eating saloon, White & Bridgens' dry goods store, and J.S. Miller, who was listed as a hardware merchant and private banker. Surviving notes are very rare.

In 1864, General Sterling Price's Confederate Army would suffer defeat at the Battle of Mine Creek, near Fort Scott, following the Battle of Westport, Missouri. After the war, the military left again, and the town was left to develop on its own. The old fort buildings continued to be used by the local citizens and gradually deteriorated. In recent years, the U.S. Department of the Interior has restored the remaining original buildings and reconstructed others to recreate the 1840s fort as a national monument.

R.D. Lender & Co.
(Merchant Scrip)

Richard D. Lender ran an eating saloon with bar "across from the *Fort Scott Bulletin* office." He first appeared in the local press on September 20, 1862. The price of a meal at his establishment was 25 cents. He issued small denomination scrip during the war. In 1863 he entered a partnership with Henry Ernich, and they ran a grocery business. Their store was located on Scott Avenue, two doors north of Locust (First) Street. In 1868, R.D. Lender commanded Company G, 19th Kansas Volunteer Cavalry Regiment, a unit formed to punish marauding Indians on the western frontier of the state.

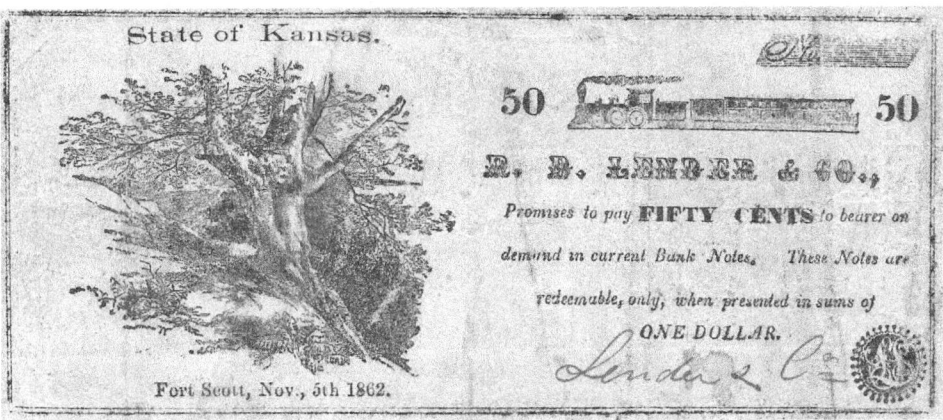

145. .50, Nov. 5, 1862. No plate letter. Uniface. No imprint . . . . Unique

J.S. MILLER
(Merchant Scrip)

John S. Miller and his family arrived in Fort Scott on March 5, 1860. Originally from Pennsylvania, he soon became involved in the business affairs of Fort Scott and Bourbon County. Miller was elected city Mayor on August 25, 1862. His business activities included a hardware store and banking. His place of business was located on the west side of William Street between Weir and Bigler. (This address today is the west side of Main between Wall and Market Streets.) He also performed contracting services for the government.

The *Fort Scott Bulletin* dated November 8, 1862, reported that several private banking offices were in operation in the town. "Among (these offices) we know of none better than that of J.S. Miller, of this city. His notes are only for the fractional part of a dollar, and were issued solely to overcome a public necessity. Mr. Miller's notes are as good as his word and every one is as safe as Uncle Sam's greenbacks." John Miller apparently spent the rest of his life at Fort Scott, since his wife passed away there in 1879.

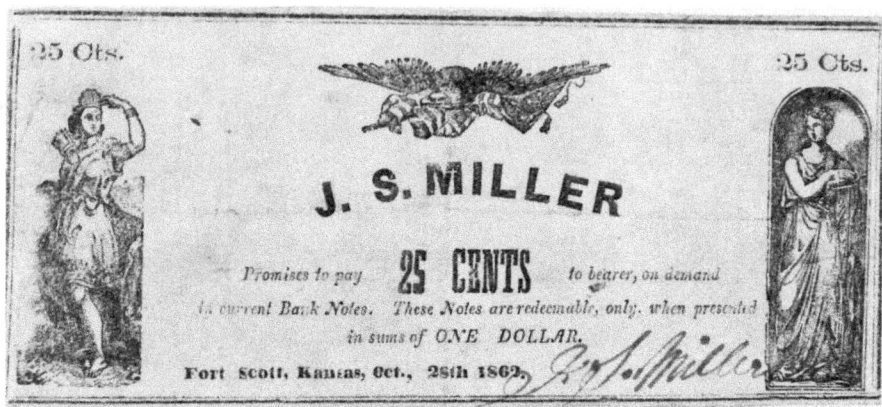

154e. .25, Oct. 28, 1862. No plate letter. Uniface. No imprint. . . . . Unique
This appears to be an incomplete note, perhaps the trial specimen or "essay." "Kansas" only appears on the date line.

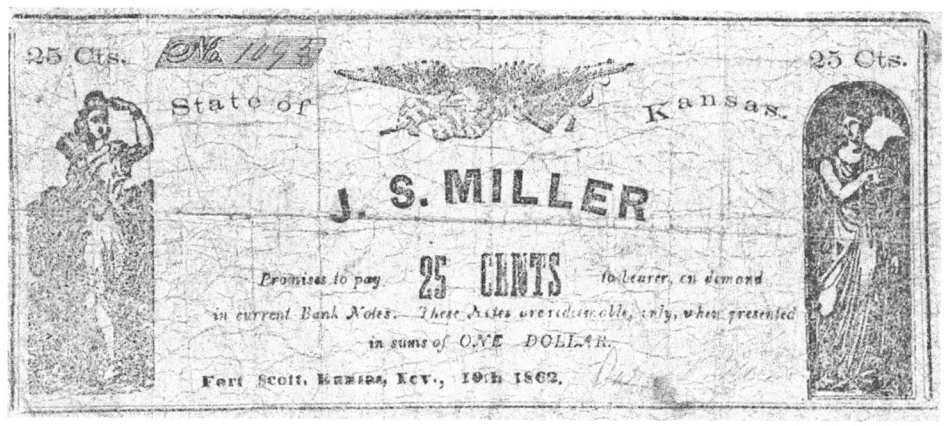

155. .25, Nov. 5, 1862. No plate letter. Uniface. No imprint. R-7

WHITE & BRIDGENS
(Merchant Scrip)

John F. White came to Kansas from Pennsylvania in June, 1858. He operated George A. Crawford's general store at Trading Post, Kansas, for two years. In 1860, he opened his own store at Fort Scott. He would later serve as Treasurer of Bourbon County. The dry goods establishment of White & Bridgens was located on Bigler Street, two doors east of the Post Office.

By 1865, John White's dry goods store was the largest of its kind at Fort Scott. "Bridgens" was undoubtedly J. Thomas Bridgens, a lawyer, who would serve as Quartermaster of the 24th Regiment of Kansas State Militia. This unit was formed at Fort Scott in early 1864 when Confederate General Sterling Price threatened eastern Kansas with an army out of Arkansas.

III. Civil War Crisis, 1861–1865

White & Bridgens issued small denomination scrip during the war, using standard Doty & McFarlan blanks that were overprinted with issuer information.

162. .05, 186_ printed, balance of date to be written in. . . . . Unique
No plate letter. Imprint; Doty & McFarlan, NewYork

165. .50, as above

ENGLEHART & FAIRCHILD
(Merchant Scrip)

Mr. Jacob Englehart and R. Scott Fairchild ran a pioneer dry goods store in Hiawatha. During the money crisis of 1862, they, like many other merchants, issued scrip in the form of $1 bills. The town declined severely during the war as most men left to join the Union Army. The local newspaper, established in the Spring of 1861, was destroyed by a fire during its first winter. It did not reopen until August 20, 1864. By 1865 with the war's end, former soldiers began returning to Hiawatha.

On January 20, 1865, an advertisement appeared in the *Union Sentinel* stating: "The Pioneer Store of Englehart & Fairchild is in full blast again." The ad was dated October 3, 1864, and listed the following goods for sale: "Staple and Fancy Dry Goods, Ready Made Clothing, Boots and Shoes, Boy's and Men's Hats and Caps, Ladies Felt and Straw Hats, Groceries, Crockery, Queensware, Glassware, Hardware, Tinware, Willow Ware and Wooden Ware, Tobacco and Cigars and Canned Fruits." Clearly the town was on the road to economic recovery.

On January 19, 1866, a notice appeared in the *Sentinel* that a new firm was to be established. "Messrs. Graves and Seburn, R. Scott Fairchild and Captain Morrill are forming a copartnership for the transaction of business on a somewhat larger scale than before...." Captain Morrill was Edmund N. Morrill who had been discharged from the Army in October, 1865. A.T. Andreas, in his *History of Kansas*, says that "Morrill went into business with R.S. Fairchild upon his return from the Army."

In the January 26, 1866, issue of the paper, the following business cards appear under merchants: "R.S. Fairchild, Dealer in Dry Goods, etc., East side of 6th Street, Opposite the Courthouse." Under Druggists and Grocers is found; "Graves and Seburn; Dealer in Drugs, etc. East of Courthouse, Hiawatha." There was also an advertisement for Fairchild, Morrill & Co., Dry Goods. Apparently Mr. Jacob Englehart had left the business by that time. Henry Graves was listed as Town Clerk from Irwin, Brown County, in 1868. Mr. W.B. Barnett had purchased the store of H.R. Dutton and B.L. Rider in 1858. He also served on the County Board of Supervisors. Harvey Seburn was the Town Clerk of Hiawatha. Edmund Needham Morrill's biography appears on page 213 of Volume X of the *Kansas State Historical Society Collections*. He served as president of the First National Bank of Leavenworth, spent four terms in the U.S. Congress and was Governor of the state of Kansas.

On January 2, 1871, W.B. Barnett, E.N. Morrill, and Lorenzo Janes, along with Jane's son Charles, opened a private bank over the stone drug store at the corner of 6th and Oregon Streets in Hiawatha. The bank was known as Barnett, Morrill & Co. A year later they constructed a new building at the same corner. In 1877, W.B. Barnett and Lorenzo Janes retired from the bank. Barnett went to Florida where he later founded the Barnett National Bank. Janes gave his interest to his son. In 1887, the firm applied for and received a state charter to incorporate as the Morrill & Janes Bank. This bank published a centennial pamphlet in 1971.

175. $1.00, 186_ printed, balance of date to be entered. Uniface, imprint R-7
M.H. Traubel Lith., 409 Chestnut St., Phila. Face in green and black. This specimen in Stack's January 18, 2005, sale brought $1,600.

Post–Civil War check drawn on Barnett, Morrill & Co., Hiawatha, Kansas

Junction City

STREETER & STRICKLER
(Merchant Scrip)

In the fall of 1857, the Junction City Town Company was organized. Treasurer of the new town Company was Robert Wilson, Sutler at Fort Riley. In 1859, Mr. William Leamer opened a dry goods establishment in the new town.

Samuel M. Strickler was born in Tennessee in 1832, and soon moved to Indiana where he grew up to attend Franklin College. After college he went to Alabama where he engaged in business for awhile before moving to Kansas in 1860. James Streeter was born in Springfield, Vermont, in 1824. He wound up in Junction at about the same time and went into business with Mr. Strickler. In 1860, the new firm bought out William Leamer's store and opened for business. In addition to selling dry goods, the business would furnish contracted supplies and transportation to government posts on the plains.

An advertisement in the *Junction City Statesman* on October 13, 1860, showed the firm located on Washington Street, between Sixth and Seventh Streets. They were dealing in dry goods, groceries, drugs, medicines, paint, stoves, nails, saddles and liquor. The approaching war brought hard times to the area. By February of 1861, the firm announced they would make no more credit sales. Interest rates were running at 20 percent per year. By September, 1861, the firm had moved to the Post Office Block, between Seventh and Eighth Streets. Milton E. Clark was manager of the store.

On September 26, 1861, the local papers announced that the new government Demand Notes, in denominations of $5 and $10, had appeared in the area. These were the first paper money issues for general circulation made by the federal government. The proposed new state banking law was also published in the press.

On November 26, 1861, a notice appeared that Streeter and Strickler had commenced construction of a new building at the southeast corner of Seventh and Washington Streets. This was the first brick building to be erected in Junction City. The building was two stories with the storeroom located on the first floor. That same month the firm advertised that they wanted to

Samuel M. Strickler

James Streeter

exchange 50,000 pounds of pork and 25,000 bushels of corn for debts owed to the firm. Sometime in 1861, James Streeter left Junction for Tennessee, where he would remain for two years.

In February, 1862, the *Junction City Union* newspaper owned by Samuel Strickler, relocated into the basement of his commercial building. By April, Streeter & Strickler were issuing scrip to meet the needs of commerce. The paper announced that the notes had been issued because of the scarcity of small change. At that time the smallest federal denomination was $5 and small change had been exported out of the country. Two notes dated May 1, and Nov. 1, 1862, have survived in denominations of .25 and $1 respectively. The notes were redeemable in U.S. Treasury notes in sums of $5. On June 16, 1862, Streeter & Strickler moved into their new building. In August, the firm exhibited examples of Confederate (i.e. southern or Rebel) money in denominations of 5 cents to $100.

On September 17, 1862, about 40 "bushwhackers" took over the town of Salina and looted supplies. The news caused much excitement around Junction City, and night guards were mounted for awhile.

On October 4, 1862, an article appeared in the *Junction City Union* expressing concern that merchants in Manhattan might be refusing to accept the "bills," i.e. scrip notes, of Streeter & Strickler. These allegations were rebutted in *The Manhattan Independent* one week later. The paper said that they had never refused the bills of any merchant in western Kansas.

In October, 1862, Samuel Strickler was elected to the Kansas State Senate. By 1863, Streeter & Strickler had taken action under Internal Revenue laws that "legitimized their issuance of scrip." Apparently there was some provision in the law that allowed scrip issue as long as federal tax was paid. Lewis Kurtz of Manhattan had also complied, so the *Union* announced that there were two houses issuing shinplasters under authority in the area, they being Kurtz of Manhattan and Streeter & Strickler of Junction City. An issue of fractional denominations, including 10-, 25-, and 50-cent notes was made by the firm in May, 1863, of which several survivors are known. In June, 1863, a notice appeared that Streeter & Strickler had sold $500 worth of Davis County scrip at par. And also in June, Mr. James Streeter returned to Junction City from Tennessee, where he had spent the last two years. He went back to Tennessee in August, but expected to return in the fall.

On August 21, 1863, Lawrence was destroyed by Quantrill's guerrillas. This led to the appointment of Samuel Strickler to organize the militia in Geary and surrounding counties. The next day Streeter & Strickler loaded 30 wagons with corn for Fort Larned. The train was scheduled to leave on September 5, and they were advertising for additional teams and drovers. On August 29, Senator Strickler took donations that had been collected for the people of Lawrence to that city.

In the fall, a competing firm applied pressure to Streeter & Strickler by preventing payment of nearly $200,000 of government drafts at Leavenworth. Strickler was able to ship $10,000 worth of clothing to Junction City which enabled his employees to get through the Winter, and thereby relieve the pressure on the firm.

On December 5, 1863, the paper announced that the "new interest bearing currency of the government had appeared at Junction." These notes were dated May 3, 1863. "The unimportant residue of the present issue of legal tenders is being forwarded to Washington in small daily sums," and "a bountiful supply of greenbacks were disbursed to the

III. Civil War Crisis, 1861–1865

Adjacent dry goods stores of James Streeter and Strickler & Church at Junction City, Kansas, c. 1870.

troops at Fort Riley last week." On December 28, Streeter & Strickler advertised to buy $200 in Davis County scrip at 75 cents to the dollar.

In January, 1864, *The Smoky Hill and Republican Union* newspaper was relocated from Strickler's basement to Eighth and Franklin Streets. Strickler remained editor and publisher. On April 16, 1864, an article in the paper noted that the price of a newspaper at Nachitoches, where General Banks' army was located, was .10 in greenbacks or $2.50 in local shinplasters. In June it was considered noteworthy that a silver three-cent piece had been seen in Junction. Its value was two and a half cents [*sic*] in greenbacks. James Streeter returned in July after an extended absence in Tennessee. On July 24 the paper reported that a soldier was in the guardhouse at Fort Riley for pilfering five and ten-cent U.S. Postage Currency notes from the cash drawer at the Post Sutler's store. Henry Mayer was Post Sutler at the time. It seems that the soldier had been able to reach the small denomination compartment of the cash register over the counter and had been doing so for some time.

By August, the firm was loading a big train with corn for Fort Larned. The train was to be well armed because of the recent Indian troubles. In October, a Confederate Army under General Sterling Price began an advance out of Arkansas and headed for St. Louis. This Confederate invasion would finally be repulsed at the battle of Westport near Kansas City, on October 29, 1864. Union forces and Kansas militia had finally brought the Confederate Army to battle along the Blue River. They continued to advance until defeated before Westport, whereupon they were forced to retreat southward along the Kansas/Missouri border until Union forces caught up with them at Mine Creek. This

Draft on the Bank of James Streeter

battle, near Fort Scott, was the largest military action fought on Kansas soil during the Civil War. Price was again defeated, and the remnants of his Army retreated into Arkansas where they remained until the end of the war.

On May 6, 1866, the firm of Hale & Kirkendall was established. This was the first bank at Junction City. It soon became known as Hale & Rice. General Rice tried to obtain a national bank charter, but the firm ran into financial difficulties after $15,000 disappeared in a nighttime burglary on March 26, 1868. The period after the war until late 1867 was a boom period in Kansas as emigration brought new business and associated commercial buildings to the area. In June, 1867, James Streeter opened a bank in company with Robert O. Rizer on Washington Street in the Streeter & Strickler block. Rizer had been discharged from the Army at Fort Riley in 1865 and settled in Junction City. He worked as a bookkeeper in the firm of Streeter & Strickler until the banking venture with Streeter in 1867. This bank was the forerunner of the first First National Bank of Junction City. Mr. Rizer was elected city mayor four times and would entertain Buffalo Bill, Sitting Bull, the Grand Duke Alexis, Wild Bill Hickok and former president U.S. Grant. He hired "Wild Bill" to clean up Junction City in the 1870s.

Between 1867 and 1871, the city issued scrip or treasurer's warrants, without much accountability, to pay for various services. No examples of this scrip have surfaced. In February, 1868 Streeter & Strickler bought out John T. Price, the sutler at Fort Riley and took over the operation at the Post. They, in turn, sold the operation to the McGonigle brothers in 1869. During 1868 and 1869 a business recession occurred. On May 15, 1869, James Streeter dissolved a partnership with David H. Smith in the Hale House. In 1870 Streeter became Treasurer in the city administration of Robert Rizer.

On January 1, 1870, the firm of Streeter & Strickler was dissolved. Strickler retired and Streeter continued to run the business. The newspaper of February 22 announced the dissolution of the merchandising part of the business, and said that Streeter was going back east to buy new supplies for the store. In March reports of failure of the business appeared, apparently brought on by the recession of 1868-1869. A Mr. A.W. Callen was called on to close out the business.

On July 9, just a few months later, a new ad appeared for Strickler & Church. Strickler was back in business, next door to the old store. Streeter's newspaper continued to run ads for his store. Strickler & Church apparently had some difficulties getting their store opened, but were finally successful. In 1871, Samuel Strickler was serving in the Kansas House of Representatives.

In the collections of the Kansas State Historical Society, there is a beautifully engraved draft drawn on the Banking House of James Streeter, dated April 24, 1871. On May 1, 1872, the First National Bank of Junction City received national charter #1977. R. McBratney was president of the newly organized bank and James Streeter was vice president. W.B. Clarke was cashier. An original series $10 national bank note issued by this bank has survived, signed by W.B. Clarke as cashier and James Streeter as vice president. The plate date on the note is May 15, 1872. On June 13, 1872, work began on a new building for the bank at the northwest corner of Washington and Seventh Streets. On June 25, 1872, the bank received its first shipment of national bank notes.

185. .25, May 1, 1862 printed date; plate B. Uniface, imprint . . . . Unique
Smoky Hill and Republican Union Print

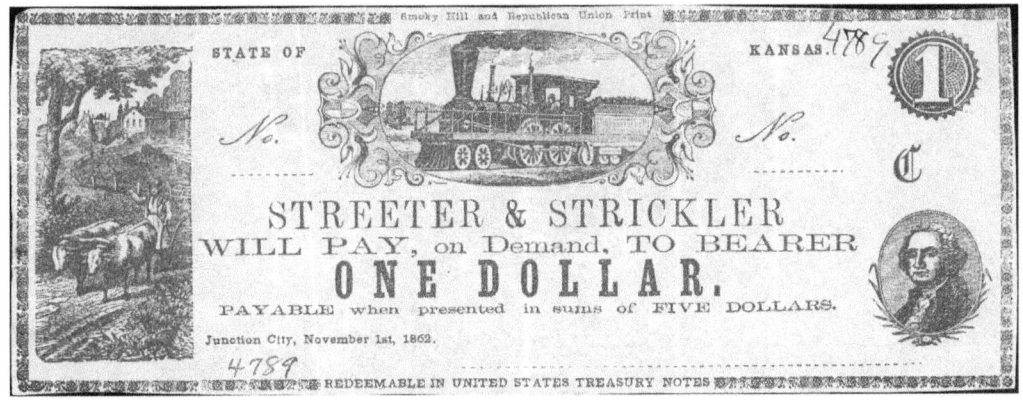

186. $1.00, November 1, 1862, printed date, plate letter C. . . . . Unique
Printed in light blue ink. Similar to # 185 above except for denomination. Same imprint

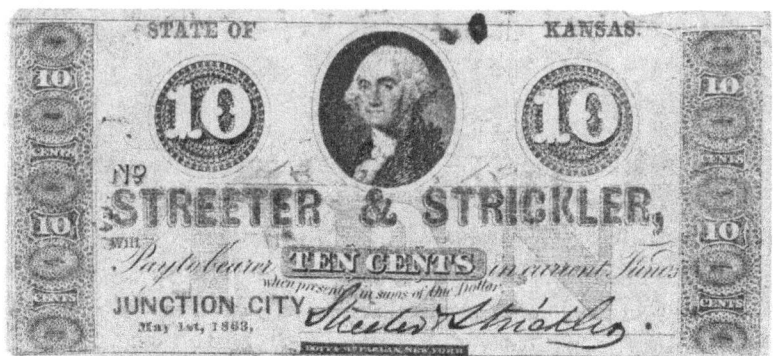

187. .10, May 1, 1863 printed date. No plate letter. Imprint: Doty & R-7
McFarlan, New York. Printed in green and black.
Back "Payable at our counter in Junction City or at the office
of N. McCracken, Leavenworth, Kans"

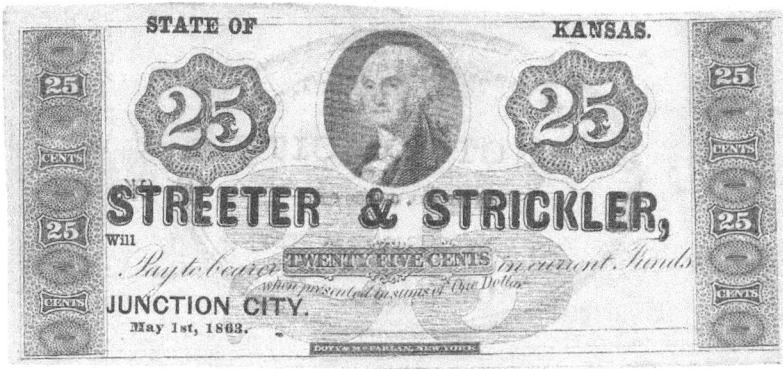

188. .25, Same as # 187 above except for denomination R-6
189. .50, Same as # 187 above except for denomination .... Unique

Manhattan

LEWIS KURTZ
(Merchant Scrip)

Lewis Kurtz opened a dry goods store in 1858 on the south side of Poyntz Avenue, near the center of the present day 300 block. His advertisements began to appear in the Manhattan newspaper in 1859.

On Saturday, November 23, 1861, a notice appeared in the *Western Kansas Express* of Manhattan titled "Missouri Money," stating "Missouri money taken at par for goods if presented soon. I redeem all my one dollar bills in gold or good eastern funds. L. Kurtz." On November 28, 1861, Kurtz advertised as a "dealer in groceries, provisions, clothing, dry goods, etc., everything usually kept in a first class country store. Will receive country produce in exchange for goods, wheat, corn, oats, pork, tallow, hides, potatoes, turnips, onions, in fact nearly everything a farmer raises." On April 1, 1862, he wanted to buy hides and furs and offered to still take Missouri money at par, if presented soon.

Lewis Kurtz advertised regularly in Manhattan and the Junction City papers. An editorial comment in the March 7, 1863, issue of the *Smoky Hill and Republican Union* of Junction City stated Kurtz was one of the best and most reliable businessmen in Manhattan. "He takes all Western Kansas shinplasters at par."

On March 21, 1863, an article appeared in the Junction City paper titled, "A reliable currency." The article stated; "Lewis Kurtz, who advertises regularly in Junction, has made his currency legitimate and accordingly extended its circulation. Mr. Kurtz has taken out a banker's license under the Internal Revenue Law and made arrangements for the redemption of his bills at Leavenworth. Our settlers who do business at Leavenworth, will thus be relieved of the inconvenience arising from the non-circulation of these notes at a distance. We now have two houses in Western Kansas issuing shinplasters under authority, which are enough to supply the demand. Settlers can therefore take the bills of Kurtz of Manhattan, and Streeter & Strickler of Junction as a reliable currency." Kurtz' ad in the same issue announced that his currency could be redeemed at his own place of business in Manhattan or at the firms of N. McCracken, and Thompson, Woodruff & Co., Leavenworth grocery dealers.

On July 4, 1863, a new notice appeared in Kurtz' advertisements as follows: "My currency is redeemable at the Banking House of Scott, Kerr & Co., Leavenworth." This notice appeared once a month until at least November, 1864. This may indicate that Kurtz' notes continued to circulate even after the new federal fractional currency became available.

After the Quantrill raid on Lawrence, the Mayor closed all Manhattan business houses for militia drill, every day from 2:00 to 4:00 P.M. Lewis Kurtz served as Secretary of the local "Governor's Guards."

By May of 1866, Kurtz had opened a branch store in St. George, a settlement located eight miles east of Manhattan on the Kansas River. He remodeled his Manhattan store that same year. Kurtz sold out his business interest in September, 1870, after complaining in the newspaper that "certain persons had been spreading rumors regarding his pending breakup for the past 3 years." He offered a reward for a stolen dog on October 21, 1870. After that, no record of Mr. Kurtz at Manhattan has been found.

A single note issued by Lewis Kurtz is known to have survived. It is a 5-cent piece. Since one of the newspaper reports referred to $1 notes he issued, the only two confirmed denominations are therefore the 5-cent and $1 note. He undoubtedly also issued other fractional values of scrip.

346. .05, January 31, 1863, printed date. Imprint: Doty & McFarlan, ... Unique
New York. "FIVE" on back in red
345. $1.00, No description . . . . SENC

John Pipher & Co.
(Merchant Scrip)

John Pipher was born August 26, 1811, in Chester County, Pennsylvania. He grew up to become a judge in Ohio and was later a member of the Cincinnati and Kansas Land Company, which purchased the steamboat *Hartford* and departed for Kansas in 1855. It was their intent to establish a settlement in support of Kansas' becoming a free state. They took with them ten pre-fabricated houses, and a meeting house to be erected at the new town.

The boat was unable to advance further up the Kansas River than the mouth of the Big Blue River. Arriving on April 26, the group joined forces with another group that had established a townsite called New Boston. The two town companies formed an association and John Pipher was elected president. The new town was named Manhattan. On June 28, 1855, John Pipher was elected as the first mayor.

Mr. Pipher acted as an agent for the land company for about a year at which time he and his son, John W., took over operation of the town's first business establishment, a dry goods store. The store, originally owned by a man named Miller, stood at present day 130 Poyntz Avenue. It seems that Mr. Miller wanted the Piphers to sell liquor, but John steadfastly refused.

John Pipher in later years

III. Civil War Crisis, 1861–1865

Manhattan, Kansas, in 1860

This disagreement eventually led to dissolution of the business arrangement and, soon thereafter, John Pipher constructed a new wooden store building near the southeast corner of present day Third and Poyntz Avenue. (Prior to renumbering of the streets in 1908, this was called Second Street.) The new dry goods firm operated under the name of John Pipher and Son.

On February 14, 1857, Manhattan was incorporated as a third class city by the territorial legislature. John Pipher was elected to the city council in the first election for the new city. From 1855 to 1860, he would also serve as Justice of the Peace. In 1860, he became the Probate Judge of Riley County, a position he would hold until 1868. John Pipher, or "the Judge" as he was referred to, also established the Methodist Church of Manhattan.

On June 2, 1860, John's brother George joined the business, which changed its name to John Pipher and Company. The firm did a general dry goods business, buying or exchanging farm produce and selling seed, implements, dishware and anything else needed to live and work at the time.

The Civil War had an early and significant effect on the area, then known as "western Kansas," as men left to join the Union Army and inflation took real money out of circulation. By the fall of 1861, hard times had caused many debtors to fall behind in their

John Pipher & Son Dry Goods store, from an 1860s map of Manhattan

obligations or not to make any payments at all. On November 23, 1861, John Pipher ran a notice in the *Manhattan Express* stating that "Persons who owe money to John Pipher & Co. will please bring in their cash, wheat and corn immediately, as we cannot allow them (unpaid accounts) to run on indefinitely." At the time Mr. Pipher was also serving as Deputy Postmaster, and later became Postmaster of the town.

In June, 1862, new advertisements appeared representing John Pipher & Co. as the "Manhattan Commercial Emporium." The variety of goods for sale, which had to be transported overland by wagon from Leavenworth, was astounding.

By July, 1861, John Pipher & Co. was issuing scrip because of the shortage of small denomination notes. A note of the $1 denomination is known bearing this date. The firm also issued fractional denomination scrip of .10, .25, and .50, dated November 1, 1862, because small change had disappeared from circulation. For some reason the scrip issues of John Pipher are not mentioned in contemporary newspaper accounts although several others do appear.

At that time, the Manhattan and Junction City newspaper editors were roundly criticizing each other over real and imagined grievances, although Manhattan merchants still advertised extensively in the Junction City paper. The *Junction City Union* ran an ad on December 27, 1862, that touted the "Farmers Store" of John Pipher & Co., at the "old stand, 353 Poyntz Avenue." (There were no building numbers in use at the time and the number "353" was actually the lot number.) These lots were wide enough to accommodate two adjacent buildings and it has not been positively determined exactly where Pipher's store stood. An illustration of his dry goods store appears on an 1867 advertising map of the city that depicts the store adjacent to a three story building to its west. That building, R.M. Elliott's Grocery Store, was later converted to a two story structure with a brick front to house the Manhattan Bank of Mr. E.B. Purcell. It stood on the eastern half of the lot adjacent to Pipher's. Therefore, it appears that Pipher's store was originally located two doors west of the corner at present day Third and Poyntz.

Two other important early dry goods firms in Manhattan were owned by Lewis Kurtz and the Higinbotham brothers, both established before 1860. Three of the Higinbothams, George W., William P., and Uriah established a store in the middle of today's 300 block on the south side of Poyntz. In 1863, Uriah left the firm to establish his own store "across the street." He died in 1864, but the other two brothers continued to operate in competition with John Pipher, Lewis Kurtz and others.

By February, 1865, brother George Pipher had branched out and was advertising a new furniture store on Poyntz above Higinbotham's. His partner in the new business was George Brown, John Pipher's son-in-law. Presumably George Pipher had given up his interest in the dry goods store because John's ads had changed to read "Jonathon Pipher and Son, The old Stand, Second and Poyntz," and "John Pipher & Son, Farmers Store on Second and Poyntz."

In the fall of 1866, a new merchant entrepreneur arrived in Manhattan. This was Mr. E.B. Purcell, from Pennsylvania. He bought out the stock of the Higinbotham's on November 14, 1866. William Higinbotham then opened a bank at the southwest corner of present day Fourth and Poyntz streets. That bank eventually became the Union Bank. It took national charter #4008 in 1889 to become the Union National Bank, which was still doing business in the 1990s. George Higinbotham would get back into the dry goods business with Mr. Purcell in 1868. In 1866, John Pipher advertised to sell carpenter's tools, tailor made clothes and miscellaneous dry goods. He also wanted to buy Pottawottamie County scrip.

On April 27, 1867, a notice appeared in the newspaper that John Pipher's store had been dismantled and would be relocated further west on Poyntz to make room for a large new building. The new building was to be erected by Mr. E.B. Purcell. Mr. Purcell built a stone building east of the old Pipher store location, on the corner, and replaced Pipher's old building with a new brick building. John Pipher's ad on June 1, 1867, stated that his goods were temporarily located at Wisner's Drug Store, across Second Street at the southwest corner of Poyntz, and that he wanted to sell them so he would not have to move them again.

The 1867 newspaper article indicates that Pipher's original building was dismantled and relocated sometime in 1867. At about the same time, Mr. Purcell began to build a new building, or buildings, on the corner lot where Pipher's store had been located.

On June 1, 1867, an advertisement appeared for John Pipher's son, John W., in partnership with Joseph Carney. The 1867 Manhattan map shows this firm's building, which stood on the north side of Poyntz in the present day 300 block. The illustration is titled "Pipher and Carneys" and the storefront is lettered "Groceries, Hardware & Queensware." Since the elder Pipher's ad, dated October 12, 1867, lists his business simply as "John Pipher" (without the "& Son"), it appears that John W. had left his father's store by that time.

The semi-centennial edition of the *Manhattan Nationalist*, dated June 16, 1910, related that Judge John Pipher sold his store and merchandise to E.B. Purcell and George W. Higinbotham in March, 1868. Higinbotham ran part of their dry goods operation from the brick building that had replaced the old Pipher store on the south side of Poyntz, while Mr. Purcell operated a store on the north side. The north side store stood at present day #302 Poyntz, on the northwest corner of former Second Street and Poyntz. The 1867 illustrated map of Manhattan also shows this building with the title "Purcell & Higinbotham."

On May 9, 1868, a notice appeared announcing the new firm of Purcell & Higinbotham at the corner of old Second and Poyntz. And, on March 20, 1869, a new firm of George W. Higinbotham & Company was announced. The "Company" consisted of Ashford Stingley and Orville Huntress. Mr. Huntress had been in business at Manhattan since 1859.

On May 7, 1870, E.B. Purcell opened a bank in conjunction with his mercantile business. This was the Manhattan Bank, located three doors west of the southwest corner of present day Third and Poyntz. The Manhattan bankers were all busy at the time buying up state scrip and treasury warrants of the various municipalities that had issued them. In the *Nationalist* issue of May 6, 1870, William P. Higinbotham was advertising to buy Price Raid Scrip, State Scrip and warrants. On September 3, 1870, a new dry goods firm, Huntress & Elliott, opened for business on Poyntz.

In January, 1871, E.B. Purcell bought out George Higinbotham's interest in their firm and began to add to his building complex at the southwest corner. He modernized the front of his bank building, as previously mentioned, and expanded the corner building to the south.

In the April, 1871, Business Directory section of the newspaper, John W. Pipher, the son, advertised that he was re-establishing himself as a dealer in dry goods. "He was formerly in business here and is well known." He advertised to sell "Wet Goods, Plows, Flour, Feed, Meal, Bran, Grain, Wooden and Willow Ware, and Heavy Groceries."

Another ad appeared on May 31, 1872, touting the "Cash House of E.B. Purcell, Merchant and Banker, Manhattan Bank; E.B. Purcell, Banker, Jno W. Webb, Cashier." The same issue of the paper reported that William Higinbotham, Banker, was an agent for the Allen Line of ocean steamers as well as the "celebrated Studebaker Wagons."

On March 14, 1873, the first First National Bank of Manhattan opened for business at lot #20 on Poyntz Avenue. Stephen French was president and J.K. Winchip was cashier. This bank, which was liquidated in April, 1877, and succeeded by the Riley County Bank, had no apparent relationship with any of the pioneer merchants mentioned here.

Then, on June 9, 1876, the papers announced that "the Judge and George were on hand again. Jno and George Pipher, three doors west of the Post Office." They were dealing in "Family and Fancy Groceries." In 1878, John Pipher was again elected to serve as Mayor of the city.

John Pipher finally retired from business activities around 1880. He continued as an influential leader in the community and church until his death on June 13, 1900. He is buried, along with his wife, in the Sunset Cemetery at Manhattan. Today the only reminder of this Manhattan pioneer and merchant is the name of a city street and a few pieces of scrip he issued during the Civil War.

The 1861 $1.00 note surfaced in the Stack's Ford Sale in 2005. Fred Marchkoff also reported a $3 and $5 denomination for Pipher in an old ANA article but these notes have not surfaced.

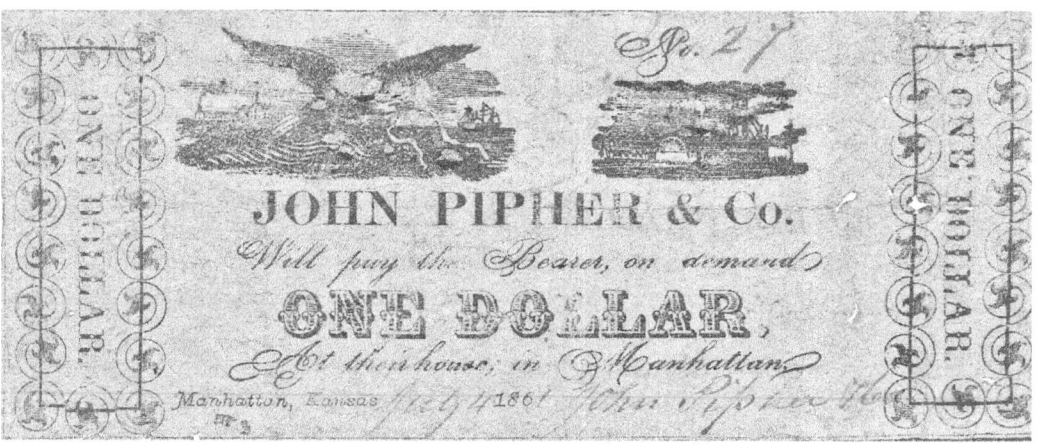

351. $1.00, 186_ printed, balance of date to be written in. . . . . Unique
July 4, 1861, seen. Newsprint, no imprint visible.
(S.N. 27 seen) (L) Eagle with spread wings,
(R) Steamboat

III. Civil War Crisis, 1861–1865

356. .10, 186_ printed, balance of date to be entered. .... Unique
    (Nov. 1, 1862 seen) Uniface, no plate letter.
    Imprint: Middleton, Strobridge & Co. Cin.

357. .25, Same as #356 above, except for denomination .... Unique

358. .50, Presumed identical to above except for denomination .... SENC

359. $1.00, 186_ printed, balance of date to be entered. .... Unique
    (September, 1862 seen) Uniface, imprint:
    Middleton, Strobridge & Co

360. **$2.00, 186_ printed as above. Center vignette differs** .... Unique
   from the $1as two stallions beside a stream.
   Uniface, imprint as above
   Note: Fred Marckhoff also reported that the $3 and $5 denominations were issued

Paola

WM. W. PINNEO DRY GOODS
(Merchant Scrip)

William W. Pinneo ran a dry goods store in Paola during the Civil War. Paola is the County Seat of Miami County in northeastern Kansas. In the spring of 1862, Pinneo issued scrip in the known denomination of $1. The notes were redeemable in sums of $5. This note surfaced in the Schingoethe sale of October 23, 2004.

Mr. Pinneo was born in Nova Scotia in 1822. He is listed in the 1865 Kansas census as living next to a store in Paola.

365. **$1.00, May 15, 1862 printed date. (L) Agriculture vignette** .... Unique
   kneeling by Indian princess; "ONE" in red above.
   (R) Milkmaid and cow; red overprinted
   "ONE DOLLAR." Uniface, no imprint

III. Civil War Crisis, 1861–1865

Paola, Kansas, in 1862

Seneca

LAPPIN & SCRAFFORD
(Merchant Scrip)

Seneca was founded in 1857 by a town company that included Samuel Lappin and Charles G. Scrafford. The original townsite had been called Rock Castle. Seneca was a stop on the Overland Stage Line from 1859 to 1867. In 1861, the town served as one of the stations on the Pony Express. The population totaled about 300 persons at the end of the Civil War. On May 17, 1870, Seneca was incorporated as a city of the third class.

Sam Lappin came to Kansas in 1854. Charles G. Scrafford was the first merchant of Seneca. He was born in New York in 1829. He came to Kansas in 1856, and settled in White Cloud, where he built the first hotel there and a sawmill. In January of 1860 he opened the first "general store" in Seneca. He soon associated in business with his father-in-law, Mr. Samuel Lappin. In 1861 they constructed a permanent store on Main Street. The local newspaper, the *Nemaha Courier*, started in November, 1863, included a large ad for the firm with a woodcut illustration of their building. Built of stone, five stories in height, the structure was located on the corner of a cross street. In August, 1862, Sam Lappin was advertising in the *Topeka Tribune* as "Land and General Agent" on Main Street in Seneca. During the small change crisis of the Civil War, the firm issued small denomination scrip using a standard Doty & McFarlan printed scrip form. Denominations of .05, .10, and 50 cents are known. The firm remained in business until about 1868/69.

Samuel Lappin as Kansas State Treasurer

In 1870 the partners established a private bank and erected a brick building to house the bank on the north

Lappin & Scrafford store in Seneca in 1863

side of Main Street. During 1872 and 1873, C.G. Scrafford served as Mayor of the city. The affairs of the bank were wound up in the mid–1870s. The State Bank of Kansas, organized in December 1874, succeeded the business and location of the Lappin & Scrafford Bank. Sam Lappin was president of the new bank and Edwin Knowles was vice president. Willis Brown, who would later be associated with the Lawrence National Bank of Lawrence, was cashier. Charles Scrafford served as a Director of the new bank. In January, 1876, both Lappin and Scrafford withdrew from the bank.

Sam Lappin served in the state legislature, and was Quartermaster General for the state of Kansas. In January, 1875, he became State Treasurer. As Treasurer he got involved in a scheme to defraud the state by purchasing forged school district bonds. He was forced to resign on December 20, 1875, and jailed at Topeka. He escaped from jail in July, 1876, and eventually made his way to Peru in South America. Arrested in Oregon in 1884, the charges against him were eventually dropped for lack of evidence. He returned to Seneca for several years before moving to

Seneca, Kansas, c. 1870s

III. Civil War Crisis, 1861–1865

370. .05, No date or plate letter. Imprint: Doty & McFarlan, New York. R-7
Uniface black and red

371. .10, Nearly identical to #370 above except for denomination .... Unique

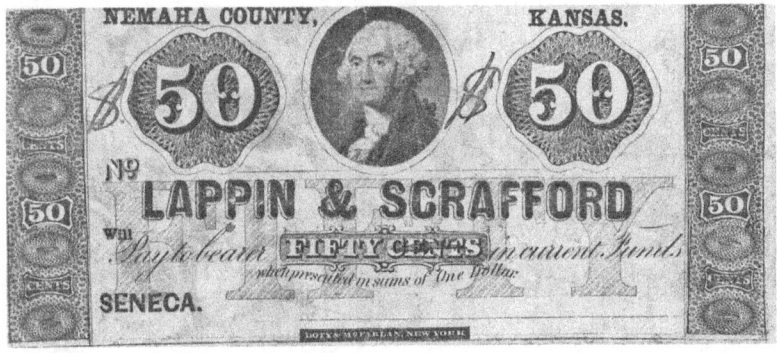

372. .50, Nearly identical to above except for denomination R-7

Washington state, where he died in 1892.

Lecompton

R.H. Farnham

(Merchant Banker)

R. H. Farnham was a pioneer dealer in land warrants and real estate. His first office was located one door north of the United States Land Office on North Elmore Street at

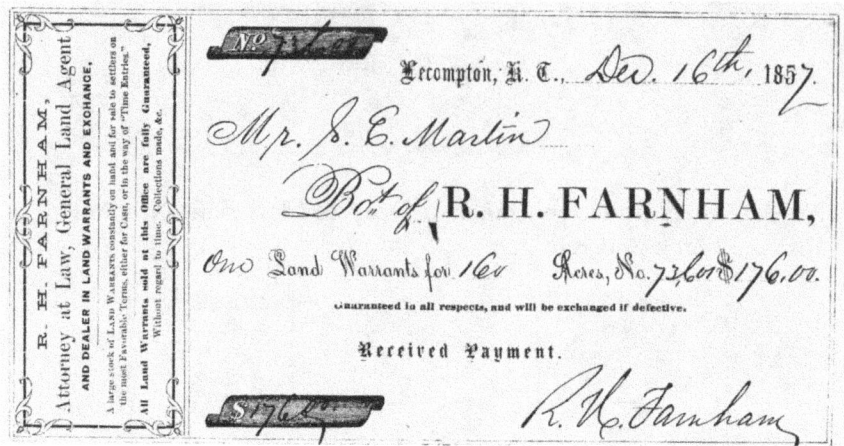

Land warrant receipt signed by R.H. Farnham, 1857

Lecompton in 1859. An advertisement in the *Lawrence Republican* newspaper, dated May 3, 1860, noted this address and the nature of his business. A land warrant receipt, signed by Farnham, reposes in the collections of the Kansas State Historical Society. The writer also has an 1859 cover postmarked at Lecompton with a corner advertisement of the firm.

In September, 1861, the Land Office was relocated to Topeka, the new State Capitol. At about the same time, Farnham apparently also moved to Topeka. This is based on the disappearance of his ads at Lecompton after 1861. On September 20, 1862, an article

Advertising cover for R.H. Farnham, Lecompton, Kansas, 1859

appeared in the *Topeka Tribune*, concerning the new U.S. Government postal currency. The article stated that, "for a year past, people have been hoarding silver, which was only sold at a premium." Shortly thereafter, Farnham introduced his own small denomination scrip to the area. Stock notes, overprinted "R.H. Farnham, Banker," and dated at Topeka, August 10, 1862, in amounts from 5 to 50 cents, were issued. Three signed examples are known to have survived with genuine signatures. The signature was "M.G. Farnham."

On August 30, 1862, an ad for one M.G. Farnham, land agent, appeared in the Topeka paper. The office was located in Gale's Block. M.G. Farnham offered to sell land warrants at a small percentage on New York prices, and wanted to buy "Kansas State Scrip, (issue of 1862), .85 @ .90; Territorial Scrip @ .50; and Shawnee County Scrip @ .50." This was obviously the same Farnham who signed the fractional notes. He is presumed to have been the son of R.H. Farnham, since census records for 1862 show M.G. Farnham as then being 28 years of age. He also appeared in the 1865 census, along with a wife and child. M.G. was listed as having been born in New York.

Another Farnham showed up in an advertisement dated October 4, 1862. This was R.M. Farnham, who was listed as an agent for the Home Insurance Company. No connection with R.H. has been determined. Research into early deed records has discovered that R.H. was actually Reuben H., and M.G. was Moulton G. Farnham.

Moulton later became associated with a man named Smith in the Smith and Farn-

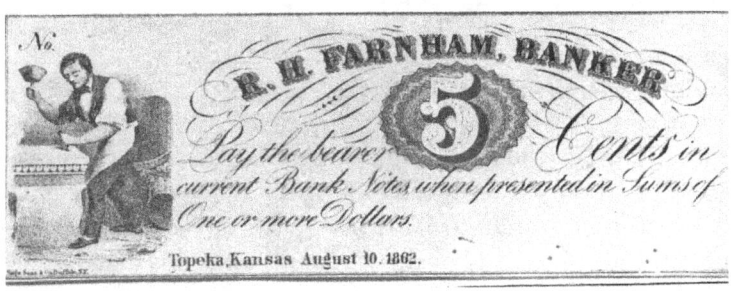

406. .05, Payable in current bank notes; imprint Sage Sons & Co. . . . . Unique
     Buffalo, N.Y.
407. .05, Payable in current funds . . . . Unique

408. .10, Payable in current bank notes . . . . Unique
409. .10, Payable in current funds R-7

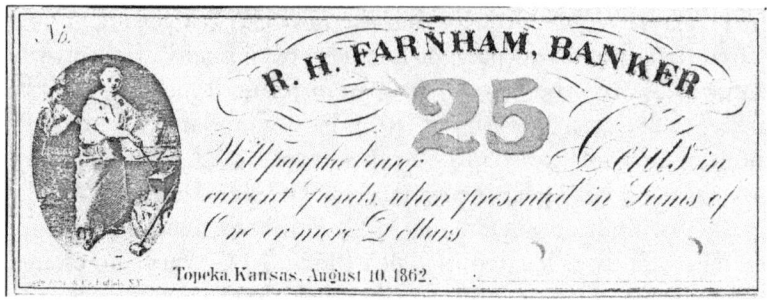

410. .25, Payable in current bank notes .... Unique
411. .25, Payable in current funds .... Unique

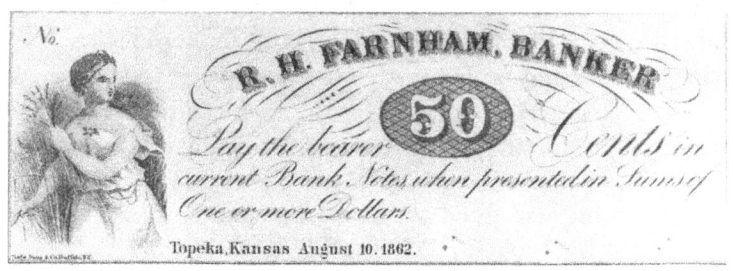

412. .50, Payable in current bank notes .... Unique
413. .50, Payable in current funds .... SENC

ham grocery firm. This firm, located in the Ritchy Block, issued a piece of advertising scrip around 1869. A standard form resembling an 1862 United States note in a "3" denomination was utilized. Moulton was then 31 years old, and listed as a grocer in census records. No information on any of the Farnhams after this date has been found.

First K.C.V. Infantry Regiment
(Kansas Colored Volunteers)
and
Harvey Spaulding, Sutler
(Sutler Scrip)

Harvey Spaulding remains an unknown, other than that he was the Sutler for the First K.C.V. Infantry Regiment, but the history of the regiment is well documented. Six companies of volunteer blacks were mustered in as a battalion at Fort Scott on January 13, 1863. Some of the recruits had seen action before the unit organization when they were attacked by nearly 500 Confederates while in camp at Butler, Missouri. During the early part of 1863, four additional companies were added to round out the Regiment. Colonel James M. Williams was commander of the unit,

Colonel James M. Williams

which was first stationed at Baxter Springs, Kansas in May, 1863, to protect local supply trains.

The First K.C.V. saw major action at Cabin Creek, Honey Springs, and Perryville in the Choctaw Nation during its first year. In 1864, a battle near Camden, Arkansas, at a place called Poison Springs, resulted in heavy casualties to the Regiment. That same

500. .25, Hand Dated June 8?, 1863. No plate letter. Uniface; . . . . .Unique
    Imprint: Kansas Tribune Print. Redeemable in
    Sutlers goods. Red/orange overprint (in an
    R.M. Smythe sale 7/11–12/06 this note realized $13,800)

year saw a number of minor actions fought near Little Rock and Flat Rock, Arkansas; and near Fort Gibson in the Choctaw Nation of the Indian Territory. The Regiment returned to Little Rock in January, 1865, where it remained until mustered out of the service on October 1, 1865. The men of the First K.C.V. had served their country well.

Atchison

THE EXCHANGE BANK
(Private Bank)

The predecessor of this private bank was probably established in 1859 at Atchison. In the 1859 city directory a listing appears for "Utley, J.N., Proprietor of Bank Exchange, corner of Third and Commercial Street." This operation probably consisted of buying and selling uncurrent bank notes and, perhaps, speculating in land warrants. It was not a commercial bank, as we understand that term today.

The operation at Third and Commercial was apparently converted into the Norton & Seley Bank in late 1859, since a local advertisement appeared for this new bank on January 2, 1860. It was located at the northwest corner of Third and Commercial Street.

William Hetherington, who has been considered as the founder of the Exchange Bank, came to Kansas in 1859 and located at Leavenworth, where he did some speculating. He moved to Atchison in 1860, and opened a dry goods store on the south side of Commercial Street between Second and Third streets.

On February 23, 1861, an advertisement appeared in the *Atchison Freedoms Champion*. It stated that an association of C.M. Seley, L.A. Alderson, and William Hetherington had formed a new firm, the Exchange Bank. Seley was president and William Hetherington was cashier. This bank was obviously an outgrowth of the Norton & Seley Bank.

The Exchange Bank issued circulating notes in 1861 and 1862, as did many other private banks and merchants, to relieve the shortage of small denomination currency. This contrasts with note issues by chartered banks of issue, which were authorized to create such money. Known denominations for the Exchange Bank include $1 and $2 bills. A one dollar note, hand dated May 5, 1861, has survived with signatures of H.B. Stirges, cashier and John Browne, president. These signatures are spurious since William Hetherington was cashier, and either Seley or Alderson would have been president at the time the note was allegedly issued. In addition, no contemporary reference to either Stirges or Browne has surfaced. Another $1 note, of a different design and with a printed date of June 1, 1861, also exists. This note has genuine signatures of William Hetherington as cashier and L.A. Alderson as president.

The partnership of Seley, Alderson, and Hetherington was dissolved April 7, 1862, when William Hetherington apparently bought out the interest of the other partners. On May 3, 1862, a new ad appeared in the paper for the Exchange Bank of William Hetherington. The ad had been written, or submitted, on April 9. Thus the bank name was changed in April, 1862, to include William's name. This is important because of the supposed existence of a check dated August 23, 1859, on the "Exchange Bank of William Hetherington."

An illustration of the check first appeared in a pamphlet published by the Exchange National Bank of Atchison in 1929, celebrating "Seventy Years of Operation." Available evidence indicates that the date on the check was incorrect, i.e. the wrong bank title and space for a revenue stamp. Such stamps were not required until 1862. The "paid" stamp appearing on the check is of a style used in the 1880s. And finally, neither the check writer, Adam Brenner, nor the payee, Mrs. Sarah Philbrick, appear in Atchison directories of the period. The date on the check was most likely a printing error. Such problems were not uncommon for the period.

Even though the check does not prove the age nor lineage of the bank, there is no reason to doubt that the bank dates to 1859. The bank always advertised "established in 1859," and its logical predecessor, the "Bank Exchange" and the Norton & Seley Bank, were organized in 1859. There still remains a controversy over exactly when William Hetherington became associated with the bank. A careful examination of evidence available indicates that William Hetherington arrived in Atchison in 1860, associated with the "Exchange Bank" in February, 1861, and became principal owner and operator in April, 1862.

The bank, with its new title, made two known issues of $1 notes in 1862. The bank, which was located at Third and Commercial, had a short life. During the winter of 1862/1863, a notorious "Jayhawker" known as "Cleveland" made Atchison his base of operations. His line of work was "disciplining" southern sympathizers in the surrounding area by stealing their property. Apparently anyone with anything worth stealing automatically became a southern sympathizer. "Cleveland" declared himself as marshal of Kansas and, since there was no one to stop him, he and his gang became the law in Atchison for a period.

It seems the "marshal," or members of his gang, made an attempt to rob the Exchange Bank in late 1862 or early 1863. This may have occurred because a "southern sympathizer" had deposited in the bank a sum of money, which the gang had expected to steal. The robbery was unsuccessful when some teamsters in the area drove off the gang. Shortly after this excitement the local citizens organized to take action against such occurrences, and lynch law restored a semblance of order in and around Atchison.

On January 14, 1863, what appears to be a letter to the editor was published in the *Atchison Freedoms Champion* under the heading Exchange Bank. The letter stated that the tax assessment rolls for Atchison County showed the Exchange Bank with only $1,050 of capital, as sworn to by the owner, and with nearly $5,000 of outstanding circulation. It goes on to say

William Hetherington

that the bank should be willing to accept its share of the tax burden, since it was being supported by the taxpayers, rather than seeking to avoid such burdens. It is not clear whether the writer was complaining about the ratio of circulation to capital or whether he did not believe the capital figure and suspected an attempt to avoid taxation. The second alternative appears more likely. In any event the letter provides an indication of the amount of circulating notes placed by the bank.

On May 21, 1863, a short article appeared about a recent gold purchase by Hetherington's banking house and then, on June 6, 1863, a notice appeared that William Hetherington was leaving for Denver on a business trip and was not expected to return for three weeks. In the meanwhile the Bank of the State of Kansas would redeem the circulation of the Exchange Bank.

In July or August 1863, the Exchange Bank apparently closed and William Hetherington moved to Missouri. Although his whereabouts for the next year and a half are not clear, it is certain that the bank was not in operation during this period. William Hetherington would not return to Atchison until the spring of 1865.

During the summer of 1864, the wholesale grocery and freighting firm of Stebbins & Porter, with operations at Atchison and Denver, opened a bank at the northwest corner of Commercial and Second Street. In the 1865 directory, this bank was listed as Stebbins & Porter, Exchange Bank. Despite the similarity of names there was apparently no relationship of this bank to the former Exchange Bank of W. Hetherington. The Stebbins & Porter Bank was converted to the First National Bank of Atchison in 1867. Mr. Stebbins became cashier of the new national bank located in the old Stebbins & Porter offices at the northwest corner of Second and Commercial Street.

As noted earlier. William Hetherington returned to Atchison in early 1865, where he apparently resumed the dry goods business. There is no evidence that he returned to banking at that time. In March, 1866, an opportunity presented itself when the Bank of the State of Kansas was liquidated and its assets were auctioned. William Hetherington bought the remaining stock and the building of this pioneer Kansas bank. The building was then located on the north side of Commercial Street, three doors west of Second. In July 1866, the Exchange Bank of William Hetherington reopened in the former state bank location, never again to close.

Even though the Bank of the State of Kansas, formerly the Kansas Valley Bank, had been a separate institution and was liquidated in 1866, its history, dating back to 1857, became part of the history of the Exchange Bank when Hetherington purchased its assets. An additional link between the two historic banks would be provided when Robert L. Pease, former cashier of the Bank of the State, would associate with the Exchange Bank as an officer and director.

Before 1866 had passed, Hetherington made a cursory attempt at obtaining a national banking charter. The effort was unsuccessful because he could not obtain the support of Senator Pomeroy, who was backing the efforts of David Auld and Henry Kuhn. Auld and Kuhn would establish the First National Bank of Atchison in 1867 by converting the Stebbins & Porter private bank.

The lack of a national charter did not hinder the success of the Exchange Bank. Construction began on a new bank building in late 1867. The new building at the northwest corner of Commercial and Fourth Street was ready for occupancy by 1869.

Further efforts to obtain a national charter were finally successful when, on July 21, 1882, the bank was granted charter #2758, becoming the Exchange National Bank of Atchison. During the interim period, Hetherington's two sons, William W. and Clifford S. had joined the firm. In 1887 the bank made a final move to its present location at the southwest corner of Sixth and Commercial Street. The present building has been extensively remodeled since 1887.

William Hetherington, Kansas banking pioneer, died at Atchison in 1890. More than 100 years later his bank was still thriving at the corner of Sixth Street.

III. Civil War Crisis, 1861–1865

21. $1.00, 1861 printed, remainder of date to be filled in. ....Unique
    No plate letter; no imprint

22. $2.00, 1861 printed as above. No plate letter. Imprint: W.H. .... Unique
    Arthur & Co., 39 Nassau and 56 Liberty Sts., N.Y

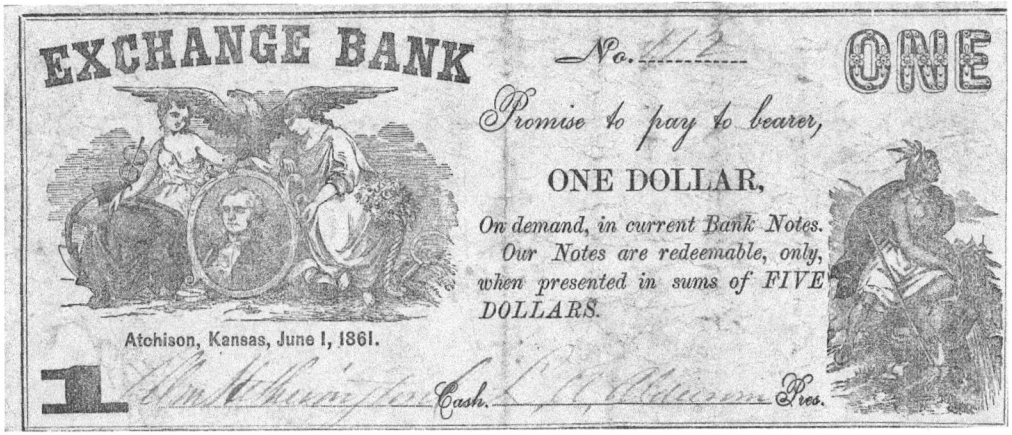

23. $1.00, June 1, 1861 printed date. No plate letter, no imprint .... Unique

THE EXCHANGE BANK OF W. HETHERINGTON
(Private Bank)

This was a title change for the Exchange Bank of Atchison that occurred in April 1862. See description under the Exchange Bank above. Became the Exchange National Bank in 1882.

31. $1.00, 186_ printed, balance of date to be written in. R-7
    No plate letter, imprint: Edw Mendel, Chicago.
    Green overprint on face

32. $1.00, 186_ printed as above. Face in green and black. Imprint: R-7
    Edw Mendel, Chicago

Former Exchange National Bank building, Atchison, Kansas, at right c. 1910

THE BANK OF WM. H.R. LYKINS
(Private Bank)

The Babcock & Lykins bank was the first real bank established at Lawrence in 1857. Carmi W. Babcock came to Lawrence in 1854 as representative of a group claiming prior rights to the townsite. He later served as postmaster and town Mayor. As a contractor he would build the first bridge across the Kansas River at Lawrence.

His partner in the bank was apparently Johnston Lykins. Johnston was a missionary to the Indians in the area and later wrote a dictionary of the tribal language. The firm erected a building adjacent to the Eldridge House, on the south side. The bank operated from "upstairs" for a few years. The Territorial Legislative session of 1857 was held in this building after reconvening from Lecompton. The financial crisis of 1857 forced the bank to close but it soon reopened. Sometime during this period Johnston's son, William became associated with the bank.

William H.R. Lykins was a member of the group claiming ownership of the land on which Lawrence was located. He was a native of South Carolina and initially a supporter of the southern position on slavery. The land claim dispute was eventually settled with an unpopular compromise that gave title of nearly half of the townsite to the Lykins group.

The bank operated as Babcock & Lykins until at least early 1861, at which time Mr. Babcock apparently separated from the organization. Soon after this the bank name was changed to The Bank of Wm. H.R. Lykins. The new bank continued to operate from its former location. During the war the bank issued small

The Lykins Bank building about 1858

Blank check for the Bank of Wm. H.R. Lykins, c. 1860s

Top: William H.R. Lykins; *bottom:* Carmi W. Babcock

denomination currency under the name of The Bank of Wm. H.R. Lykins. One signed copy is known to exist, dated June 2, 1862. Two more issues dated February and December, 1862, show the name as Wm. H.R. Lykins, Banker.

During the infamous Quantrill raid of August 21, 1863, the bank was robbed. The building was destroyed in the general conflagration of the business district. For some unknown reason the home and other property of William Lykins were spared during the attack. It is known that the raiders had lists of persons to be killed at Lawrence, and they may also have had lists of persons to be spared. In any event there were rumors that Quantrill had protected Mr. Lykins.

The bank reopened after the raid in a corner of the Jacob House building. This building, one of two that survived the raid is likely still in existence today at #731 Massachusetts Street. Shortly thereafter, Lykins erected a new bank building at present day 743 Massachusetts Street. This building, completed in 1865, also survives to the present.

In 1865, William Lykins applied for a national banking charter. A Mr. Washington Hadley from Indiana, apparently supplied the capital for the new bank. They organized the National Bank of Lawrence, which opened for business on January 2, 1866. The new bank was located at the southwest corner of Massachusetts and Winthrop (Seventh) Street on the ground floor of the newly reconstructed Eldridge Hotel. Washington Hadley was president, William Lykins was vice president and Ethan A. Smith, former cashier of the Lawrence Bank in 1860 and 1861, was cashier of the national bank. Lykins continued to operate his private bank. In

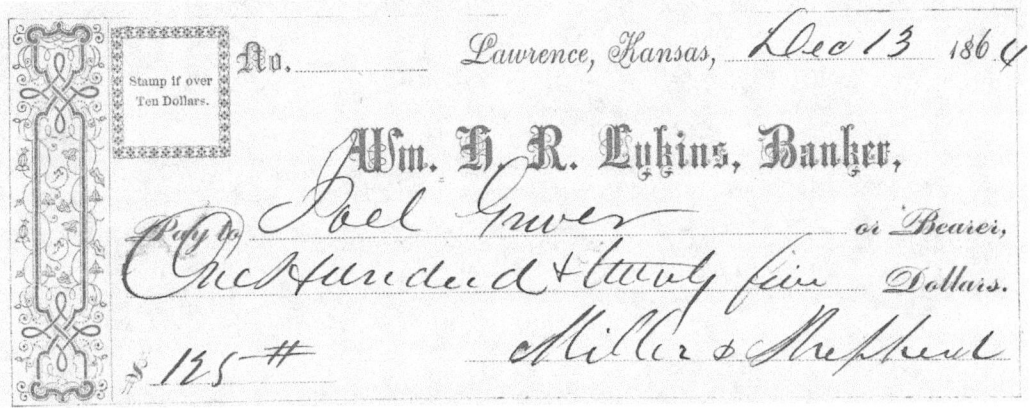

Check drawn on the Bank of Wm. H.R. Lykins, Dec. 13, 1864

August, 1866, Ethan Smith retired from the bank to become manager of the Eldridge Hotel and Washington Hadley became cashier. William Lykins became president of the National Bank, and remained in that position until October, 1867. (Remarkably a first charter $1 national bank note with Lykin's signature as president has survived, and is shown here.) William G. Coffin of Leavenworth was appointed president on October 11, 1867. William Lykins made arrangements to sell his private bank building to the National Bank.

A general business depression followed the war and conditions grew steadily worse until late 1867. The private bank of William Lykins gradually became overextended and finally failed. The bank closed for good in May, 1868, nearly a total loss to its depositors and creditors. Lykins left Lawrence then and may have settled in Oklahoma. The National Bank relocated into the former Lykins Bank building in May of 1868, and remained at that location until 1872. At that time it made a final move into newly erected quarters at the northwest corner of Massachusetts and Winthrop Street.

225. .05, December 30, 1862 written date. Uniface, ... Unique
no maker's imprint, printed in red ink

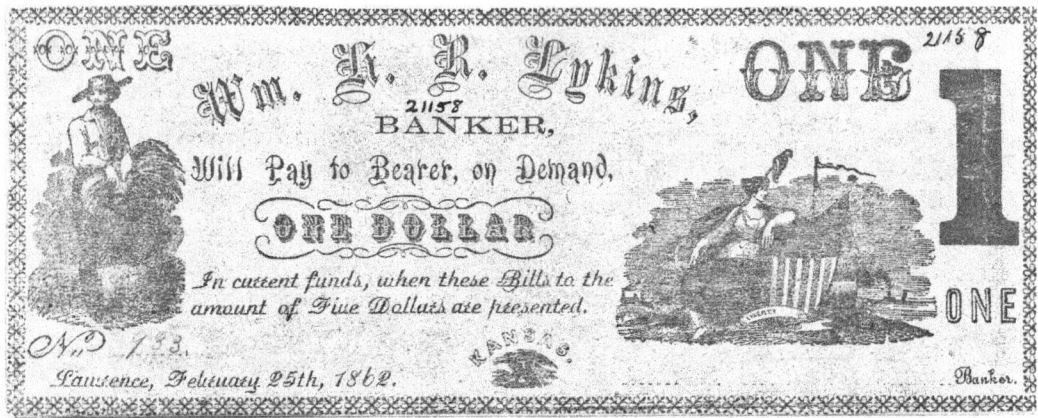

226. $1.00, February 25, 1862, printed date. No plate letter, ... R-7
no maker's imprint. Printed in pale green ink
on pinkish paper

227. $1.00, 186_ printed, balance of date to be entered. .... Unique
No plate letter, imprint: B.F. Corlies & Macy,
Stationers, 33 Nassau St., N.Y.
Green "ONE" overprint

III. Civil War Crisis, 1861–1865

228. $2.00, 186_ printed, as $1 above except for denomination R-7

229. $3.00, 186_ printed, as $1 above except for denomination R-7

Original Series, First Charter $1 National Bank Note signed by Wm. H. R. Lykins

THE SIMPSON BROTHERS BANK
(Private Bank)

The three Simpson Brothers established this bank in 1858. All had arrived in Lawrence during 1854. Samuel Simpson, a preacher, was the first to arrive after walking from St. Louis! He was soon involved in most of the significant border warfare troubles around Lawrence. Samuel probably arranged the eastern financing of the bank. Henry was a lawyer by trade. The third brother, William, was the banker. William served as president of the bank until the partnership was apparently dissolved in 1869.

The bank was located at the southwest corner of Massachusetts and Winthrop (Seventh) Street. A successful business was conducted by loaning money to merchants, farmers and cattle dealers. Most of the loans were for small amounts and the periods averaged 90 to 120 days. Two signatures were required to borrow money. Rates ranged from 3 percent to 10 percent per month.

Left: Samuel N. Simpson; *right:* Henry M. Simpson

III. Civil War Crisis, 1861–1865

Simpson Bros. Bank as it appeared in 1869, after the raid

During the small note shortage in 1862, the bank issued $1 notes. Several unissued notes and one correctly signed note have been documented. Four different printers apparently produced the notes. Since the amount circulated would have been small, the use of four printers raises questions. Four of the identical known surviving notes appear on an unusual thick paper, and may have surfaced together around 1956. They were originally dispersed among the Western Reserve Historical Museum in Cleveland, the Boys Town Museum in Omaha, the Kansas State Historical Society Museum in Topeka, Kansas, and in a private collection. These examples may have been produced or reproduced in the late 1930s on book paper. (Correspondence seen from D.C. Wismer warned a collector about reproductions produced for collectors.) Four other observed examples appear on contemporary period bank note or newsprint paper.

On August 21, 1863, William Quantrill's guerilla raiders burned the bank after they were unable to open the safe. Within a week following the raid, a temporary wooden structure had been erected over the ashes of the former building and the bank was back in operation. Eventually a permanent brick structure was erected at the same location.

The bank was forced to close again for about four weeks during the fall of 1864 when General Sterling Price led a Confederate army out of Arkansas to eventually threaten Lawrence. Two of the brothers served in the Kansas militia, and were called up during the crisis. Before they left Lawrence, the brothers took the bank records and other papers to the farm of Dr. Samuel Prentiss, then located west of town, and buried "the bank" at various locations. After Price's army was defeated at the battle of Westport and headed back south, the Simpsons returned to Lawrence, dug up the bank assets and reopened the bank. (I wonder if they might have overlooked one of the locations and whether a stash could still be buried there...?)

An incident concerning the bank in 1868 illustrates some of the risks of banking in the 1860s. The *Kansas Daily Tribune* reported on May 5, 1868, on "Forgery on Simpson Bros. Bank." A man named W.J. Parker had applied for $3,000 in credit at Field, Leiter & Co., a wholesale dry goods house in Chicago, using a draft for $13,050 drawn by Simpson Brothers on Hanes & Macy. The Chicago firm was suspicious and telegraphed the bank to verify the draft, whereupon it was revealed to be a forgery. Mr. Parker then forwarded the draft to the Simpson Brothers, along with a nasty letter in order to avoid suspicion of the Chicago authorities.

In 1869, William Simpson apparently bought the interests of his brothers and relocated the bank to the northwest corner of Massachusetts and Henry (Eighth) Street. The bank name was changed slightly at that time to The Simpson Bank. William remained as president and H.W. Chester became cashier. In 1873 J.J. Crippen bought an interest in the bank and assumed the position of vice president. He replaced Mr. Chester as cashier around 1875.

In 1874 and 1875 Kansas suffered from terrible drought and grasshopper plagues. Crops were destroyed and land values plummeted. The entire country was in the grip of a serious depression at the same time. The Simpson Bank, like many others operating on limited capital, gradually became overextended. That December the bank's correspondents at Kansas City, St Louis, and New York City all failed. On December 10, 1877, the Simpson Bank was placed in the hands of a receiver. According to William Simpson in 1915, the

Blank Deposit slip, c. 1860s

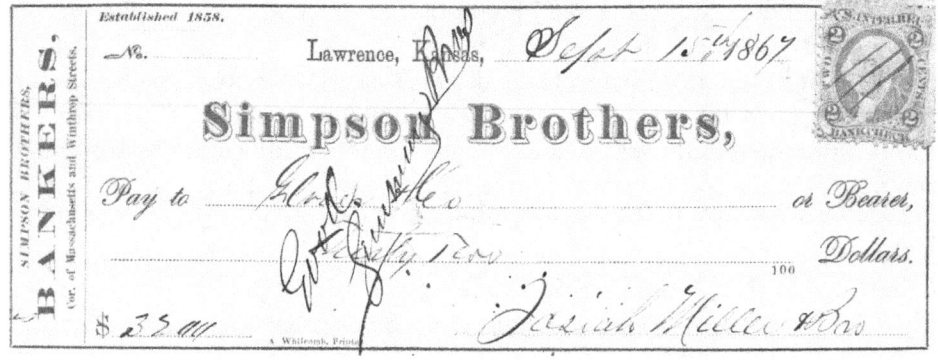

Certified check on the Simpson Brothers bank, dated 1867

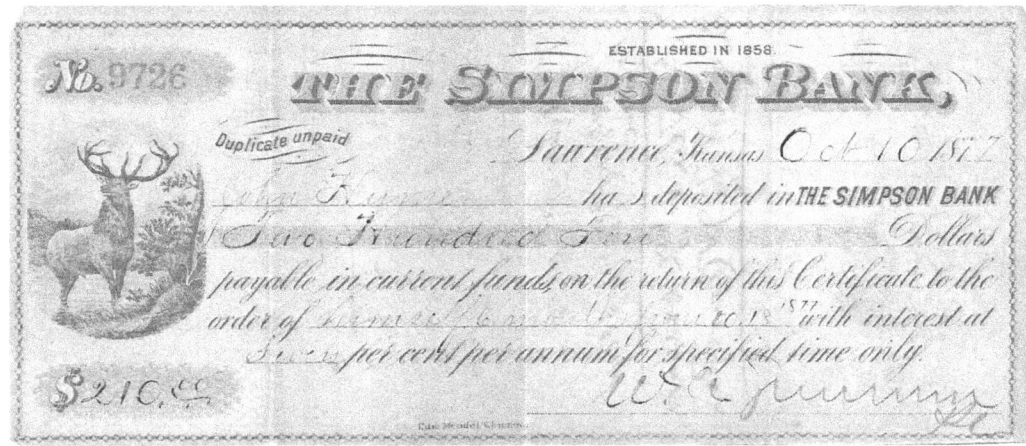

Certificate of Deposit on The Simpson Bank, 1877

receiver James S. Crew was able to collect enough of the bank's assets to cover over 95 percent of the bank liabilities. However, large legal expenses and hefty fees charged by the receiver resulted in depositors recovering only 35 percent of their claims.

The receiver, James Crew, became president of the National Bank of Lawrence on March 13, 1878. William Simpson became vice president of the bank at the same time. The National Bank of Lawrence was the only bank in the city to survive the crisis. Because of the officer change it would appear that much of the former business of the Simpson Bank was moved to the National Bank. In any event, William Simpson and James Crew formed a connecting link between the pioneer Simpson Brothers bank and the National Bank of Lawrence.

Samuel Simpson eventually preached in the west. Henry and William moved to Kansas City, Kansas, where William remained in the financial business.

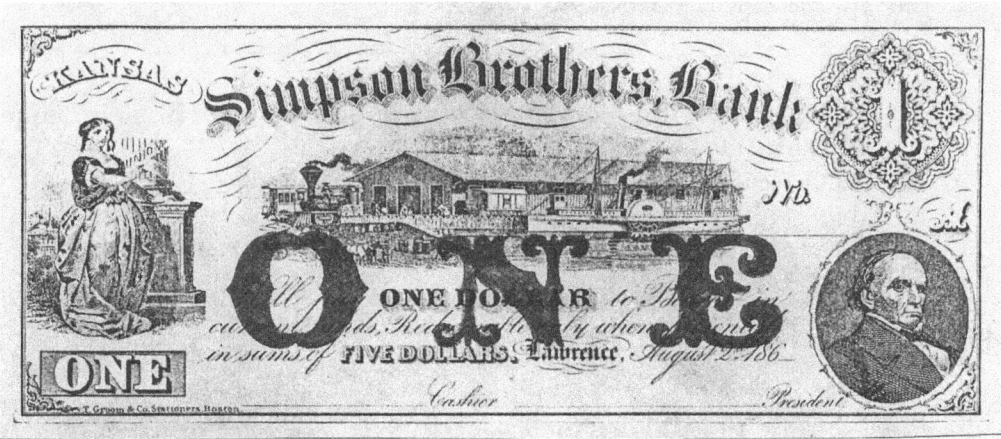

252. $1.00, August 2, 186_ printed, balance of date to be entered. . . . . . . .Unique
   (R) Portrait of Daniel Webster. Plate letter A. Uniface,
   Imprint: T. Groom & Co., Stationers, Boston.
   "ONE" overprint in red

253r?. $1.00, As above, except printed on thick paper. No overprint and R-7
incomplete redemption clause. May be a reproduction,
or possibly a proof. (Four known)

254. $1.00, As 253 above with slight layout variations. Plate letter B. .... Unique
Imprint: B.F. Corlies & Macy, N.Y.
"ONE" overprinted in red, bank note paper

255. $1.00, July 3d, 186_ printed. Uniface. Plate letter A. . . . . Unique
Mirror image of red "ONE" overprint appears
on back. Imprint: T. Holland Lith.,
12 School St. Boston

256. $1.00, 1862 printed. Uniface, black, or dark blue, on white; . . . . Unique
redeemable in "current funds," in sums of $5. (L) Farmer
plowing with two horse team, "1" on rosette above.
(C) Train, imprint: State Journal Print., Jun 14 date
on only note seen. S.N. 217. This note turned up
at a Missouri coin dealer's in 2000

Leavenworth

CLARK, GRUBER & CO.
(Private Bank)

Milton E. Clark arrived at Leavenworth in the spring of 1855, and opened a grocery and dry goods store on Cherokee Street. On March 8, 1859, he opened a bank in partnership with his brother Austin, who had been associated in the grocery business, and Emanuel H. Gruber. E.H. Gruber had worked for the banking firm of Isett, Brewster & Co., predecessor to the Scott, Kerr bank in the city. The Clark, Gruber bank was located where #303 Delaware Street is located today. It is likely that the grocery firm had also performed many banking services for customers before the bank was started. The new bank would become one of the most important banks at Leavenworth and in Kansas during the territorial and early statehood period.

On February 20, 1860, the Territorial Legislature granted a charter of incorporation to the Leavenworth, Pikes Peak Exchange Co., with A.M. Clark and E.H. Gruber as incorporators. This new firm was established to take advantage of gold discoveries near Pikes Peak. It was authorized to buy and sell exchange and gold dust for conversion into ingots. The issue or circulation of any form of paper currency was expressly prohibited in the charter. It appears that the firm never operated under this exact name, but a branch office of the Leavenworth bank was opened at Denver City, then part of Kansas Territory, with Milton Clark in charge. Additional branches were later established at Central City and Salt Lake City, Utah.

At Denver, between 1860 and 1863, the Clarks established a bank and private mint, which produced gold coins and ingots. The mint was later purchased by the United States government to become the nucleus for the Denver mint. The bank was converted into the First National Bank of Denver in 1865.

Clark, Gruber & Co. issued $1 notes during 1861 and 1862 at Leavenworth. The Denver branch issued $5 notes, redeemable in gold. In fact the Denver notes were preferred by the public over federal notes at the time. The charter provision against issue of currency obviously was not enforced while the country was occupied with the Civil War.

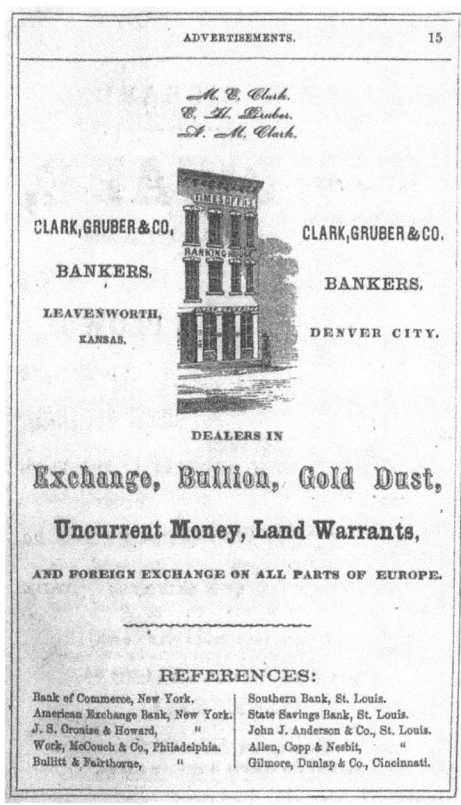

City directory ad, 1860–1861

Left to right: Austin M. Clark, Milton E. Clark and Emanuel H. Gruber

III. Civil War Crisis, 1861–1865

In May of 1864, E.H. Gruber dissolved his partnership in the operation and, in association with M.D. Whitridge, opened his own bank at Leavenworth. Gruber's bank was located at the southeast corner of Main and Delaware Street. The former Clark, Gruber bank then became the Clark & Co. Bank and continued to operate at the former location.

E.H. Gruber's bank failed in 1866, apparently as a result of mismanagement. Gruber may have left Leavenworth at that time, and later turned up banking in Virginia City, Montana. In 1865 the Clarks, in association with Jenkin W. Morris, established the Second National Bank of Leavenworth. This was accomplished by converting the private bank of J.W. Morris into a national association. Austin M. Clark was president of the new bank. J.W. Morris served as vice president. The separate firm of Clark & Co. continued to operate as a private bank.

In 1874, the Second National Bank was liquidated by Austin Clark and the business of the bank was transferred to the private firm of Clark & Co. This happened in spite of the cashier's complaints to the Comptroller of the Currency. Shortly after the Second National was closed Milton Clark became associated with the German Bank of Leavenworth.

The German Bank was established in 1869, by Simon Abeles, as the German Savings Bank. Originally located at the northwest corner of Cherokee and Third, it relocated to the southeast corner of Delaware and Fourth Street in 1872. In 1874, the German Savings Bank was converted to a commercial bank and changed its title. Milton Clark, became cashier, and several other employees from the liquidated Second National also took positions in the reorganized German Bank.

In 1876 Jenkin W. Morris joined the German Bank as cashier. He remained in the position for about a year. In 1877 Austin Clark died at Leavenworth. In the following year the Clark & Co. bank was liquidated and absorbed by the German Bank. Milton Clark became president of the German Bank at that time. The Clark bank, which had been in continuous operation since 1859, was undoubtedly a victim of the 1870s depression. M.E. Clark remained as president of the German Bank until 1882, when poor health forced his resignation. He had been active in Leavenworth banking for 23 years when he retired. He passed away in 1904. He and his brother had constructed and lived in a magnificent mansion that remains a private home in Leavenworth today.

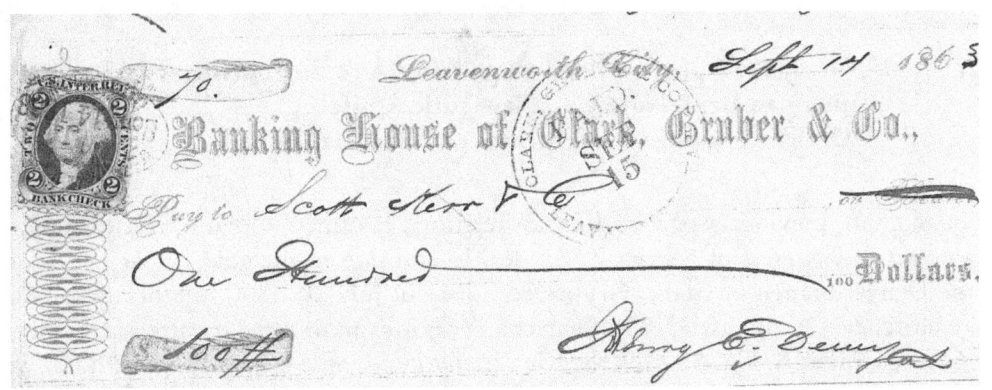

Check drawn on the Banking House of Clark, Gruber & Co., Leavenworth City, Kansas, 1863

Finally, in 1877, to complete the chain of pioneer banking associations at Leavenworth, the German Bank was absorbed and liquidated by the First National Bank.

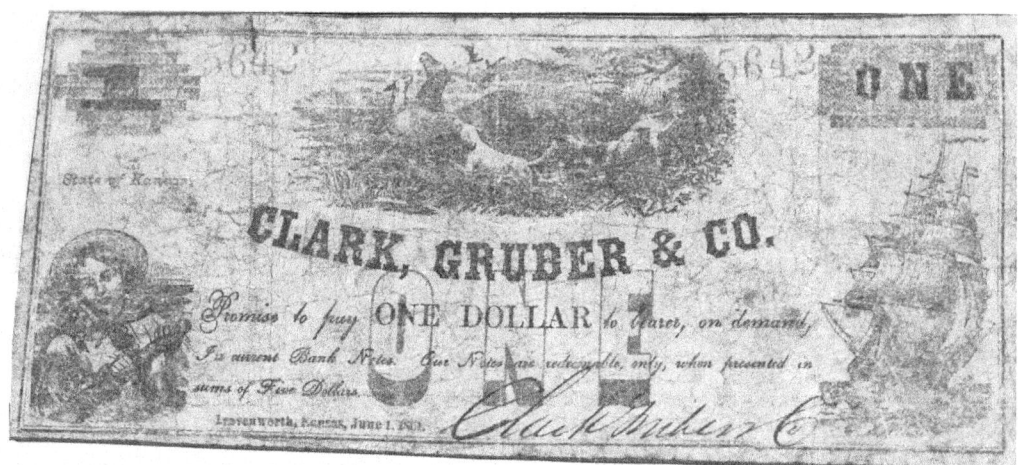

301. $1.00, June 1, 1861 printed date. No plate letter, uniface, ... R-7
no maker's imprint. Green "ONE" overprint

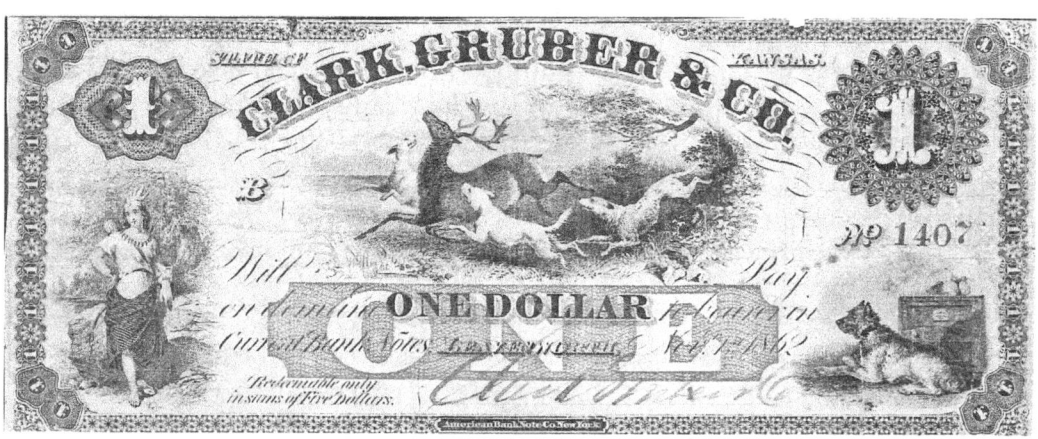

302. $1.00, Nov. 1, 1862 printed date. Plate letter A & B. Imprint: R-7
American Bank Note Co., New York. Uniface,
"ONE" in red panel overprint. 12,500 sheets issued

Colorado, previously part of Kansas Territory, became Colorado Territory by the organic act of Congress of February 28, 1861. In addition to the gold coinage circulated by the Denver branch of Clark, Gruber & Co. from July 20, 1860, the firm also issued paper currency. On August 3, 1861, Denver's *Rocky Mountain News* reported favorably on the Clark, Gruber & Co. $5 bills then in circulation. These elegant uniface notes were produced by the American Bank Note Co. The portrait at right is the first governor of Colorado Territory William Gilpin. They were "payable [on demand] in Denver Coin at their Bank in Denver." It is believed all issued notes were redeemed or destroyed, since

III. Civil War Crisis, 1861–1865

F.O.C. Darley vignette used on Denver Clark Gruber notes

no issued notes are known to have survived. At present only two proofs and five remainders (unissued notes) are known. In recent years these Clark, Gruber & Co. notes have claimed the title of "King of U.S. obsolete notes," with prices ranging up to six figures at public auction.

Due to the cooperation of the auction companies which have sold three examples of these choice Clark, Gruber & Co. notes in recent years, we are enabled to share them with readers. Seven Clark Gruber $5 Denver notes are known in total.

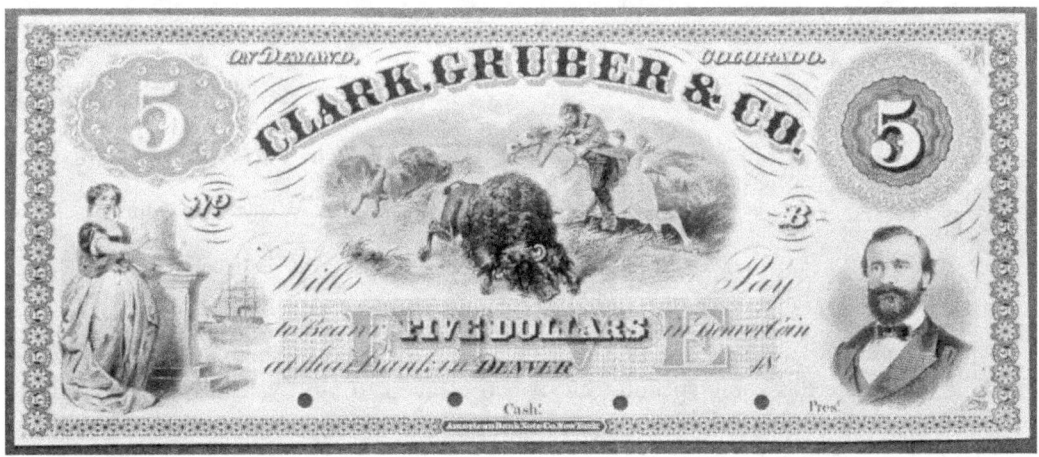

This proof $5 note of Clark, Gruber & Co., Denver brought $77,625 in a January 18, 2005, Stack's auction

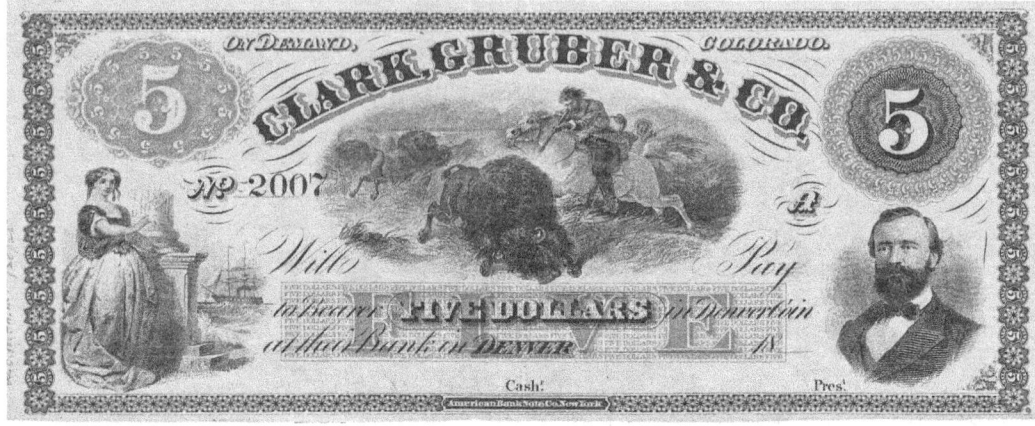

This $5 remainder of Clark, Gruber & Co., Denver brought $60,375 in a June 17, 2005, R.M. Smythe auction

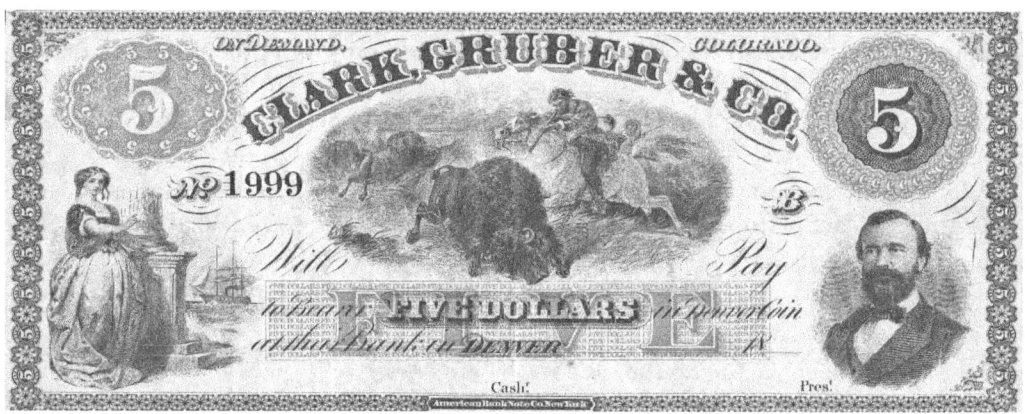

Another remainder $5 of Clark, Gruber & Co., Denver brought $126,500 in a January 9, 2008, Heritage auction

THE BANKING HOUSE OF J.W. MORRIS
(Private Bank)

Jenkin W. Morris was a medical doctor who came to Leavenworth from Des Moines, Iowa, in 1857. He did some speculating in real estate and land warrants for some time prior to 1862, when he opened a private bank. The Banking House of J.W. Morris was located at the northwest corner of Delaware and Main Streets, fronting on Delaware.

Morris issued scrip in 1862 and 1863, when there was a critical shortage of small denomination currency. Known issues include a $1 note dated Nov. 1, 1862, and a 5-cent note, dated Jan. 1, 1863.

In 1864, J.W. Morris became vice president of the First National Bank of Leavenworth, which was then located directly across Main Street from his private bank. In 1865, the Clark brothers from Clark & Co., successors to the firm of Clark, Gruber & Co., obtained a charter for the Second National Bank of Leavenworth. The new national bank was established by converting Morris' private bank. Austin Clark served as president, J.W.

Morris was vice president and Henry S. Bulkley was cashier of the national bank. William P. Borland replaced Bulkley as cashier soon after the bank organized.

Jenkin Morris remained as vice president of the Second National until 1868, when he apparently sold his interest in the bank. At that time the bank was relocated to where #223 Delaware Street is today. This building, used by the bank from 1868 until 1874, still stands on lower Delaware Street. In 1974 it was being used as the American Legion Hall.

Austin Clark remained as president of the Second National until 1871 or 1872, when James C. Stone replaced him. Stone had been associated with the Clarks in banking since the territorial period. A.M. Clark returned to the presidency shortly before the bank was liquidated.

The Second National had done a large business after the Civil War, but appears to have overextended its resources during the economic crisis that began in 1873. In August, 1874, Austin Clark placed a notice in the *Leavenworth Times* stating that depositors' accounts and deposit certificates of the Second National Bank would be assumed by the private bank of Clark & Co. William Borland, cashier of the Second National, wrote to the Comptroller of the Currency on August 8, 1874, to protest that Mr. Clark was liquidating the bank without authority of the stockholders. Mr. Borland accused Clark of using this method to obtain the assets of the Second National without having to pay for them. It is unknown whatever became of Mr. Borland's charges, but in any event the Second National was liquidated and its business was taken over by Clark & Co.

Jenkin W. Morris

Jenkin Morris returned to banking at Leavenworth in 1876 when he became cashier of the German Bank. In later years he became a director of the Manufacturers National Bank of Leavenworth. He probably was associated with banking in the city for the rest of his life. During the period from 1862 to 1877, he was a link between his own private banking enterprise of the Civil War, the Clark brothers, the First and the Second National banks, and the German Bank, which in turn was absorbed by the First National in 1887.

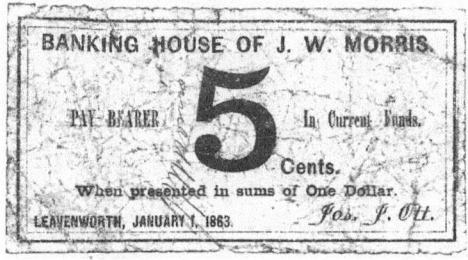
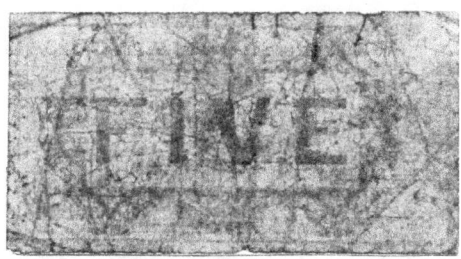

311. .05, January 1, 1863 printed date. No imprint, no plate letter. . . . . . . Unique
    Back "FIVE" in frame in red
312. $1.00, Nov. 1, 1862, (L) deer. (C) Indian Maidens, ... Presumed unique
    shield and eagle. (R) Dog on safe. No other information

SCOTT, KERR & CO.
(Private Bank)

In the summer of 1856 the firm of Isett, Brewster & Co. of Des Moines, Iowa, opened a banking office at Leavenworth. The owners were T.M. Isett and W.C. Brewster. John Kerr was the "company," i.e. manager of the Leavenworth office. Between 1857 and 1859, Emanuel H. Gruber, later a partner in the famous Clark, Gruber firm, was a clerk in the Isett, Brewster bank. The office was located on the north side of Cherokee Street, between Main and Second Street.

In August 1858, Lyman Scott, Sr., bought out the interest of Isett and Brewster, and in company with John Kerr formed the bank of Scott, Kerr & Co. Mr. Scott Sr. had been an iron manufacturer in Philadelphia, who came to Kansas in 1857. His two sons would manage the bank. Lucien arrived at Leavenworth in 1857 from Cincinnati, and his brother Lyman Scott, Jr., arrived that same year from Philadelphia.

The new bank moved to a two story brick building at the southeast corner of Delaware and Second Street in 1860. This building was the earliest bank building in the state, and survived virtually unchanged until 1974, when a remodeling removed the second story.

Scott, Kerr & Co., like many private banks and merchants, made at least two issues of $1 notes during the Civil War. The first issue, dated July, 1861, used the title The Bank of Scott, Kerr & Co. The second issue, dated in 1862, used an abbreviated title to Scott, Kerr & Co. The first printing of the second issue of notes had the town name spelled incorrectly, without an "A." The spelling was corrected for the second printing, thereby creating two varieties of these magnificent American Bank Note Company products. The bank probably placed about 20,000 to 25,000 of these notes in circulation. The Scott, Kerr Bank also acted as the place of redemption for some of the Kansas merchants who produced wartime scrip. Lewis Kurtz of Manhattan is one example.

As stated previously the two Scott sons, along with John Kerr, ran the bank. Lucien served as president. In 1863, the Scotts applied for a national banking charter. This was for the first charter granted in Kansas, a particular objective of Lucien's as reflected in his correspondence to the Comptroller. Thus began the First National Bank of Leavenworth, a separate bank from the private firm of Scott, Kerr & Co., although the two banks operated in close association. Thomas Carney, state governor during 1863 and 1864, became

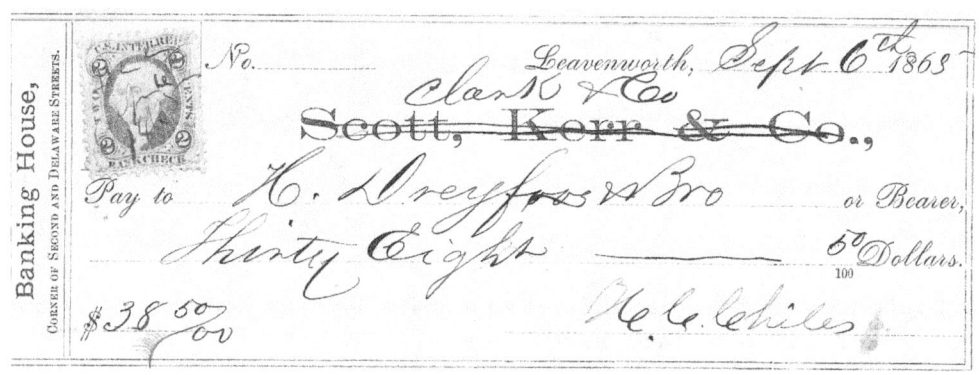

Check drawn on Clark & Co. overwritten on printed Scott, Kerr & Co. form, 1865

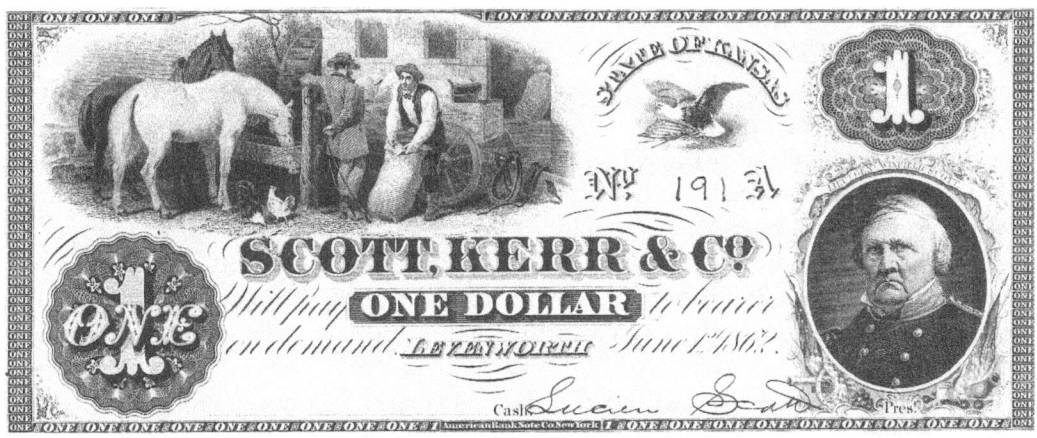

Proof of Scott, Kerr & Co. $1 note with the location misspelled LEVENWORTH

the first president of the new national bank. Lucien Scott was cashier and Jenkin W. Morris, who had a private bank across Main Street from the First National, became vice president. The bank was located at the northeast corner of Main and Delaware Street.

In 1864, John Kerr became president of the First National, and Greenup Bird took over as cashier. Mr. Bird would later have the historical distinction of being cashier of the Clay County Savings Association at Liberty, Missouri, when it became the first bank in the country to be robbed in daylight by the James gang. Apparently the Scotts were busy with other concerns for the following two years. Lyman Sr. had gone to New York before 1863 and was very ill, which might explain the sons' absence from Leavenworth.

In 1866, Kerr sold his interest in the banks and resigned as president of the First National. The private bank changed its name to Scott & Co. and Lucien Scott took over as president of the national bank. He would hold that office for nearly twenty years, until his death. John Kerr may have gone to New York to reassociate with his former employers since there was an Isett, Kerr Bank in that city for many years.

In 1868, the First National Bank moved from its original location to a magnificent

Vignette "Men at Mill" employed on some banknotes

three-story building at the northeast corner of Fourth and Delaware Street. This building remained virtually unchanged on the outside until 1956, when the top story was removed in an ugly remodeling. This remnant of a formerly impressive piece of architecture still stands at the same corner.

The private bank of Scott & Co. continued to operate until 1874, when it failed despite rescue efforts of the First National. The bank was liquidated, and what remained was absorbed by the First National. The national bank may have had difficulties of its own during September, 1873, as there is a report that the bank closed its doors for several days at that time. In any event, the bank survived. In 1877 it absorbed the last successor to the pioneer banks of Leavenworth, when it took over the liquidating German Bank.

The First National absorbed other banks, not mentioned here, throughout its long history. It remained at Fourth and Delaware until 1966, when it relocated to its location at Seventh and Delaware. In the 1990s, the bank was purchased by the historic Exchange National Bank of Atchison. The First National played an important and long role in the economic development of the state. It was a principal correspondent for many of the pioneer banks of Kansas. It remains in business today as one of the historic links to the territorial period of banking in the state.

321. **$1.00, July, 1861, printed date. (L) Woman feeding horse.** .... **Unique**
    (R) Cattle drinking from stream. Uniface, orange
    and black. Plate letter A
    Imprint: may be Mendel, Chicago

322. $1.00, June 1, 1862 printed date. (L) Mill scene, ... R-6
(R) Portrait of Lieut. General Winfield Scott.
Incorrect spelling of "LEVENWORTH"
Plate letter A. Uniface. Proof known.
High # seen — 8771

323. $1.00, As above, except town spelled correctly as "LEAVENWORTH" ... R-6
Plate letter A High # seen — 19204

BANK OF THE STATE OF KANSAS
(Chartered Bank, Civil War Crisis Period)

This bank was a continuation of the Kansas Valley Bank. The legislature passed an act on January 25, 1861, just prior to statehood, changing the name of the bank. The bank issued notes with the new name under provisions of its state charter extension, in denominations of $3, $5 and $10. Few of these notes may have reached circulation before federal notes were available to replace them. For information about these notes and the territorial issues of this bank refer to the chartered bank section under the territorial and statehood period.

The small denomination crisis of the Civil War period caused the legislature to

Vignette: "The Safe Guard"

amend the charter of this bank by allowing the issue of $1 and $2 bills. The original and extended charter had prohibited any note issues smaller than the $3 denomination. The American Bank Note Company prepared a new plate for the $1 note and these notes were issued beginning in the spring of 1862. They are known with plate letters A and B. The $2 denomination was not used.

55. $1.00, 18__ printed, remainder of date to be written in. Plate letters R-7
A and B. Face in green and black. Uniface. Imprint: American
Bank Note Co., New York. Proof known with plate letter A.
At least four issued notes are known

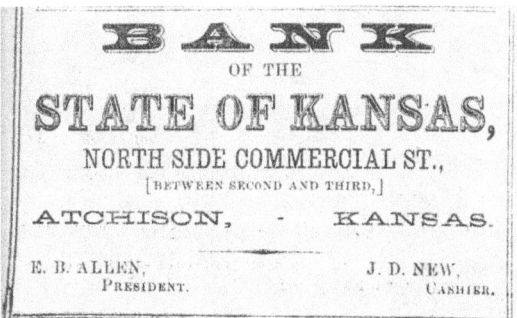 

Left: City Directory ad, 1865; *right:* Bank scene from *Harper's Weekly*, 1866

Unissued remainder, $1, Bank of the State of Kansas

THE LAWRENCE BANK
(Chartered Bank, Civil War Crisis Period)

When Kansas became a state in 1861, the Lawrence Bank reorganized under the provisions of the new state constitution. Notes were issued to replace the territorial period issues as early as July, 1861. As the shortage of small denomination currency worsened in 1862, the bank sought to place an issue of small notes into circulation. Most of the $5s from the issue of July, 1861, still resided in the bank so they were turned in at Topeka and replaced with an issue of $1s and $2s on November 1, 1862. A total of $3,273 was issued. This issue was caused by the Civil War crisis, and therefore is included in this section of the catalog. For details about the bank and other note issues refer to the sections on chartered banks during the territorial and statehood periods. It is possible, but highly unlikely, that the $3 note was also reissued in 1862. None are known to exist and several unissued half sheets with $1 and $2 notes only have survived.

213b. $1.00, Same as #213, except hand dated Nov. 1, 1862 .... R-7

214b. $2.00, Same as #214, except hand dated Nov. 1, 1862 .... R-7

IV

Post–Civil War Period, 1866–1879

During the Civil War the federal government took over the issue of paper currency through the National Banking system and by issuing "greenbacks." An effort was made to force all state banks to either convert to the national system or cease to issue currency. In 1865 Congress passed a confiscatory tax to be collected every time a state bank note was used. This tax, of 10 percent, was to take effect on March 1, 1866. At the same time it became illegal for merchants and corporations to issue paper substitutes for money. The tax effectively ended the issue of private and chartered state bank notes. Therefore, banknote engraving companies were forced to pursue other markets. There was no prohibition against local governments issuing scrip, or treasury warrants, and many cities and towns did so beginning during the financially distressed period of the late 1860s. Several Kansas towns are known to have issued tax warrants. These were either lithographed or engraved and had a similar appearance to the former state bank notes. Issues are known from Chetopa, Independence, Leavenworth, and Wyandott.

The state government also made an issue of printed denomination scrip, commencing in 1867, to pay certain expenses incurred by the state during the Civil War and for Indian expeditions in 1864. This scrip was to pay 7 percent interest and would be redeemed when and if the federal government paid the war expense claims of Kansas.

On February 29, 1868, the Kansas Legislature passed an act authorizing the charter of savings banks. Several savings banks were chartered under this act, including the Atchison Savings Bank, the Topeka Bank & Savings Institution, and the Kansas State Savings Bank at Wyandott. Savings banks soon came up with a clever method to create money using paper notes by issuing engraved "Certificates of Deposit" that looked like money even to having dollar denominations printed on them. Money was created when such certificates were issued without demanding a corresponding deposit by the recipient. A single chartered savings bank, the Kansas State Savings Bank at Wyandott is known to have used this method to get around federal restrictions on the issuance of paper money.

UNION MILITARY SCRIP
(State Scrip)

The Kansas State legislature authorized the issue of this scrip in 1867, to pay claims against the state arising from the Indian campaign of 1864 and the Confederate invasion of the same year. The scrip was to bear interest and would only be redeemable if the United States government reimbursed the state for war-related damages and other expenses.

Confederate General Sterling Price led an army out of Arkansas toward St. Louis in the fall of 1864. His objective was to gather recruits and obtain supplies. Eventually he turned west toward Kansas. After a number of engagements he finally met defeat at the battle of Westport near present day Kansas City. Kansas State militia played a large role in the action. Price retreated south along the Kansas border and was again brought to battle at Mine Creek, near Fort Scott, Kansas. This was the largest Civil War battle fought in Kansas. Again defeated, the Confederates retreated into Arkansas.

Prior to these Confederate troubles, Indians on the western frontier of Kansas had initiated a series of raids on local settlements. This resulted in military expeditions against the Indians. They were singularly unsuccessful, but resulted in many expenses and claims against the state for various services and supplies.

The total amount of scrip issued was approximately $500,000. In addition to the printed denomination notes described here, there was a write-in denomination form prepared (apparently locally). The write-in forms were probably used after the printed denomination notes were used up. In 1872, the federal government paid the state $337,000 against these claims. Certain expenses, including all Indian expedition costs and interest were disallowed. Even so, the state treasurer paid out notes as they were presented, causing many legitimate claims to go unredeemed. He would later be forced to resign in lieu of impeachment for his actions. A number of state-appointed commissions were established in later years to examine the claims and apparently many were eventually paid by the state. A quantity of redeemed notes reposes today in the collections of the Kansas State Historical Society museum, which of course are no longer redeemable.

The notes were prepared and printed by the Continental Bank Note Company of New York. Several notes are known that appear to be specimens and a single cut sheet of green essay notes is known. A number of modern reprints have also been made of these notes by American Bank Note Company. All notes bear engraved signatures of the then Governor Samuel J. Craw-

Top: Vignette: "Cavalry Trooper"; *bottom:* Vignette: "Indians Attack Miners"

ford, and Secretary of State, R.A. Barker. The notes are dated June 1, 1867. They are hand-signed by various Treasurers as the notes were issued between 1867 and 1873, when the last of these notes were paid out. (A later Kansas Treasurer who was also involved with the issue of Kansas obsolete notes, was Samuel Lappin of the Seneca firm Lappin & Scrafford. He was State Treasurer from January, 1875, until December 20, 1875.)

The *Junction City Weekly Union* dated Feb. 1, 1868, carried a notice stating "Military Scrip issued for service in the Price Raid and the various Indian expeditions, is finding its way into this neighborhood. The patriotic Plum Hunters (a local military outfit), whose heroic deeds shed luster all over the West, are now reveling and dissipating in consequence of this visit of the Paymaster. We understand that ten cents on the dollar has been paid for this scrip, and consequently the money market is easing up. The value of the scrip depends entirely upon whether Congress assumes its payment, about the probability of which, there is a variety of opinions."

State of Kansas 7 percent bond issued to pay off the costs of fending off Indian raids and expeditions against Confederate General Sterling Price's invasion in 1864.

Left to right: U.S. General Samuel R. Curtis; Governor Samuel J. Crawford; Confederate General Sterling Price

Write-in Union Military scrip

Treasurers who signed these notes were in office as follows:
- Martin Anderson Jan., 1867–Jan., 1869
- George Graham Jan., 1869–Jan., 1871
- Josiah Hayes Jan., 1871–Apr. 30, 1874 (resigned)

421. $1.00, Plate letters A, B, C, D. High # seen 25533 .... R-4

421s. $1.00, Specimen; Plate letters B and C seen. Notes are R-7
hole punched at signature; no serial #, no signature

422. $5.00, Plate letters A and B. High # seen 13014 .... R-4

423. $10.00, High # seen 14669 .... R-4

423e. $10.00, Essay in green ink .... Unique
423r. $10.00, Modern reprint on thick paper

424. $20.00, High # seen 6953 .... R-5

IV. Post–Civil War Period, 1866–1879

424e. $20.00, Essay in green ink . . . . Unique
424r. $20.00, Modern reprint on thick paper

425. $50.00, High # seen 1531 . . . . R-5
425s. $50.00, Specimen, hole punched at signature space; no serial #, . . . Unique
    no signature
425r. $50.00, Modern reprint on thick paper
425r2. $50.00, Reprint produced by ABNCo for series "The Old West"
    in 1985. Copy statement on back

426. $100.00, High # seen 905 .... R-5
426r. $100.00, Modern reprint on thick paper

THE KANSAS STATE SAVINGS BANK
(Chartered Savings Bank)

The Kansas State Savings Association was chartered by the state legislature on February 8, 1868. The bank, located in the Levee Block of Wyandott, was to experience a short career, as it would be forced into liquidation in the fall of 1872. John Arthur was first president and Peter Connelly was first cashier. Arthur was a medical doctor and good friend of the father of Jesse and Frank James. In fact, he had delivered both of the babies. John Arthur was an entrepreneur and adventurer. After selling some slaves in Texas during the Civil War, he put the money into cattle and drove the herd to New Orleans, where he received payment in Confederate notes. He held the notes when he returned to Kansas and they eventually became worthless. He also developed property and acquired large land holdings in Wyandotte County. In later years he got involved in navigation on the Missouri River and land reclamation along its banks.

Moses M. Broadwell was first vice president and E.M. Bartholow, who also banked at Lawrence, served as one of the directors. In 1869, Peter Connelly left to open his own banking office in Wyandott and would later become cashier of the First National Bank of Wyandott. W.H. Shackleford, Sr., replaced him as cashier at the Savings Bank. In 1870 J.P. Broadwell became president of the savings bank and W.T. Wheatly became cashier. In 1872 the bank closed.

The bank's advertisements appeared regularly in the *Wyandott Gazette* beginning in December 1868. The bank office was located in the "Levee Block," close by the Missouri River. The Kansas State

Vignette: "Indians Ambush Wagon Train"

IV. Post–Civil War Period, 1866–1879

Earliest known legitimately signed Kansas State Savings Bank circulating certificate of deposit

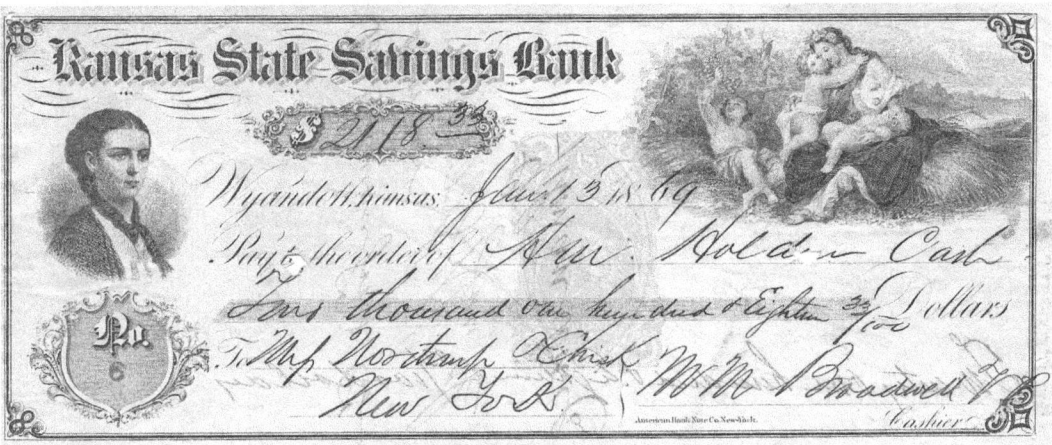

Kansas State Savings Bank draft

Savings Bank issued certificates of deposit designed to look like bank notes. By issuing certificates without requiring an offsetting deposit, the bank could create money. This is exactly why federal prohibitions existed against private note issues. Around 1875, the government finally put an end to such issues.

The notes were printed in green and black ink by the Continental Bank Note Company, and R.P. Studley & Co., Agents at St Louis. None of the notes bear a plate letter. Circulating notes have a red serial number. The earliest known, genuinely signed, note bears serial #5, dated Nov. 16, 1869, and is signed by M.M. Broadwell as president and Peter Connelly as cashier. Most notes are found with false signatures added and well worn, to create the impression they had circulated. This was all part of a scam to pass the notes after the bank had failed.

A cut sheet of proofs or essays is known for the bank. They are uniface and have no green overprint nor red serial number. They also have a slightly different obligation as "pay to h__ order" rather than bearer on the regular certificates. The $1 was cut from the sheet circa 1980.

448. $1.00, Date 18__, balance of date to be entered. R-4
Back ornate green design. High # seen 9351

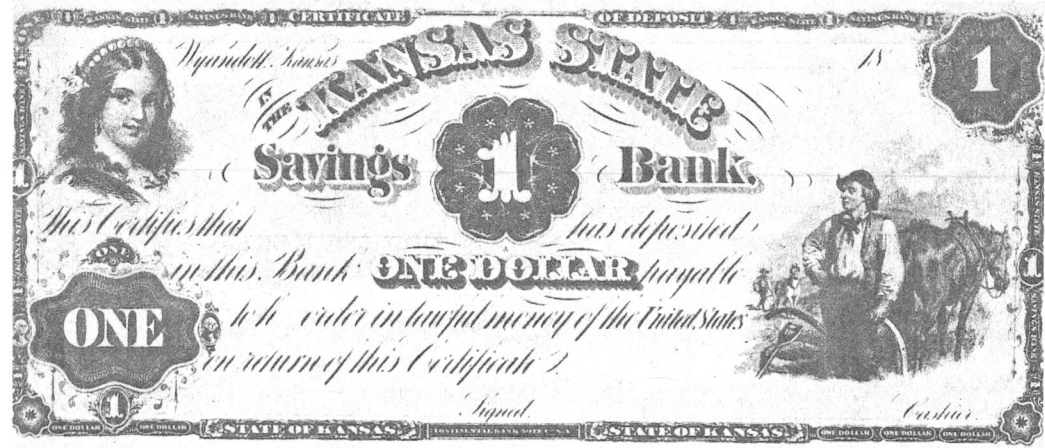

448p. $1.00, Proof or trial. Uniface no overprint .... Unique

IV. Post–Civil War Period, 1866–1879

449. $2.00, Date 18__, balance of date written. Back as illustrated. R-4
High # seen 9992

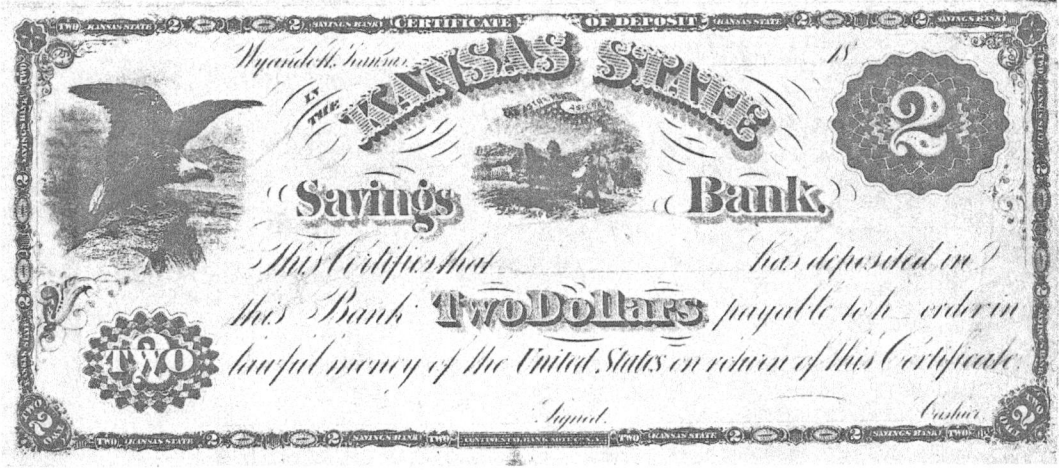

449p. $2.00, Proof or trial. Uniface, no overprint .... Unique

450. $3.00, Date 18__, balance written. Back as R-4
illustrated. High # seen 8964

450p. $3.00, Proof or trial. Uniface, no overprint .... Unique

IV. Post–Civil War Period, 1866–1879

CITY OF CHETOPA
(Municipal Scrip)

Chetopa is located in southeast Kansas, near the Oklahoma border. The area was first settled around 1857. The name comes from the Osage Indian language, meaning "the site of four houses." This referred to the homes of the chief's four wives located there.

The town was burned in 1863 by Union soldiers to prevent it from falling into enemy hands. After the war, the area was resettled and became a city in 1869. The first city election was held on April 4, 1870, with F.M. Graham elected Mayor. H.R. Dobyns became city clerk at that time. The Missouri, Kansas and Texas Railroad reached Chetopa that same year.

Chetopa in 1871

During the hard times of the 1870s, Chetopa, like many other cash strapped western towns, issued demand notes on authority of the Board of Supervisors. A single $2 note is known with genuine signatures.

70. $1.00, No date, no plate letter. "ONE" overprinted in red. R-7
    Back ornate design in green. Imprint: the R.P. Studley Comp'y, St Louis.

71. $2.00. No date, no plate letter. Similar to $1 above, green back. R-6

THE CITY OF INDEPENDENCE
(Municipal Scrip)

The City of Independence was founded in 1869 by a group of men led by Robert W. Wright. Wright later became a leading merchant in Dodge City. His store would be located next door to the Long Branch saloon. In January, 1872, a railroad branch line connected Independence to distant markets. A government land office was located there the same year. Population at the time had reached nearly 2,300 persons.

180. $1.00, 187_ printed, balance of date to be written in. .... Unique
Known date is March 5, 1875. (L) Two Indians; "1" on oval above. (C) Cowboy on horse with cattle, "CITY WARRANT" above (R) Woman feeding chickens. "1" on rosette above. Imprint: American Bank Note Co., N.Y. Back ornate design with "1"s at left and right and "ONE" on "1" in fancy rosette at center. Note is green and black. Serial # 3429

The first city Mayor was J.B. Craig; city clerk was C. M. Ralstine. Independence, like many other western cities, faced a severe cash shortage during the depression years of the 1870s. In 1873 a school was constructed at a cost of $23,000. To pay bills the city fathers authorized an issue of warrants that were receivable for taxes. A single note is known from this issue. The note is green and black, with a green back design. It was produced by the American Bank Note Company of New York, and bears the signature of James DeLong, mayor in 1875.

CITY OF LEAVENWORTH
(Municipal Scrip)

An article in the *Kansas City Journal Post*, on Feb. 6, 1927, was titled "Currency Issued by Leavenworth, Kansas, 56 years ago, Still Bobbing up to Worry Town Officials." It was accompanied by an illustration of a $5 note of the 1871 issue of Leavenworth City scrip.

The article pretty well covered the issue of this scrip and what happened to it. Kansas and other mid-western towns had similar experiences in the 1870s. The Leavenworth City Council meeting minutes for 1871 showed that by May 16 of that year, outstanding city scrip (possibly a hand written variety) had depreciated to 75 cents on the dollar and further decreases were expected. In fact, the value continued to decline until it brought only 30 cents on the dollar, at which point it was redeemed, and withdrawn from circulation by the city treasurer. The article noted that "even today (1927), stray outlawed pieces of city scrip continued to pop up all over the country."

The writer apparently was discussing what were undoubtedly two different issues of scrip. What had depreciated by May 16, 1871, was an issue that preceded the attractive notes known to modern collectors. The council authorized a new scrip issue on May 16, 1871, which date appears on the note illustrated in the article. And, on June 10, 1871, the council authorized the expenditure of $1,000 for the cost of printing $50,000 of new scrip by the Continental Bank Note Company of New York. These notes were printed four to a sheet as $1A, $1B, $2, and $5 for a sheet value of $9. To print $50,000 worth would have required 5,555 sheets. The highest serial number recorded for these notes is currently #2663. During the month of April, 1871, the city had issued $8,470.41 of the earlier issue scrip.

The deflationary period following the Civil War proved extremely difficult for the early cities and towns in Kansas. Real money was scarce and many towns issued paper scrip to meet their financial obligations. The article reported that a thick packet of these notes was in the possession of a Kansas City woman who had formerly resided at Leavenworth. Since the bills bore a certain resemblance to federal currency of the period, it was fairly easy to pass them off to unsuspecting recipients. Only recently a carnival playing in Texas had taken in one of the $5 notes and forwarded it for redemption to the Leavenworth City auditor. And, not long after that a local citizen presented a $1 note for redemption. Of course the notes were not redeemed because they were then worthless However, it did not help the city's image that these notes kept surfacing.

The holder of the hoard had obtained it from a former African slave. This man had served her family for many years after the war. "Uncle Wilson" as he was known, resided in a shack on the former family place in Leavenworth. He occasionally did odd jobs for the city mayor. When Uncle Wilson died, the family went through his belongings. In the attic of the shack they found a tin box, bulging with Leavenworth scrip in unsigned, new notes. Many of the notes were still banded in paper wrappers. The total amounted to between $8,000 and $10,000 in denominations of $1, $2 and $5.

The Leavenworth City council at their regular meeting on May 16, 1871, had authorized this scrip. Of particular interest were the following excerpts from recommendations of the ways and means committee:

1. The city clerk was to draw all scrip to order and enter the purpose for which it was issued.

2. The city treasurer was instructed not to endorse any scrip presented after May 16, 1871.

3. The treasurer was also instructed to pay no interest, on city scrip, either old or new, from and after May 1, 1871.

Vignette: "The War Alarm"

The report went on to detail amounts of scrip then outstanding, and the current depreciated value of same. It urged the council to pay city obligations in cash whenever possible to avoid the cost of the inevitable discount on scrip. If scrip could only be passed by the city at 50 cents on the dollar, the cost of whatever they were buying was in effect doubled. Acting mayor, Levi Houston was in the chair for this meeting, and William W. Creighton was city clerk. Mayor at the time was John A. Halderman, later U.S. Minister to Siam.

The council agreed that scrip was a poor idea; nevertheless, they authorized the engraving of $50,000 in city warrants, "suitable for a circulating medium." City scrip was then being used for expenses of the general fund for fire department, streets, culverts and bridges, gas and the pest house (whatever that was), at a rate of $8,000 to $9,000 a month.

The article also stated that when the old city hall was razed to make room for the new structure, a large amount of this scrip, in uncut sheets, was found. The sheets were destroyed and today only a single uncut sheet is known. Another hoard was found when an old brick building was torn down for a street widening in 1912. Supposedly these were the notes that found their way to many different parts of the country. From accounts of hoards of this scrip found in later years, it is obvious that a major portion was never issued. A local citizen stated that a court ruling finally prevented further issue. A judge had ruled that the city did not have authority to legally issue "money." The same individual thought that some of this scrip was used to encourage railroads to build through the town. A number of people indicated that Leavenworth City scrip did not see much general circulation. Of the notes known in collections today, only a single correctly signed and issued note has been observed.

IV. Post–Civil War Period, 1866–1879

Leavenworth mayors during the period were:

John A. Halderman	1870–1871
D.R. Anthony	1872–1873
J.L. Abernathy	1874–1876

City Clerks were:

W.W. Creighton	1870–1873
W.B. Challacomb	1874–1876

274p. $1.00, As above. Face proof on card stock R-7

274. $1.00, May 16, 1871 printed date. Plate letters A and B. R-4
Ornate green back design. Imprint Continental
Bank Note Co., New York, high # seen 2552

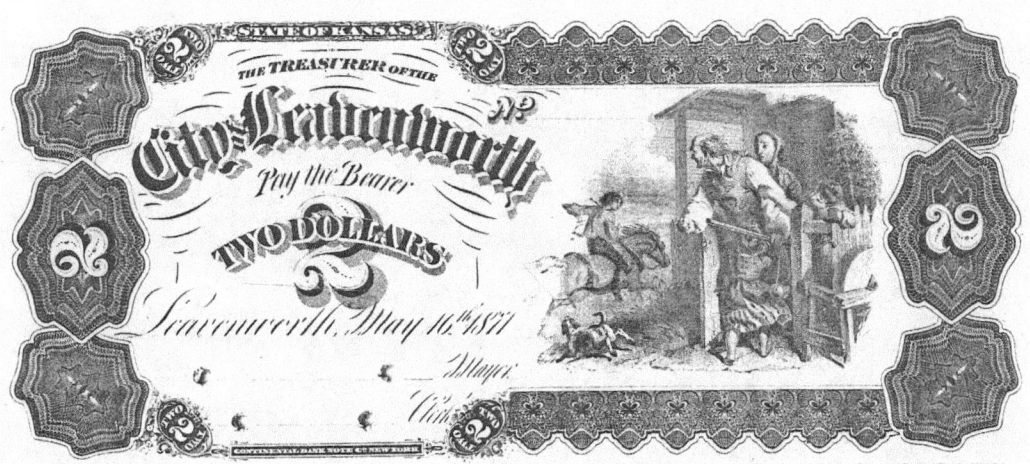

276p. $2.00, As above, face proof R-7

276. $2.00, As above. Central vignette "The War Alarm" by F.O.C. R-4
No plate letter. Green back, high # seen 2506

277p, $5.00, As above, face proof R-7

277. $5.00, As above. No plate letter. Green back, high # seen 2663 .... R-4

277pb. $5.00, Different back design proof than issued R-7

IV. Post–Civil War Period, 1866–1879

THE CITY OF WYANDOTT
(Municipal Scrip)

Wyandott was named for the "Wyandot" Indian tribe, which was resettled in the area from the eastern states before Kansas became a United States Territory. The town site was surveyed in 1857, and by the end of that year the population had reached 1,000 persons. The old City of Wyandott fronted on the Missouri River, and is now part of downtown Kansas City, Kansas, along Minnesota Avenue. In 1886 the separate cities of Wyandott, Armourdale, "Kansas," and old Kansas City, Kansas, were combined to become the present day city. The old name survives today as the name of the county, Wyandotte [*sic*].

In the 1870s city warrants were issued to pay for services. These notes were lithographed by the K.C. Litho. Co., Kansas City, Mo. The central vignette on the notes represents the city as seen from across the river in 1869. These notes are normally found unsigned.

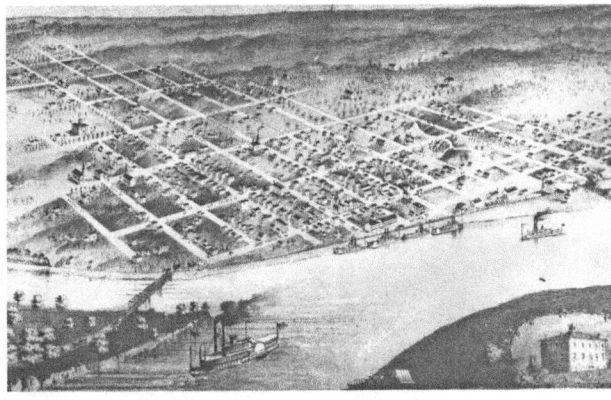

Wyandott, Kansas, 1869

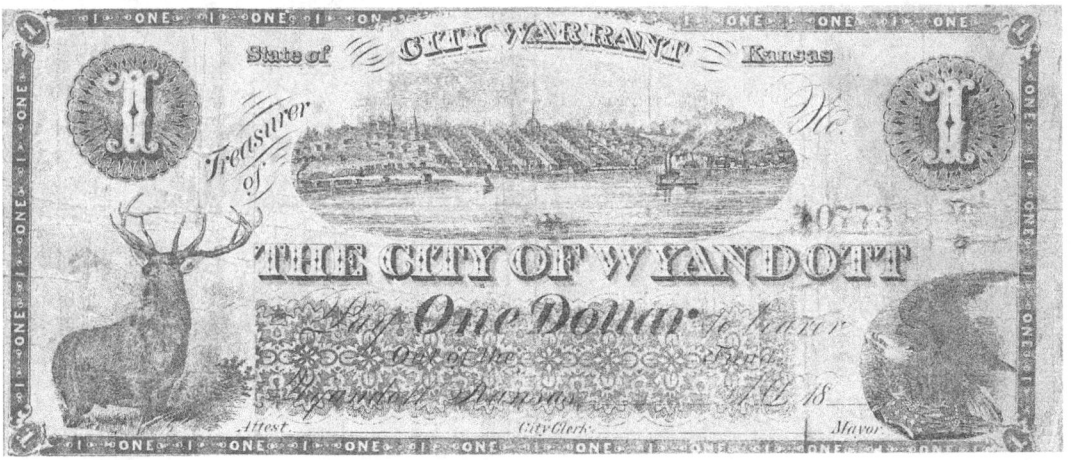

436. $1.00, No date, no plate letter. Face has a green panel and border R-6
overprint. Back ornate design in green. Imprint:
K.C. Litho. Co., Kansas City, Mo. High # seen 19776

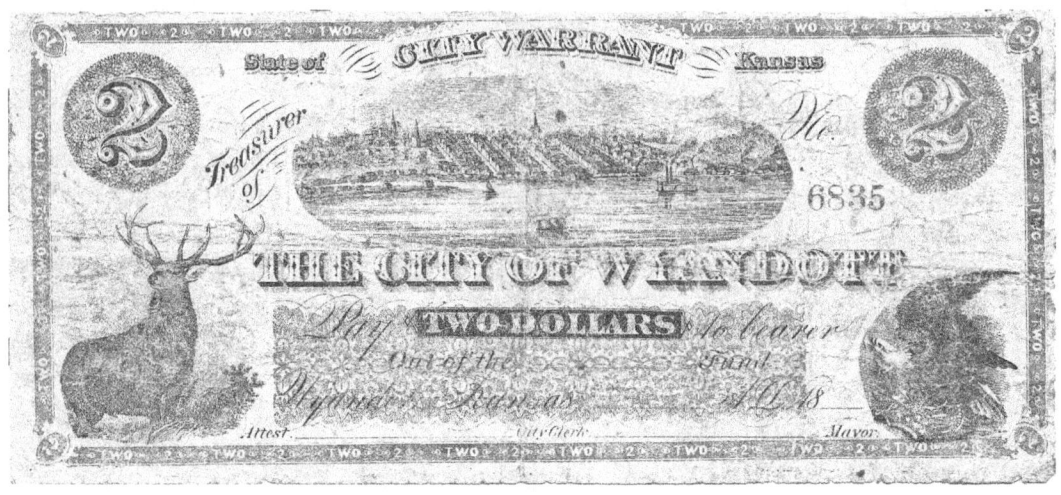

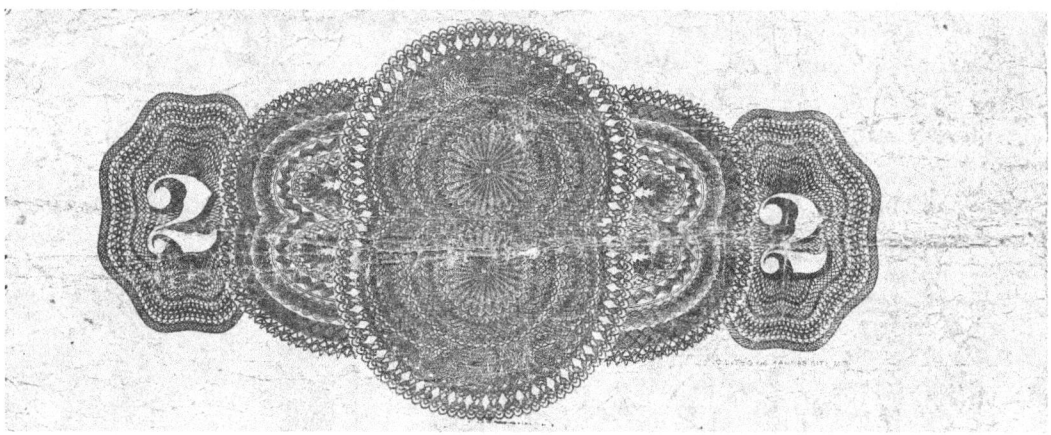

437. $2.00, As $1 above except for denomination High # seen 6835 . . . . R-6

V

Miscellaneous Scrip Period, 1870s–1930s

Paper money, or pieces of paper that look like bank notes, has been used for many purposes besides representing a store of value or substitute for real money. Merchants in America issued scrip notes as early as the Colonial period. They soon found that small advertisements designed to resemble money were likely to be retained by customers. Sometimes there was an added discount or partial redemption value for this type of scrip, which made it even more likely to be retained. In addition to advertising, an early need was recognized to train future business persons in the handling and use of money. Business colleges resulted and "College Currency" was developed as training tools. Many of these notes were elaborately printed and often produced in color.

Various business enterprises made significant use of scrip for their employees as captive customers. Railroads and coal companies provide examples of this practice. Miners were often paid in scrip redeemable only at the "company store." Railroad scrip looked like banknotes except that denominations often purported to represent miles of railroad travel rather than dollars so as not to violate prohibitions of U.S. law.

Depressions and various economic crises often created a need for substitute currency. The national depression that began in 1893 brought on widespread issue of "Merchandise Due Bills" in Kansas. Although specifically stated on the notes that they "were not to be used as substitutes for money" that is exactly what their intent was. Most of these notes wound up being seized by the United States Secret Service. In 1907 a banking panic and the 1914 outbreak of World War I caused the issue of many items collected as depression

Miscellaneous scrip, type not included

scrip. The great depression of the 1930s was widely addressed with scrip, mostly issued during the banking crisis of March 1933.

There are other examples of "miscellaneous Kansas paper money"; such as Postal Currency, insurance certificates, play money, theater and stage scrip, Labor Exchange Scrip, lottery tickets, raffle tickets, advertising coupons and various other items collected as adjuncts to the hobby. Typical examples of Kansas' miscellaneous scrip are illustrated and discussed in this section.

Advertising Scrip

Note: This type of scrip normally has no unit of U.S. monetary value stated thereon. More of these stock ad notes turn up every year. They were widely used during the latter half of the nineteenth century and into the twentieth. No attempt to list ad scrip after the 1880s has been made as the scope would be too large. These notes are all currently R-7 to Unique. For additional information refer to Bob Vlack's book titled An Illustrated Catalogue of Early North American Advertising Notes (R.M. Smythe, 2001).

Lookalikes of U.S. Fractional Currency

D.S. Ames, Fort Scott, Jeweler

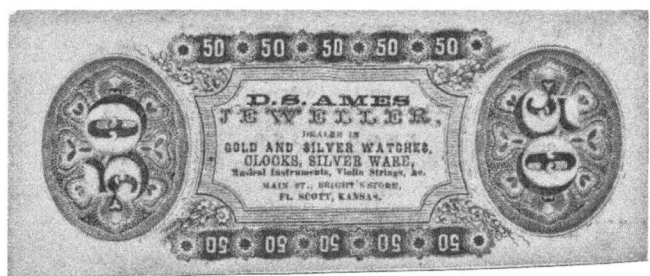

1. **"50," Similar to third issue U.S. fractional currency; lookalike** .... **R-7 also seen from other states, circa 1870.**

V. *Miscellaneous Scrip Period, 1870s–1930s* 155

DURFEE HOUSE, LAWRENCE

E.A. Skinner Proprietor. Located at the corner of New Hampshire and Pinckney (present day Sixth Street).

2. "50," Similar to Ames "50" above. R-7

M. NEWMARK, LAWRENCE, DRY GOODS DEALER

3. "50," Similar to Ames "50" above R-7

LOUIS ROCHAT, ATCHISON, WATCHES AND CLOCKS

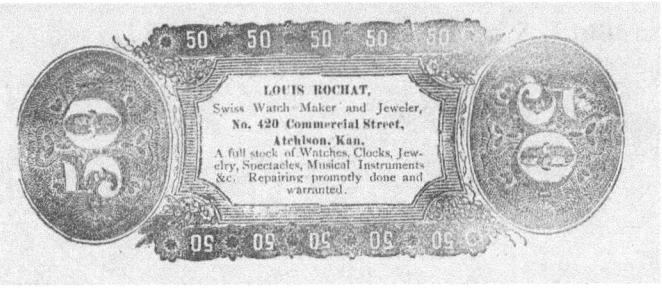

4. "50," Similar to above fractional look-alikes R-7

Lookalikes of U.S. Federal Currency

M.D. Calkins & Co., Garnett,
Metal Tipped Boots and Shoes

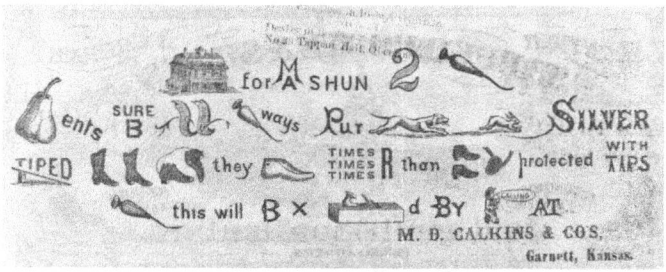

5. "1," U.S. Capitol on face similar to $2 Legal Tender note, ...R-7
   rebus on back, Imprint: W. Swaty, Dealer in Books
   and Stationery, No. 29 Tappan Hall, Oberlin, Ohio.
   Rebus back. Also seen from other states. *(bottom bill at 54% to match top)*

Beechler & Lewis, Leavenworth,
Boots and Shoes

6. "3," Similar to 1861 U.S. $5 Demand notes. Also seen R-7
   from other states.

ULMER SMITH & CO., INDEPENDENCE, FURNITURE DEALER AND UNDERTAKER

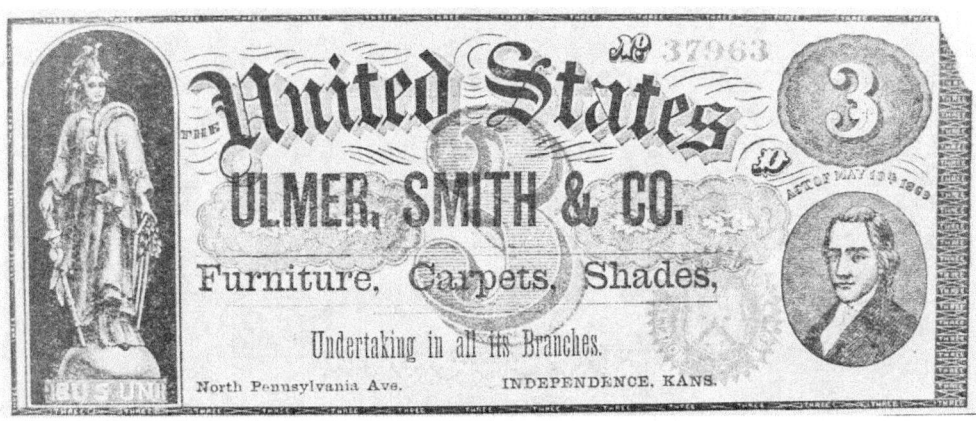

7. "3," Similar to #6 above R-7

SIPPLE BROS., PARSONS, DEALERS IN STAPLES AND FANCY GROCERIES

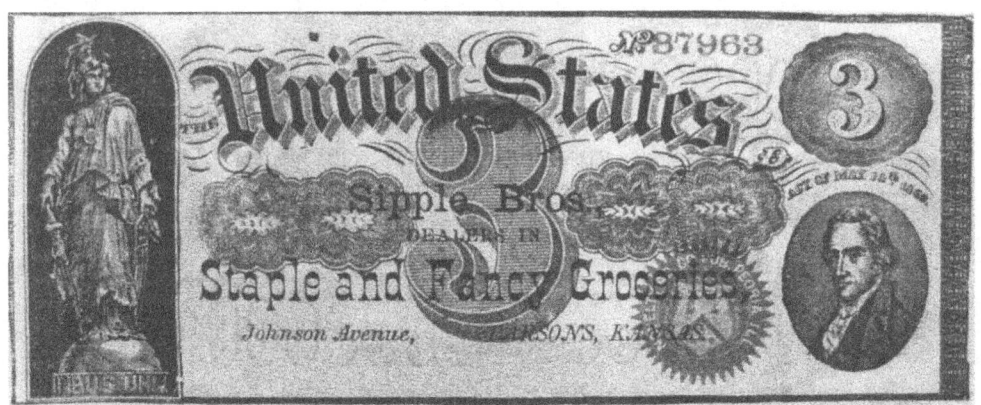

8. "3," Similar to #6 above R-7

Wm Hudson, Winfield, Watches, Clocks and Jewelry

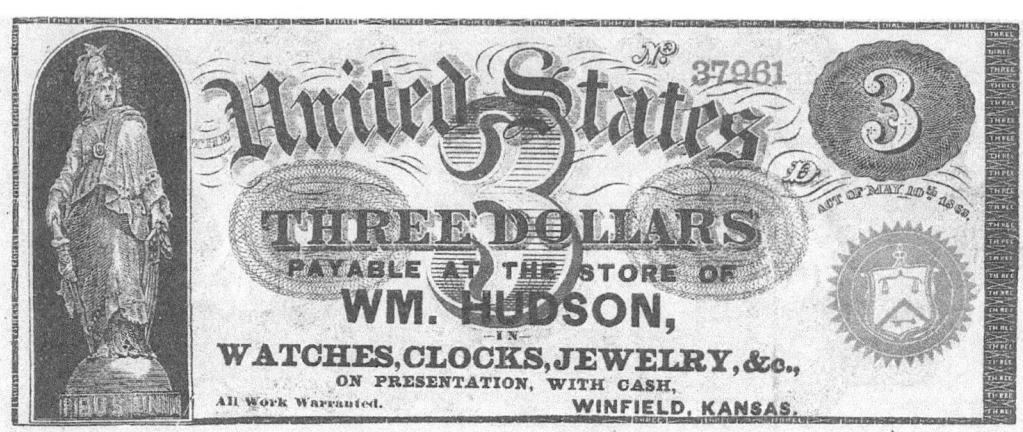

9. "3," Similar to #6 above, but no portrait of Alexander Hamilton R-7

Parker & Giles, Topeka, Groceries and Provisions

10. "3," Similar to #6 above R-7

Frizell Hardware, Larned

11. "3," Similar to #9 above R-7
    Oildorado Dry Goods & Groceries,

Kansas Branch Bridge, Oildorado

12. "3," Similar to #6 above R-7

The Economy Clothing, Dry Goods and Shoe Store, Garden City

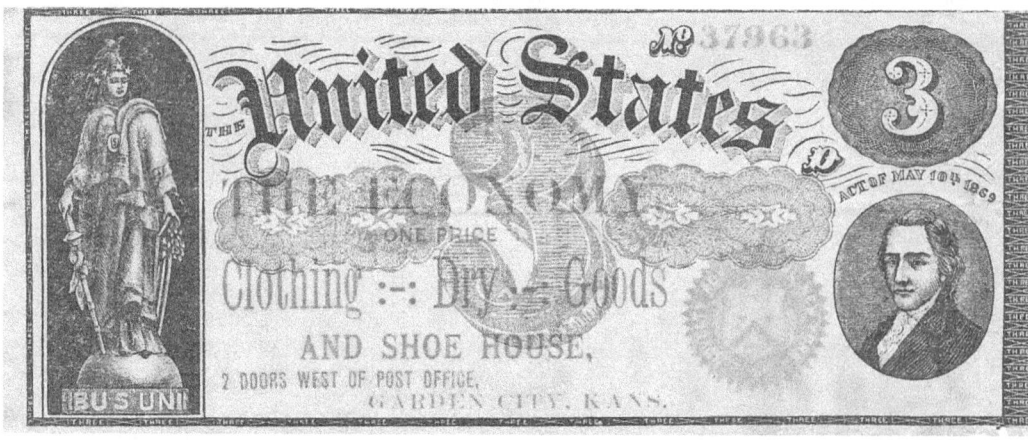

KAW VALLEY HOTEL, NORTH LAWRENCE

13. "3," Similar to #6 above R-7

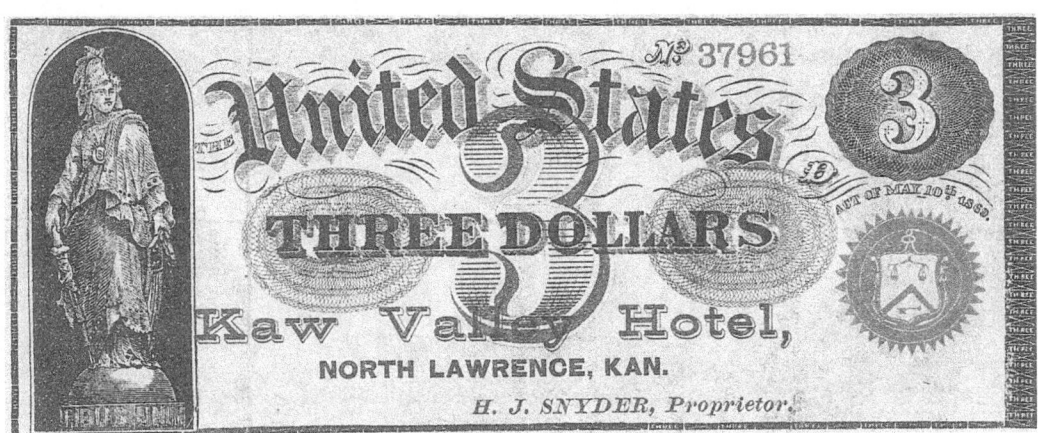

OAK HALL CLOTHING HOUSE, C.M. SALINGER, LEAVENWORTH

15. "3," Similar to #6 above R-7

Standiford, Youmans & Eldred, General Merchandise, Medicine Lodge

16. "3," Similar to #6 above R-7

V. Miscellaneous Scrip Period, 1870s–1930s

D.C. McMurtrie, Stove and Tin Ware, Emporia

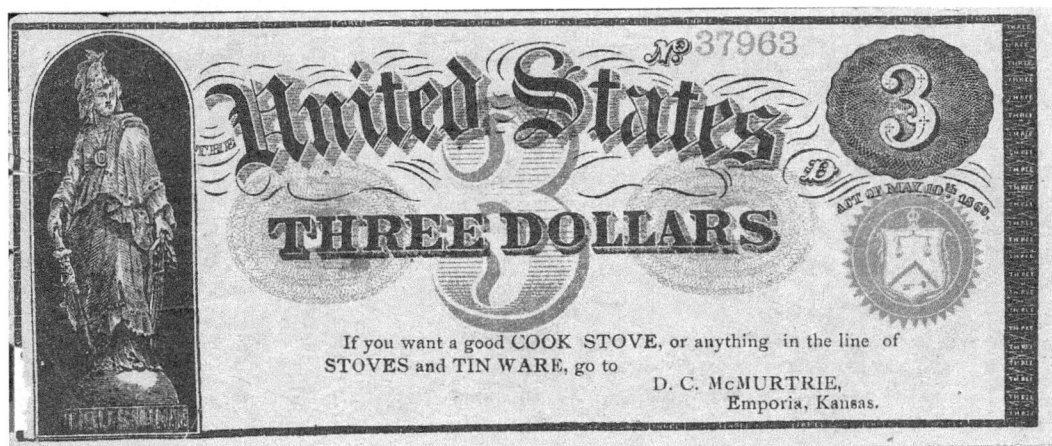

17. "3," Similar to #9 above R-7

Palace Drug Store, Olathe

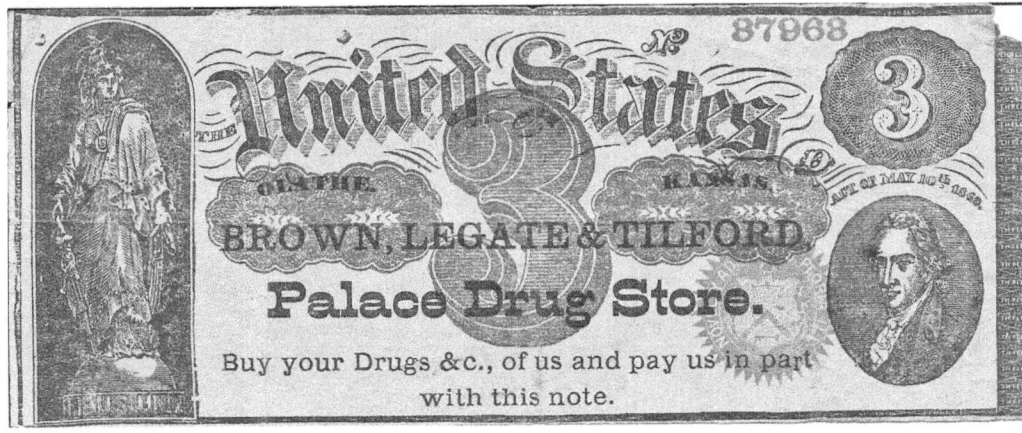

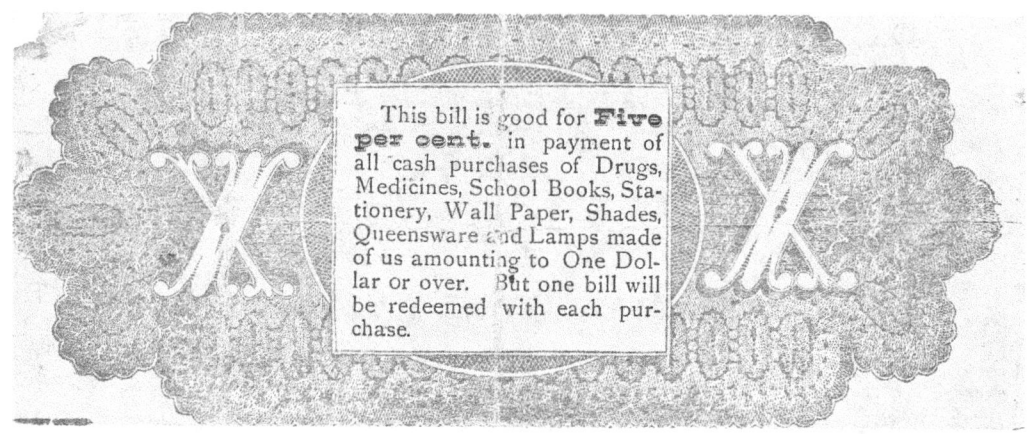

18. "3," Similar to #6 above R-7

Morris Kohn, New York Store, Wichita, Corner Douglass Ave., and Main Street

19. "1," Black, with green back. Vignette (L) Salesman showing coat . . . . Unique
to customer; Bottom center, Dog and Safe. Imprint: I.P. Barnes,
Printer, 16 Cortlandt Street, New York

Kansas Pacific Railroad, T.J. Anders, Local Agent, Topeka

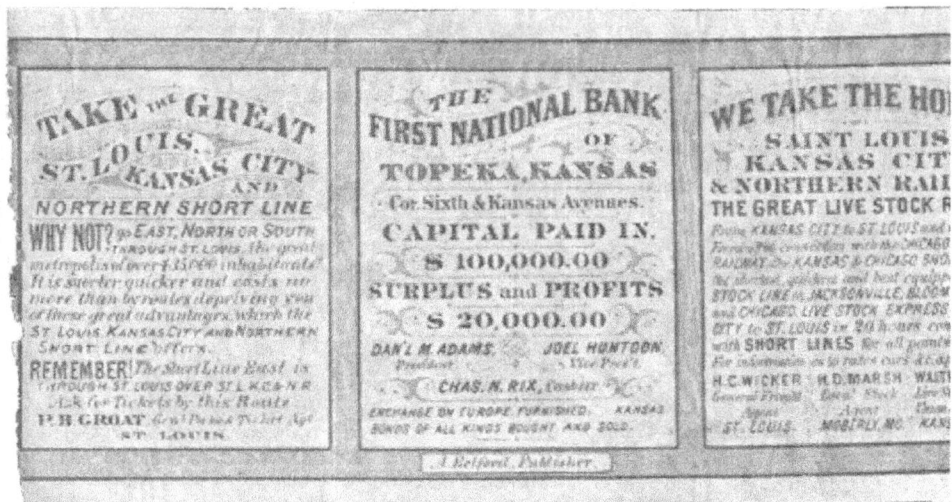

20. "5," Center, Steer Head on yellow paper. Imprint: A. Gast & Co., ... Unique
St Louis. Back: 3 ads in green by A. Belford, Publisher.
Center ad is for First National Bank of Topeka,
Daniel M. Adams, President and Charles M. Rix, Cashier.
Only example known is clipped.

Note: The first National Bank, Charter # 1660, took this title and failed in 1873. Therefore the note was issued by 1873.

Baseball Advertising Notes

Lewis & Edwards, Merchant Tailors, Emporia

V. Miscellaneous Scrip Period, 1870s–1930s 165

21. **National Baseball League Advertising note, 1888. Portrait of manager W.H. Watkins. Back shows Detroit Wolverines Baseball Club players** R-7

STAR CLOTHIERS, HUTCHINSON

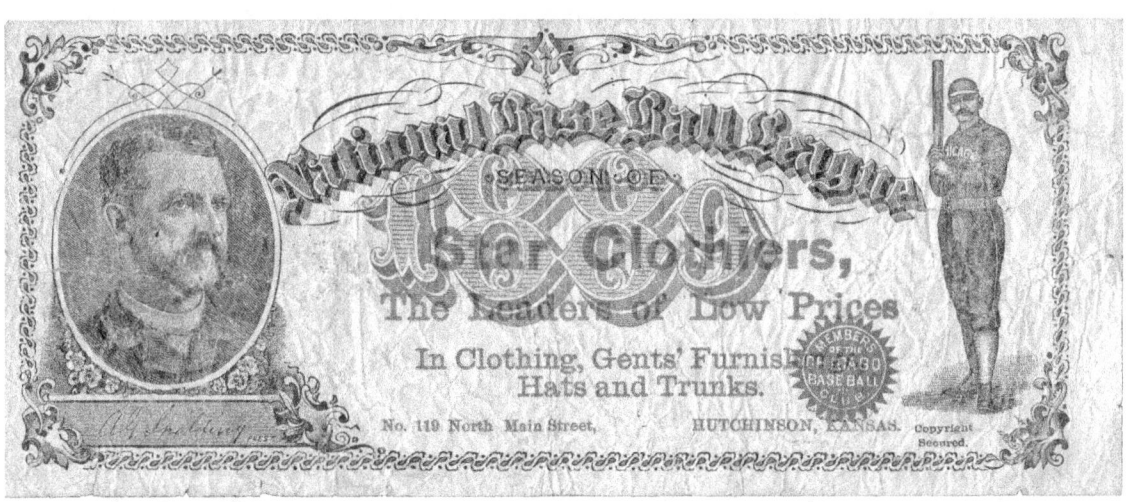

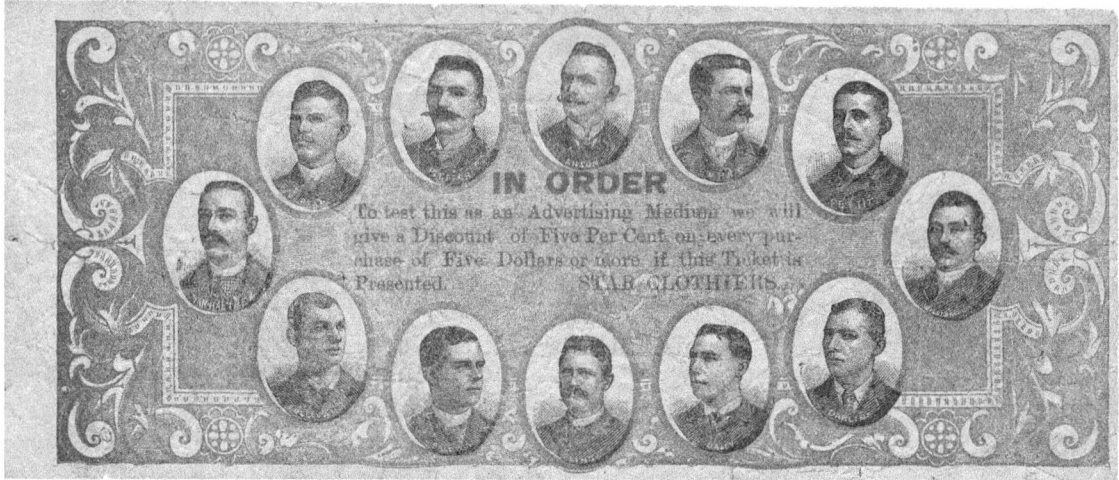

22. National Baseball League Advertising Note, 1889. (L) Portrait of A.J. Spaulding. (R) Baseball Player at bat. Back shows Chicago White Stockings Baseball Club players

TAYLOR & TAYLOR, PEOPLE'S PHARMACY, FRANKFORT

23. National Baseball Association Advertising note, 1887. Back shows R-7
St. Louis Browns baseball players in striped caps.

Confederate Lookalikes

W.E. HOWARD & SON,
MONUMENT WORKS, HUTCHINSON

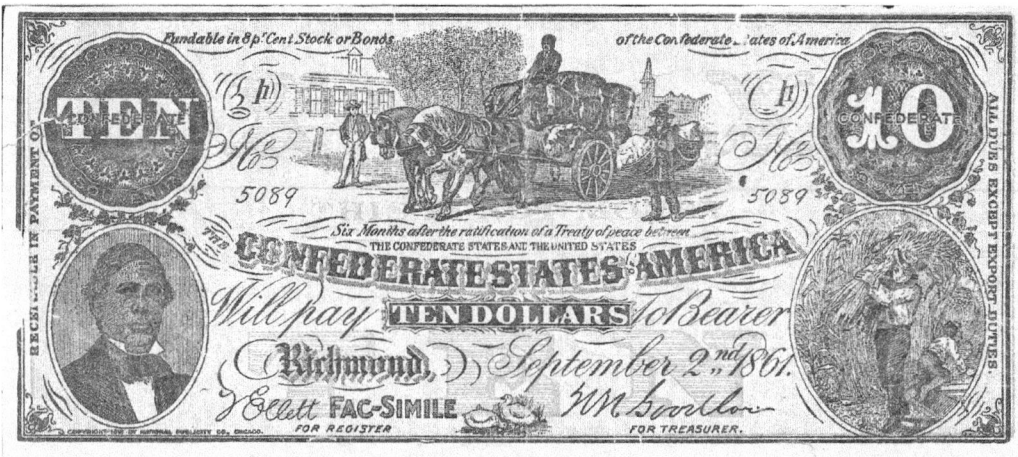

V. Miscellaneous Scrip Period, 1870s–1930s

OUR SALESMAN

This Certificate will entitle you to a credit of $10.00 on any Monument of $100.00 or over.

Do not fail to see us or write us while the big sale is on.

If you do not need a Monument, or have one, kindly give this to a friend that can use it for it is worth TEN DOLLARS in trade with

The W. E. Howard & Son Monument Works
Hutchinson, Kansas

Two Blocks East Santa Fe Depot   Office Phone 931; Residence 3060

24. Advertisement on the back of a facsimile Confederate note. R-3
Copyright by National Publicity Co., Chicago. Many more similar notes exist.

W.F. Dean, Dry Goods, Dodge City

25. Coupon for $1, Eagle with banner left; all blue. . . . . Unique

 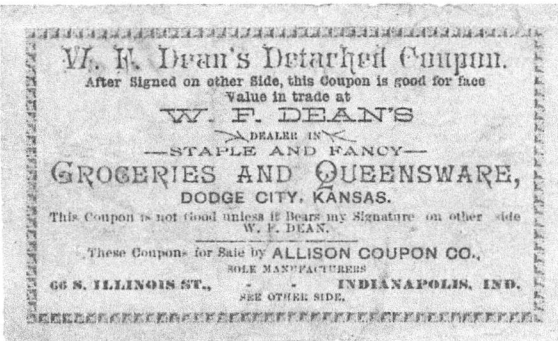

Note: Hugh Shull turned up this unusual piece. No other info.

Drover's Bank Notes
Overprinted with Advertising Messages

The territorial notes of the Drovers Bank of Fort Leavenworth and Leavenworth City, which are overprinted with various advertisements, could also be included in this section.

Boyer & Gallotti, Winfield
Overprinted with Advertising Messages

BOYER & GALLOTTI
Have Now a Very large Assortment of
FIRST CLASS DRY GOODS
At Prices to Suit Panic Pockets
When We fail to Suit others need not try,
Our Prices and Material are Guaranteed
WINFIELD, KANSAS

A $1 "Centennial Promissory Note" produced by the Illustrated Ad Co of N.Y. appeared in an R.M. Smythe Auction (lot 3500, January, 2001) credited to "Boyer & Gallotti of Winfield, KS."

Coal Company Scrip

In 1859, coal was discovered near Leavenworth deep beneath the surface. In 1866, near surface beds were found in Cherokee County, southeastern Kansas. The first coal town, Weir City, was established in 1871 by T.M. Weir. Soon thereafter Pittsburg, about nine miles northeast of Weir, was founded. In 1876, the Girard and Joplin railroad reached the area and provided a transportation link, which allowed full scale development of coal operations. Osage, Leavenworth and Franklin counties soon followed. By 1888, Pittsburg

Pittsburg, Kansas, deep shaft coal mine

had 10 coal companies in operation with stores and houses for workers. Peak production of coal in Kansas occurred in 1904, after which time it steadily declined.

It is expected that additional denominations, to $100, were printed by several of the known issuers; that more companies issued scrip, and that new coal scrip notes will surface over time.

G.W. FINDLAY & CO., FORT SCOTT (CIRCA 1880s–1890s)

George W. Findlay established coal operations at Godfrey and Clarksburg, near Fort Scott, Kansas. He served as the Kansas state mine inspector from 1887 to 1889 and died around 1900.

1a. .05, Uniface, no imprint (no city or state location appears on note) R-7

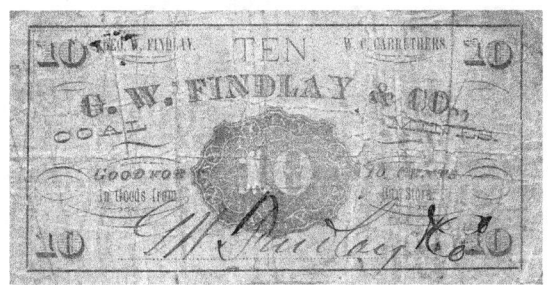

1b. .10, Uniface green ink, no imprint (no city or state location appears R-7
on note)

ROGERS COAL CO., PITTSBURG & LITCHFIELD (1885)

Rogers Coal Company was an outgrowth of the Oswego Coal Co. around 1885. David Ramsay was superintendent and about 400 men were employed at the company.

2a. .05, 188_ printed, known date Sept 11, 1885, no imprint, face blue on . . . R-7
white, back brown on white
2b. .10, Same as 5 cent above R-7
2f. $2.00, Brown ink, large size note, Imprint St Louis B.N. Co. R-7
Red SN 313?, back brown

WEAR COAL CO., PITTSBURG (1897)

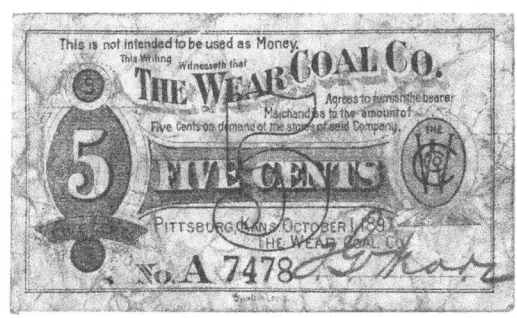

3a. .05, Oct 1, 1897 printed. Brown face and back. Imprint St Louis?
   Red SN A7478
3b. .10, Oct 1, 1894 printed, as above. Red SN A3583

OSWEGO COAL CO., WEIR CITY (1881)

4a. .05, Aug 7, 1885. Black on white, back brown. Identical to R-7
   Rogers Coal Co. scrip. (July 8, 1886 date also seen)
4b. .10, As above R-7
4c. .25, As above R-7
4d. .50, As above R-7

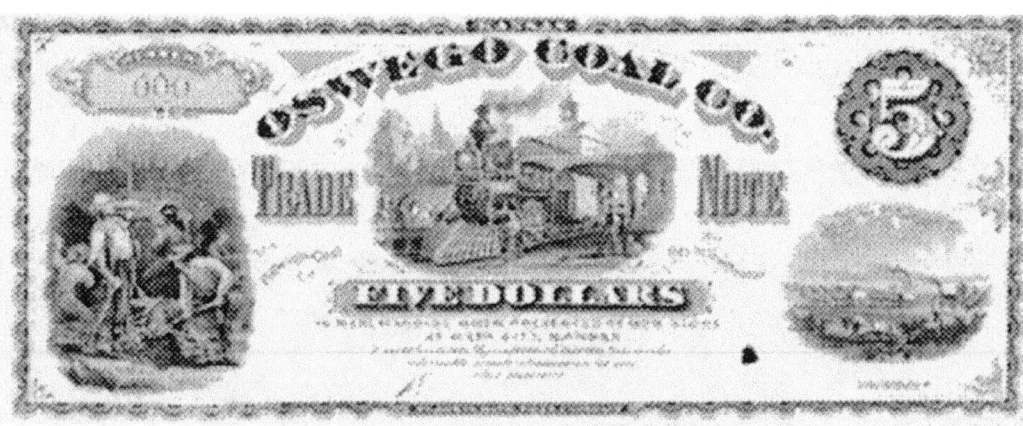

4gp. $5.00, proof (L) Mining Scene (C) Railroad Scene (R) City View. ... Unique
   Face in brown ink. Imprint: St Louis Bank Note Co.

LARSON BROS., WEIR CITY (CIRCA 1904/7?)

Round Cardboard Tokens. The tokens are uniface, signed on the back "John Larson, Weir" and hand dated Jan 1, 1904 or possibly 1907.

5b. .10, Black on light violet. "Good for 10 cents in merchandise," 38 mm ... R-7
5d. .50, Black on orange, 38 mm. "Larson Bro." on face R-7
5e. $1.00, Black on white? Soiled, 40mm R-7

City Hall, Weir City, Kansas, c. 1905

MILLER BROS. & CO., MULBERRY, (CIRCA 1910)

The Millers were among the first settlers to the area. They were involved with numerous business activities, including general merchandise, coal mining and banking. Mulberry, evolved from a coal camp originally called Mulberry Grove. It survived the closing of the shaft mining era and is located northeast of Pittsburg, on the Kansas/Missouri border, in Crawford County.

6a. .05, Payable in general merchandise; presumably at the ....Unique
company store. The note is printed black on white
with red overprinted "5s" and serial number.
Upper (L) vignette of coal mining. Back is ornate
design in black. Imprint: Gast Bank Note Co., St. Louis

College Scrip

For more information about these notes, refer to College Currency, Money for Business (BNR Press, 1993) by Herb and Martha Schingoethe. Shingoethe numbers are used where available.

FLORENCE PUBLIC SCHOOLS, FLORENCE

KS-100-10. $10, Generic note with overprint, "For use in the public R-7
Schools of Florence, Kansas" Black with back design

KANSAS NORMAL SCHOOL COLLEGE BANK, FORT SCOTT

KS-150-.05. .05, Nov. 10, 1880. Black with green back R-7
KS-150-.25, .25, Nov. 10, 1880, no imprint, back design, no plate letter R-7
KS-150-5. $5, Nov. 10, 1880, no plate letter. Imprint: Braden & R-7
Burford, Lith. Inds
KS-150-50. $50, List of Presidents of the U.S. on back R-7

V. Miscellaneous Scrip Period, 1870s–1930s

COMMERCIAL INSTITUTE, HOLTON

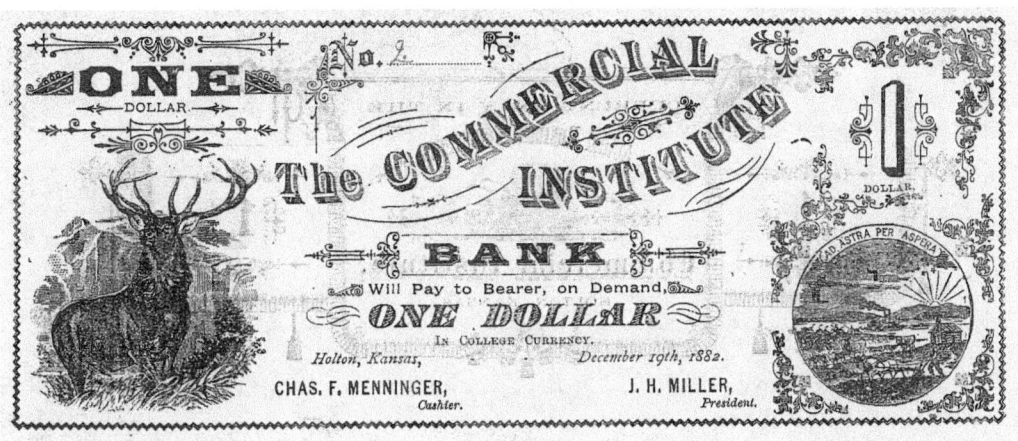

KS-200-1. $1, Dec. 19, 1882 Black on white. (L) Monarch of the glen. R-5
Back design, no plate letter

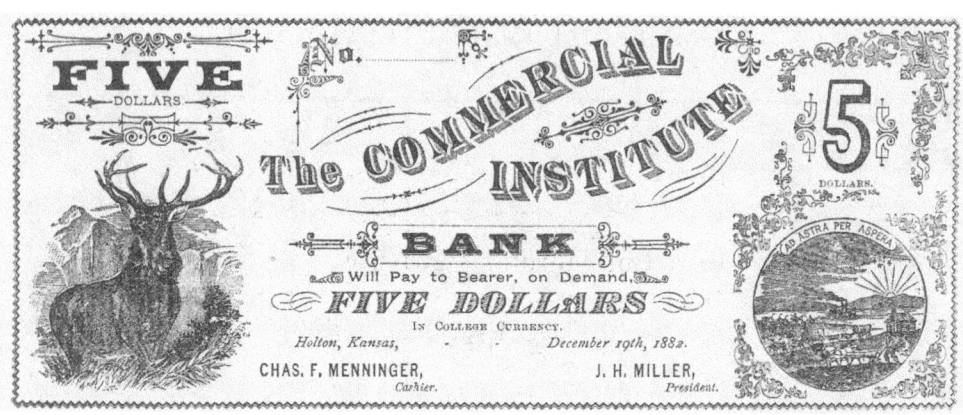

KS-200-5. $5, As above R-5
KS-200-10. $10, As above R-5
KS-200-50. $50, As above R-6
KS-200-500. $500, As above R-7

First National Bank
of Macaulay's Commercial Institute, Lawrence

KS-250-3. $3, 87_ Black with green overall undertint. Back design R-7
in green. Imprint: A. Gast & Co. Lith. St. Louis

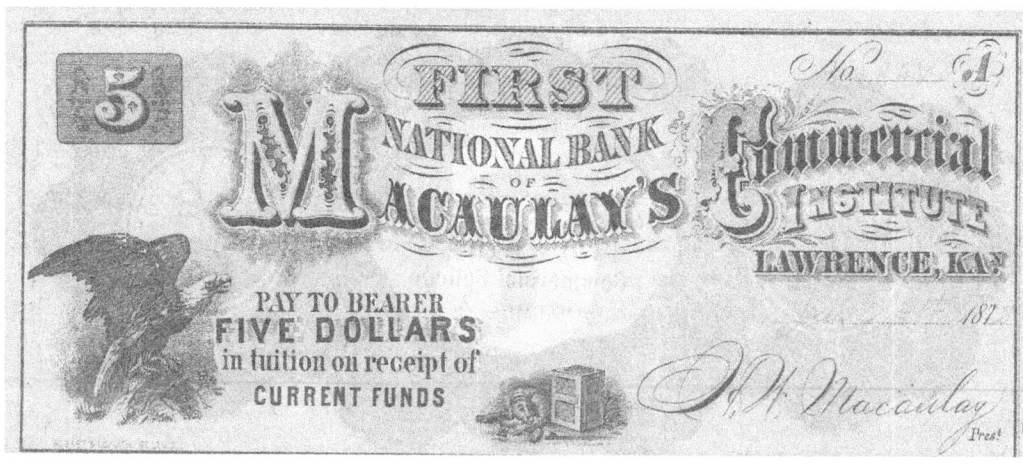

V. Miscellaneous Scrip Period, 1870s–1930s

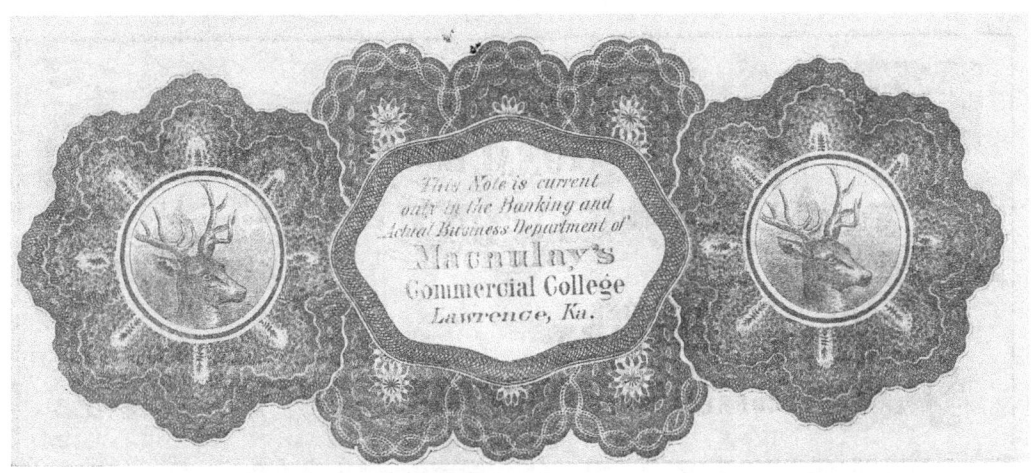

KS-250-5. $5, 187_ printed, known date Jan., 1872 .... R-7
KS-250-10. $10, As above R-7
KS-250-100. $100, As above R-7

THE BUSINESS COLLEGE BANK, LAWRENCE
(SUCCESSOR TO MACAULAY)

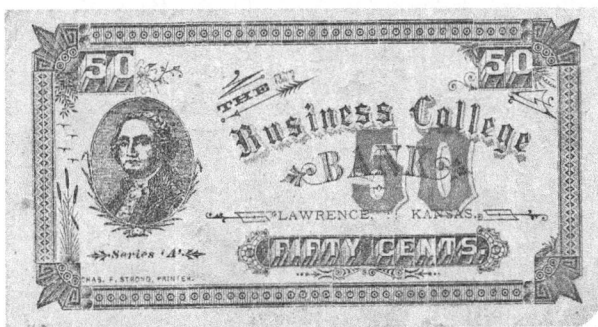

KS-265-.10. 10¢, Black on white with red overprinted "10." Uniface, ... R-7
    Imprint: Chas. F. Strong, Printer
KS-265-.50. 50¢, As above R-7

LAWRENCE, KANS.   Lawrence National Bank Bldg.

Lawrence Business College was upstairs in the National Bank of Lawrence

First National Bank of Western Business College, Leavenworth

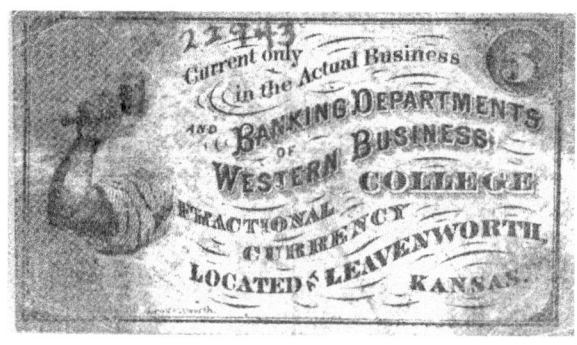

KS-275-.05. .05, (L) Arm and Hammer, Imprint ? Lith, Leavenworth R-7

V. Miscellaneous Scrip Period, 1870s–1930s

KS-280-5. $5, Jan. 1, 1873. Imprint: C.J. Smith & Co., Lith. Leavenworth ... R-7
KS-280-20. $20, Similar to $5 above R-7

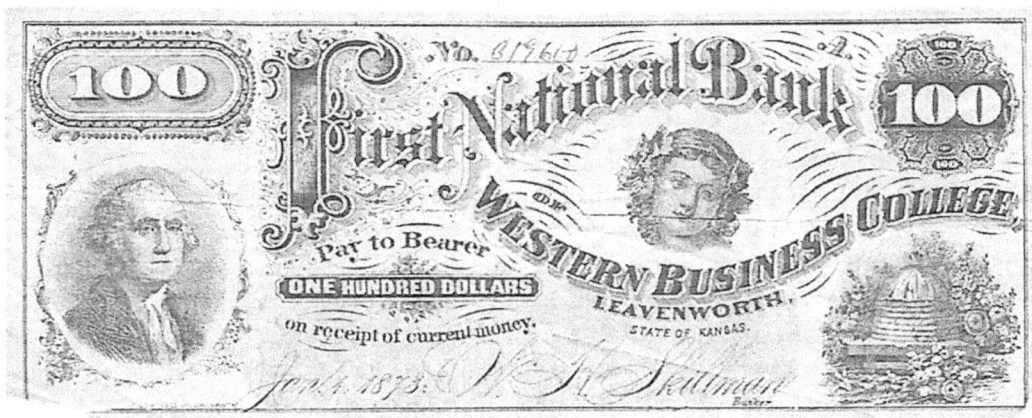

KS-280-100. $100, Similar to $5 above R-7
KS-280-500. $500, Similar to $5 above R-7

SOUTHWESTERN BUSINESS COLLEGE, WICHITA

Established in 1885 by E.H. Fritch. Taken over in 1895 by the Wichita Business College. The College also utilized colored cardboard commodity cards.

KS-300-.01. 1, CENT R-7
KS-300-.03. 3, CENTS R-7
KS-300-.15. 15, CENTS R-7

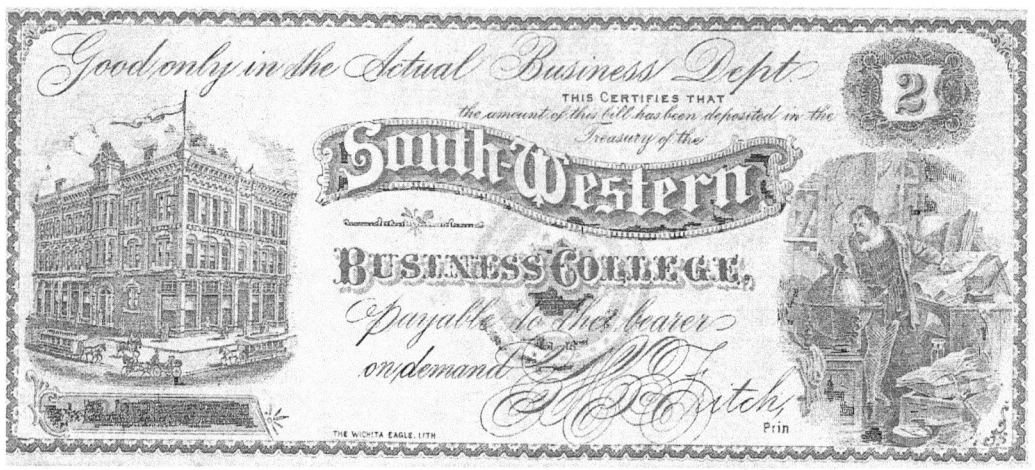

KS-300-1. $1, Uniface. Greenish Black. Vignettes (L) College Building R-6
(R) Explorer with Globe. Imprint: The Wichita Eagle, Lith.

KS-300-2. $2, Same as $1 above R-6
KS-300-5. $5, Same as $1 above R-6
KS-300-10. $10, Same as $1 above R-6
KS-300-50. $50, Same as $1 above R-6
KS-325-.05. 5, CENTS Black. Generic Ames, New York form with R-7
   Fritch signature
KS-325-.20. 20, CENTS Same as 5 Cent note above R-7
KS-325-5. $5, Same as 5 Cents above R-7
KS-325-10. $10, Same as 5 Cents above R-7
KS-325-20. $20, Same as 5 cents above R-7

FIRST NATIONAL BANK OF NATIONAL BUSINESS COLLEGES, ST. JOSEPH, MO AND TOPEKA, KS

MO-200-20. $20, Green on white, back green. Imprint: Hatch & Co. R-7
   Trinity Building, 111 Broadway, N. York
MO-200-50. $50, As above R-7

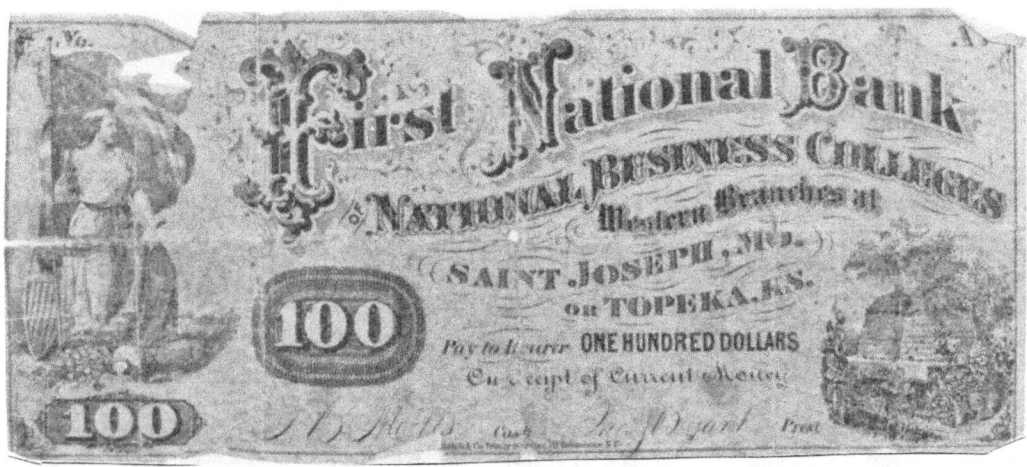

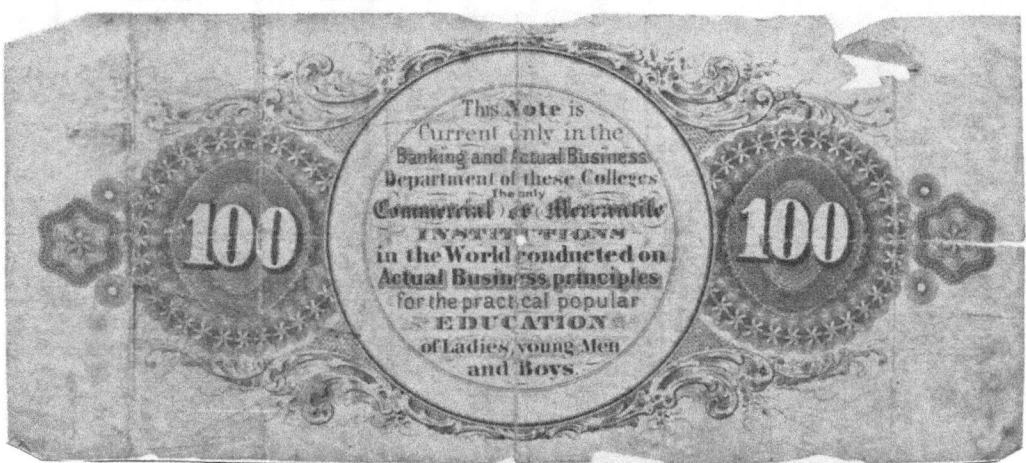

MO-200-100. $100, As above R-7

Depression Scrip, 1907–1914

During the "Banker's Panic" of 1907 more than 200 cities in 41 states issued clearing house certificates for circulation. Many other types of emergency currency were also issued. When World War I broke out in 1914 a brief panic ensued. Several cities issued certificates, which were soon withdrawn. *Note:* It is expected that more issuers, along with currently unreported denominations of known issues, will surface in the future.

Atchison

THE ATCHISON SAVINGS BANK CIRCA 1907

Cashiers Checks with rubber stamped dates of Nov. 19, 1907–Dec 17, 1907. Imprint: Trade Print.

1a. $1.00 .... R-7
1c. $5.00 .... R-7
1d. $10.00 .... R-7

EXCHANGE NATIONAL BANK

Cashiers Checks, blue on white. Portrait of Wm. Hetherington at left. Uniface. Imprint: Union Bank Note Co., K.C. Mo.

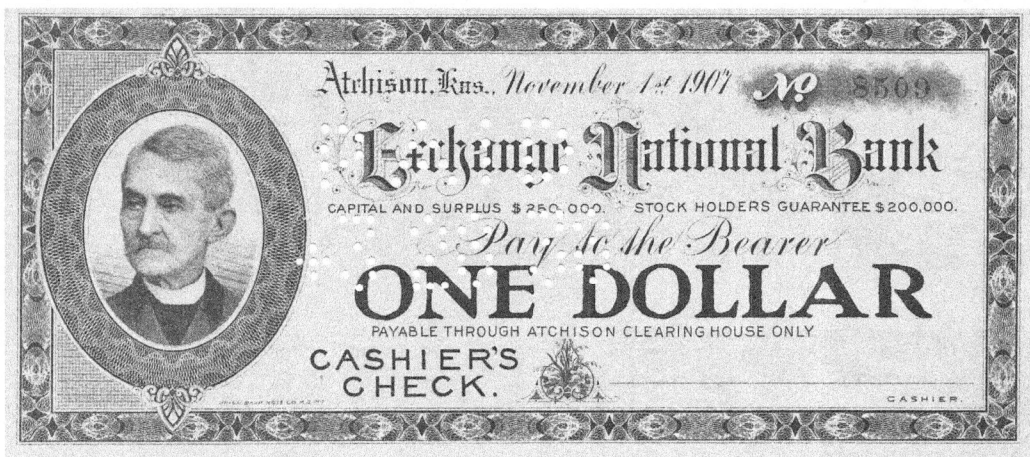

2a. $1.00 .... R-6
2b. $2.00 .... R-6
2c. $5.00 .... R-6

Exchange National Bank, Atchison, Kansas, in 1907

V. Miscellaneous Scrip Period, 1870s–1930s 181

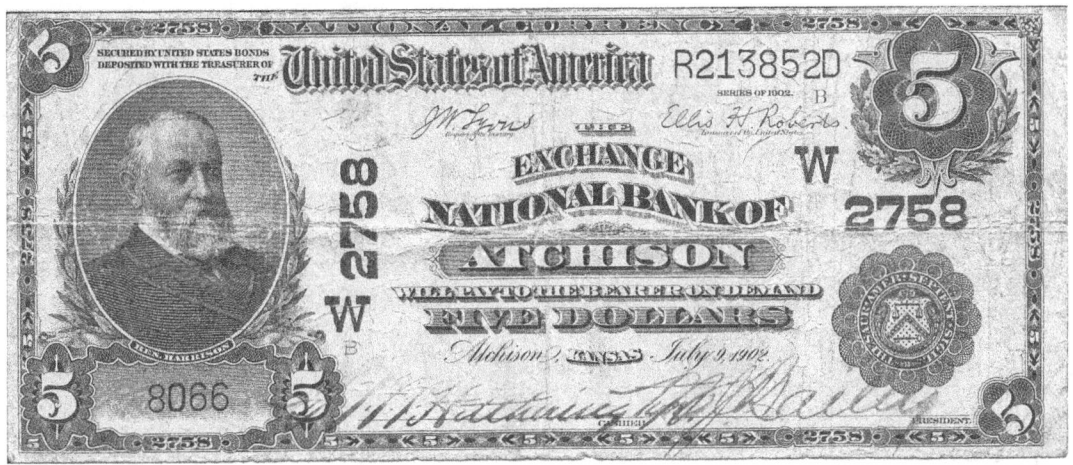

First National Bank

Cashiers Checks, black on white. Two quail at bottom, uniface. Imprint: Union Bank Note Co. K.C. Mo.

3a. $1.00 .... R-7
3b. $2.00 .... R-7
3c. $5.00 .... R-7
3d. $10.00 .... R-7

Garden City

The U.S. Sugar & Land Co.

Ninety-day 7 percent certificates. Printed black on orange-yellow paper. Imprint: Trade Mark Registered in U.S. Pat. Office.

7d. $10.00 .... R-7
7e. $20.00 .... R-7

Independence

Citizen's National Bank

Cashiers Checks. No date, circa 1907; Imprint: Combe Litho, St. Joseph, Mo.
10c. $5.00 .... R-7
10e. $20.00 .... R-7

The Commercial National Bank

Cashiers Checks. Portrait of Washington at left. Imprint: Combe Litho, St. Joseph, Mo.
11d. $10.00 .... R-7
11e. $20.00 .... R-7

The First National Bank

Cashiers Checks identical to commercial National and Citizens National items above.
12a. $1.00 .... R-7
12b. $2.00 .... R-7
12c. $5.00 .... R-7
12d. $10.00 .... R-7

Newton

Clearing House Certificate of Newton Banks

Dated Aug 4, 1914. Payable on or before Jan. 1, 1915. Imprint: Kansas Printing Co., 2569.
15a. $1.00 .... Unique

Parsons

Parsons Commercial Bank

Cashiers Checks, Seal of the state at left. Black on white with green back design. Imprint: Union Bank Note Co., K.C. Mo.

V. Miscellaneous Scrip Period, 1870s–1930s

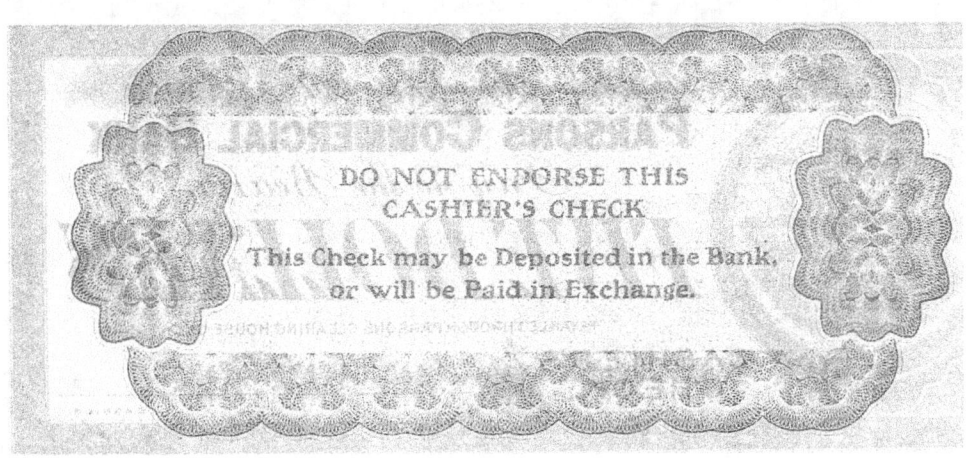

18c. $5.00 .... R-6
18d. $10.00 .... R-6

THE FIRST NATIONAL BANK

Dated Nov. 12, 1907. Cashiers Checks, similar to Parsons Commercial Bank checks.
19a. $1.00 .... R-7
19c. 5.00 .... R-7
19d. $10.00 .... R-7

Pittsburg

ASSOCIATED BANKS OF PITTSBURG

Certificates payable at the banks in Pittsburg. Imprint: Western Bank Note & Eng. Co., Chicago.
22a. $1.00 .... R-7
22b. $2.00 .... R-7

22c. $5.00 .... R-7
22d. $10.00 .... R-7

Topeka

The Associated Banks of the City of Topeka

Clearing House Certificates. The $1 and $2 are black on white. The $5 and $10 are black on light blue paper. Payable through Clearing House only. Imprint: Hall Litho Co., Topeka.

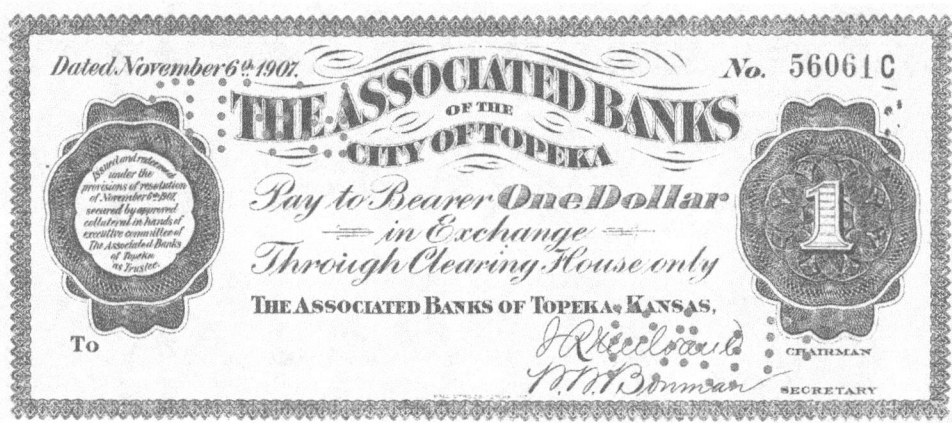

25a. $1.00 .... R-7
25b. $2.00 .... R-7
25c. $5.00 .... R-7

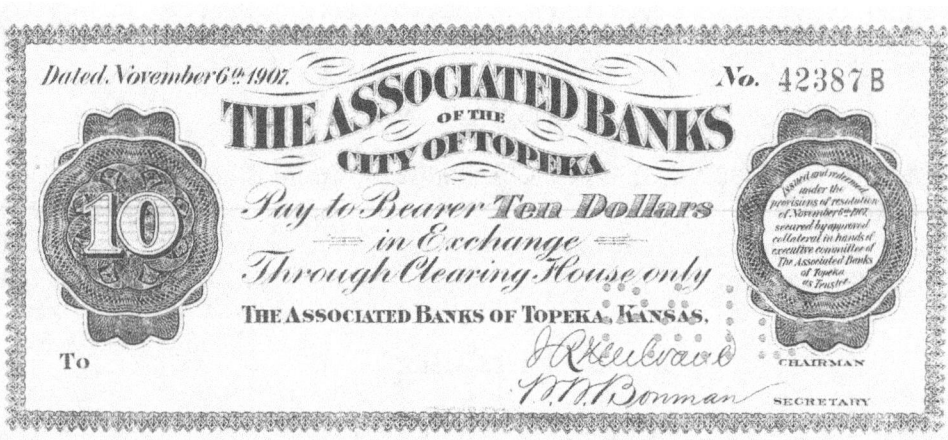

25d. $10.00 .... R-7

Wichita

Citizens State Bank

Circa 1907. No location is shown on this note (Chase Museum in 1941)

28a. $1.00 .... Unique

National Bank of Wichita

Cashiers Checks. Dog's head at lower center. Black on white with fine green line overprint. Imprint: Western Litho Co., Wichita.

29a. $1.00 .... R-7
29b. $2.00 .... R-7
29c. $5.00 .... R-7
29d. $10.00 .... R-7

National Bank of Wichita

Cashiers Check. Nov. 1, 1907. Imprint Claude D.? Funk Printing Co., Wichita.

30f. $25.00 .... Unique

Wichita Clearing House Association

Certificates. Dated Nov. 20, 1907. Black on white, back Green with spread Eagle. Imprint: Western Litho Co., Wichita.

31a. $1.00 .... R-6
31c. $5.00 .... R-6
31d. $10.00 .... R-6

WICHITA CLEARING HOUSE ASSOCIATION

Dated Aug. 3, 1914. Face identical to 1907 issue except for date. Back orange with young girl's portrait in center. Imprint: Western Litho Co., Wichita.

32a. $1.00	R-7
32c. $5.00	R-7
32d. $10.00	R-7

1930s Depression Scrip

For additional details on these notes refer to the standard catalog of *Depression Scrip of the United States, of the 1930s, including Canada and Mexico* by Ralph A. Mitchell and Neil Shafer (Krause Publications, 1980). Mitchell/Shafer catalog numbers are used.

Atchison

CHAMBER OF COMMERCE

| KS51-.10. .10, Feb 18, 1933 | R-7 |
| KS51-.50. .50, Feb 7/18, 1933 | R-7 |

Bunker Hill

THE BUNKER HILL COMMUNITY CLUB

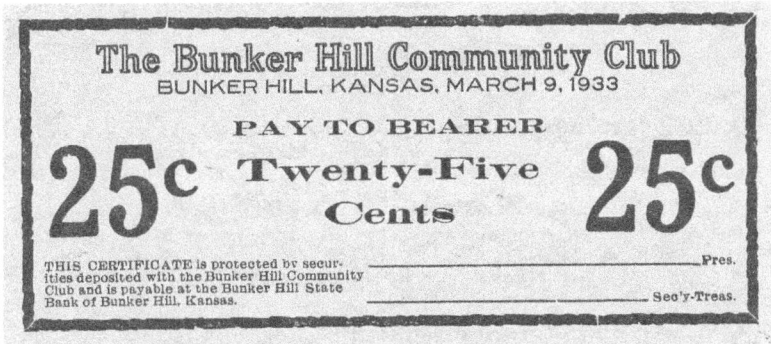

KS60-.25. .25, Mar 9, 1933 .... Unique

Clay Center

CHAMBER OF COMMERCE

KS80-.05. .05, Mar 10, 1933 (red/orange) R-4
KS80-.50. .50, Mar 10, 1933 (brown) R-4
KS80-1.A. $1.00, Mar 10, 1933 (green) R-4
KS80-1.B. $1.00, Same except "Script" R-4

Chanute

THRIFT DOLLAR (?)

KS90-1. $1.00, 1932 (green on white) R-4

Council Grove

MERCHANTS EXCHANGE

KS100-.10. .10, Mar 7, 1933 (green on green) R-4

Garden City

MUNICIPAL UTILITIES CERTIFICATE

The scrip notes of Garden City include a portrait of C.J. "Buffalo" Jones. Jones was an early buffalo hunter who became a great conservationist working to save the buffalo. Teddy Roosevelt appointed Jones as the first warden of Yellowstone National Park in 1902. He met Zane Grey, who wrote about Jones' life in *The Last of the Plainsmen*. In 1959, "Buffalo Jones" was among the first inductees into the National Cowboy and Western Heritage Museum in Oklahoma City.

KS125-1. $1.00, Mar 10, 1933 (blue on yellow) R-5
KS125-5. $5.00, Mar 10, 1933 (black on pale green) R-6

Gardner

CITY WARRANT

KS140-.25. .25, Mar 7, 1933 (black on yellow) R-7
KS140-.50. .50, Mar 7, 1933 .... R-7
KS140-1. $1.00, Mar 7, 1933 .... R-7

Great Bend

CITY OF GREAT BEND

KS155-.50. .50, Mar 1, 1933 (green on yellow) R-7

Hillsboro

BONUS DAY CERTIFICATE

KS170-1.A. $1.00, ND (black on light green) R-7
KS170-1.B. $1.00, ND (black on yellow) R-7

Holton

JACKSON COUNTY CHAMBER OF COMMERCE

Total issue: $1,000
KS185-.25. .25, Mar 11, 1933 (black on green underprint) R-7
KS185-.50. .50 .... R-7
KS185-1. $1.00 .... R-7

MAYORS SCRIP

Total issue: $500.
KS190-.25. .25, Dec 9, 1937 (black on yellow) R-7
KS190-.50. .50, Dec 9, 1937 .... R-7
KS190-1. $1.00 .... R-7

Independence

GUARANTEED SCRIP

KS200-1. $1.00, Redemption after June 1, 1933 (brown on light brown) R-7

Johnson County

CHAMBER OF COMMERCE

KS205-.25. .25, 1933 .... R-7

Kansas City, Kansas

CLEARING HOUSE CERTIFICATES

Total: $900,000 printed by Burd & Fletcher Printing Co., Kansas City. All destroyed except 100 of each denomination.

KS225-1. $1.00, 1933 (green on white) R-3
KS225-5. $5.00, 1933 (green on white) R-3

KS225-10. A$10.00, 1933 (green on white) R-3

KS225-10. B$10.00, 1933 (black on white) R-7

Kansas City, Kansas and Missouri

Goodwill Barter and Exchange Centers

KS220-.10. .10, ND (black on green) R-6
KS220-.25. .25, ND R-6
KS220-.50. .50, ND R-6
KS220-1. $1.00, ND R-6

Lawrence

Lawrence Clearing House

KS235-1. $1.00, Series 1933 .... R-7

KS235-5. $5.00, Series 1933 .... R-7
KS235-10. $10.00, Series 1933 .... R-7

Luray

Chamber of Commerce

KS255-.25. .25, Mar 6, 1933 (black on white) R-7
KS255-.50. .50, Mar 6, 1933 (yellow paper) R-7
KS255-1. $1.00, Mar 6, 1933 (gray paper) R-7

Neodesha

Chamber of Commerce

KS285-.05. .05, Mar 8, 1933 (purple underprint) R-5
KS285-.10. .10, Mar 8, 1933 (dull red underprint) R-5
KS285-.25. .25, Mar 8, 1933 (blue underprint) R-5
KS285-.50. .50, Mar 8, 1933 (orange underprint) R-5
KS285-1. $1.00, Mar 8, 1933 (brown underprint) R-5

KS285-5. $5.00, Mar 8, 1933 (green underprint) R-5

Ness City

Farmers Cooperative Grain & Supply Co. (Due Bill)

KS305-.25. .25, Mar 10/11, 1933 (black on white cardboard) R-7
KS305-1. $1.00, Mar 10/11, 1933 (black on orange cardboard) R-7
KS305-2.5. $2.50, Mar 10/11, 1933 (black on peach cardboard) R-7

Oswego

American State Bank

KS315-1. $1.00, Mar 10, 1933 (black on white) R-5
KS315-5. $5.00, Mar 10, 1933 (black on white) R-5

The

KS315-10. $10.00, Mar 10, 1933 (black on white) R-5

First National Bank

KS325-1. $1.00, Mar 10, 1933 (black on white) R-7
KS325-5. $5.00, Mar 10, 1933 (black on white) R-7

Parsons

Parsons Commercial Bank

KS335-5. $5.00, Mar 10, 1933; similar to American State Bank scrip, ... R-7
Oswego

Russell

City of Russell

KS360-.50. .50, Dec 22, 1932–Jan 20, 1933 (black on pink) R-7

Sedan

Chamber of Commerce

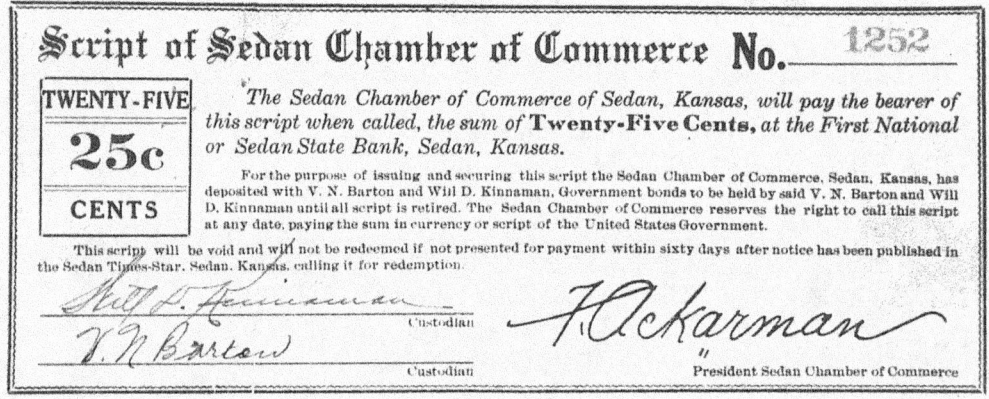

KS385-.25. .25, ND (1933) (black on yellow) R-7

Topeka

The Associated Banks of Topeka

KS410-1. $1.00, Mar 6, 1933 (green and blue) R-7
KS410-5. $5.00, Mar 6, 1933 (blue and dark blue) R-7
KS410-10. $10.00, Mar 6, 1933 (orange and blue) R-7
KS410-20. $20.00, Mar 6, 1933 (gray and blue) R-7

Topeka Clearing House Association

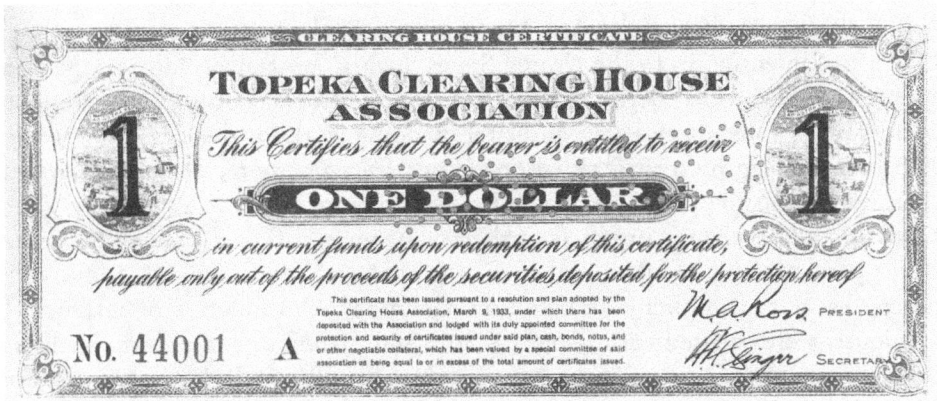

KS415-1. $1.00, Mar 9, 1933 (green and black on white) R-7
KS415-5. $5.00, Mar 9, 1933 (green and black on greenish) R-7
KS415-10. $10.00, Mar 9, 1933 (green and black on yellow) R-7

Waverly

Waverly Scrip Money

KS440-.05. .05, Mar 7, 1933 (black on yellow) R-7

Wichita

Unemployed Trading Post

KS485-.05A. .05, ND (1933) (blue and brown on green) R-7
KS485-.05B. .05, ND (1933) (tan safety paper) R-7
KS485-.05C. .05, ND (1933) (red and green on gray) R-7
KS485-.05D. .05, ND (1933) (blue and brown on gray) R-7

Labor Exchange Scrip

G.B. DeBernardi of Independence, Missouri, started the Labor Exchange movement in 1893. An Italian emigrant to the United States, he lost most of his farm property as a result of the Depression that began in 1873. He became a social activist at that time, first as a member of the Greenback Party, and later by doing work for the Grange movement. In 1890 he wrote a lengthy treatise titled *Progressive Thought and the Dawn of Equity*, and soon thereafter began the Labor Exchange Branch program.

Workers could exchange products of their labor for certificates, valued in fractional or multiple parts of a day of labor, rather than for paper money. This valuation method was chosen so as not to conflict with U.S. laws regarding the production of currency. The notes obviously were equated with their U.S. coin and currency counterparts, such as $5/100$ equal to five cents, etc. The certificates were produced by T. or F.B. Eng, K.C., and have slightly varying designs. These certificates could be exchanged for other goods or services in the Exchange. The movement spread rapidly and eventually included more than 300 Exchange branches in 34 states and Canada, with more than 15,000 individual members. Headquarters of the movement was at Kansas City, Missouri. Very little of this scrip has surfaced to date, but more is expected to turn up as collecting interest spreads, for example following the R.M. Smythe sale of the Schingoethe obsolete notes part #9.

Kansas had at least 12 Exchange Branches established in various towns, including the only colony, established as an Exchange, at Freedom, Kansas, near Fort Scott. Only six Kansas notes from three different locations have been seen to date. Kansas towns with Exchange Branches and notes reported are as follows:

#6. **Olathe**	SENC
#38. **Olathe**	SENC
#54. **Pittsburg**	SENC
#131. **Salina**, $1/100$	Unique
#140. **Harding**	SENC
#197. **Edwardsville**	SENC

V. *Miscellaneous Scrip Period, 1870s–1930s*

#199. Freedom, ⅒, ¼, ½ and 1 unit R-7
#223. Osage City, ⁵⁄₁₀₀ unit .... Unique
?. Beloit .... SENC
?. Fort Scott .... SENC
?. Peterton .... SENC
#?. Turner .... SENC

By the turn of the century, the results of the Spanish American War and adoption of the gold standard had the country on a firm financial footing, largely obviating the need for the Exchange movement. Interest waned and DeBernardi passed away in 1901. Although a few Exchanges continued to operate into the teens, most of them soon faded into oblivion.

Other Miscellaneous "Kansas Money"

There have been various other Kansas paper documents that are similar in appearance to bank notes produced. These items are often included as part of paper money collections. These include things like insurance policies, lottery tickets, raffle tickets, political receipts or political messages, Merchandise Due Bills, and others, many of which have a similar appearance to various period bank notes. Several Kansas examples are included in this section, but no attempt to document all material that fits this category is made here.

LIFE INSURANCE

Leavenworth $100. 18__ printed. The Missouri Valley Life Insurance Co. of Leavenworth, Kansas. A life insurance policy made to look like a $100 bank note.

RAFFLE TICKETS

Such tickets often bear a relation to currency. Hard-times lotteries were used to sell items that were otherwise impossible to sell. Another popular use was to raise funds for public works projects or churches. Large amounts of money could be raised through numerous small donations. This is still done, most recently to sell houses and other properties. Lotteries that promise great riches have also always been popular where legal.

 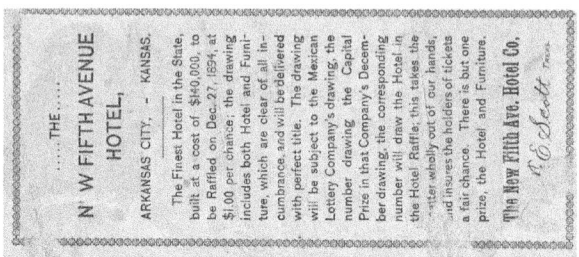

$1.00 Raffle Ticket for The New Fifth Avenue Hotel, 1894, Arkansas City, KS

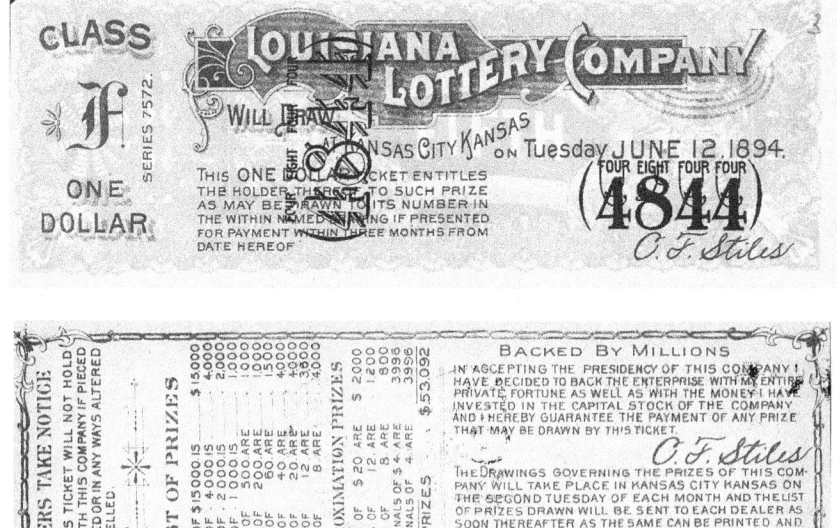

$1.00 Lottery Ticket; Kansas City, Kansas; 1894 (Louisiana Lottery)

POLITICAL SCRIP

Political party messages have often been published as lookalike bank notes. The Greenback Party of the 19th Century, leaflets bearing anti-gold standard messages, others published against the Bank of the U.S. and other causes, have all employed the banknote format to get their message across. Another use has been in the form of receipts for political donations.

V. Miscellaneous Scrip Period, 1870s–1930s

$1.00 Political Receipt, the Kansas Republican Party, 1938. Orange back border.

ADVERTISING COUPONS

Coupons that promise discounts or just advertise a business are still widely used. The idea was that people are more likely to look at, and save, something that resembles money than a simple printed message.

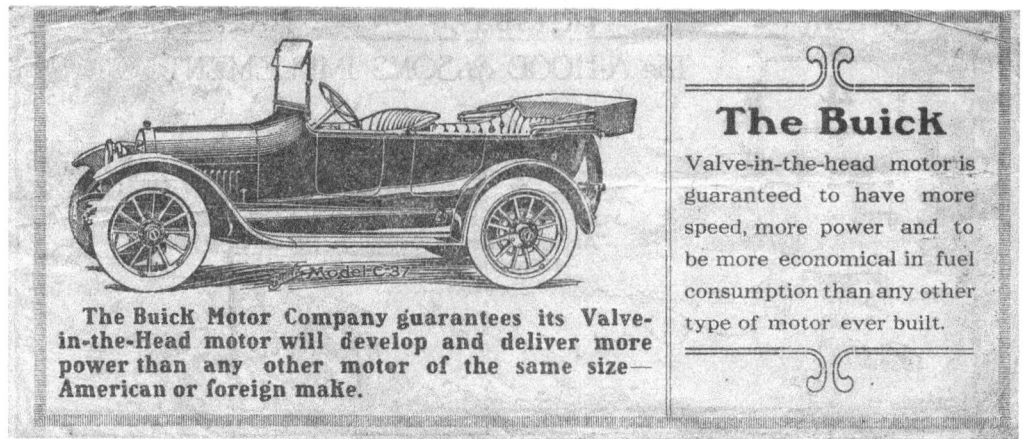

The A. Hood & Sons Implement Co., various locations. "1" blue on white and "4" green on white seen, probably others were printed. Advertising coupons, circa 1920.

COLLEGE BOND SCRIP

In 1870 the Kansas State Agricultural College at Manhattan issued bonds in $100 denominations that came to be known as "college greenbacks." They were redeemed by the state in 1880 at a total cost of $40,000.

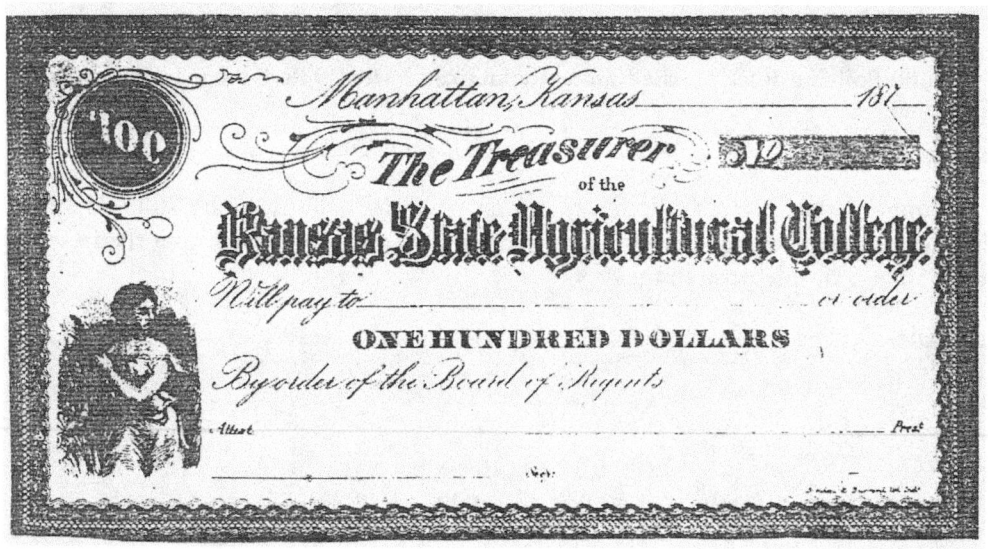

$100, Manhattan, Kansas _____ 187_. The Treasurer of the Kansas State Agricultural College will pay _____ One Hundred Dollars, By order of the Board of Regents.

MERCHANDISE DUE BILLS, OR INTERCHANGEABLE DUE BILLS

These bills were purportedly not intended as substitutes for real money. However, they were redeemable in goods valued at common U.S. coin and currency denominations

V. Miscellaneous Scrip Period, 1870s–1930s

such as five cents, ten cents, etc. Blanks could be signed by anyone and many of the signatures seen today were probably added years later. More of these notes (with currently unlisted issuer names) will undoubtedly turn up as time passes. They could possibly be considered examples of 1893 depression era scrip. An article in *Banker's Magazine* for September, 1894, reported: "U.S. Secret Service confiscates 70,000 due bills passing as currency in the small towns of Kansas. Seized at Topeka. Size of 10 Cents currency of the past. Paid to farmers for crops, redeemable at face value for goods. Ordered to stop the business."

Due Bills were stock notes, all of similar design, produced by Padgett & Bro., of Topeka. There appear to be two basic designs, one with an eagle on the face and another without vignette. They have been seen in green, blue, red and reddish brown on white and have surprisingly ornate backs. They were to be signed by individual issuers. Several legitimate signatures of the firm represented by the note are known. Many more of these notes have appeared with suspicious signatures, which may or may not be contemporary.

One Jack issued by Merchants of Wilmore, Kansas, "good only for purchase of merchandise...."

Ten Cents Merchants Daily Savings Club check issued by Albert H. Schuler, Valley Falls, Kansas.

Riley, Kansas

Kaup & Trumbull

1a. .05, Green on white R-4
1b. .10, Green on white R-4

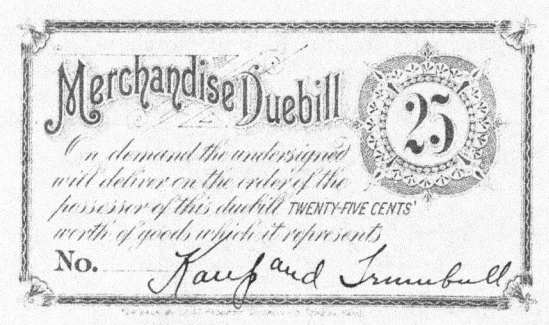
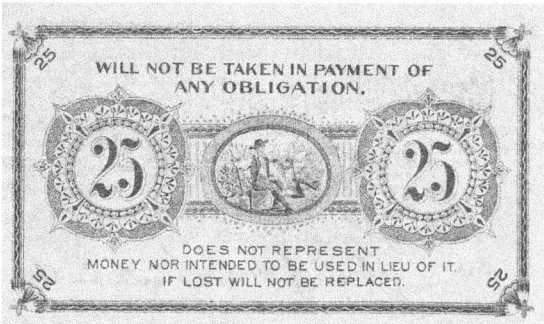

1c. .25, Green on white; also appears in blue on white R-4
1d. .50, Green on white R-4
1e. $1.00, Green on white; also appears in red on white R-4

Wichita, Kansas

V.F. Ferguson

The 1905/06 City Directory listed Virgil F. Ferguson, Union Pacific Tea Co., 1007 and 501 W. Douglas, Wichita. Red brown on white. Eagle left.

2c. .25 .... R-7
2d. .50 .... R-7
2e. $1.00 .... R-7

Location Unknown

William A. Voigt

Eagle left. Backs are blue on white.

3a. .05	R-7
3b. .10	R-7
3c. .25	R-7

J.B. Strickland

4b. .10	R-7

Cook & Hopkins

5a. .05, Violet on white	R-7

Landbloom & Roseberg

6f. $2	R-7

Herman & Schlane

7a. .05	R-7

A.C. Andrews & Co.

8b. .10, Eagle left, green on white. Interchangeable R-7

A.D. Wertenberger

9b. .10, Interchangeable R-7

Cribbs & Kennedy

10b. .10, Eagle left R-7

Alex Landers

11b. .10, Face in red ink Similar to #1 above R-7

H.J. Chase

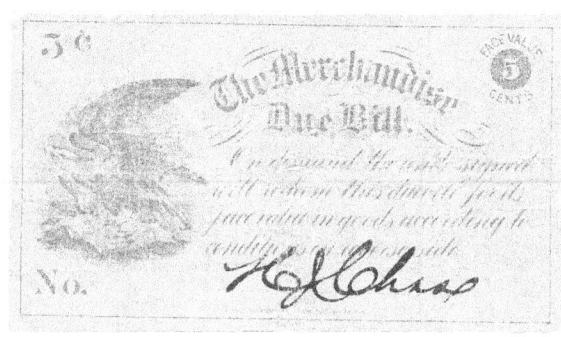

12a. .05, Face in green ink Similar to #1 above R-7

A. Hubet

13d. .50, Violet on white Similar to #5 above R-7

Postal Notes

The United States ceased production of fractional denominated currency notes in 1879, when the country returned to resumption of specie payments. The small notes had proved so popular to the citizenry for the mailing of small amounts of money that the Post Office Department came up with the idea of small denomination money orders. These were called Postal Notes, and produced in several series. Most surviving examples were purchased by collectors of the period, and thus not redeemed. Other examples were misplaced as book marks, etc. The illustrated example was dated 1894 at Hays City, Kansas.

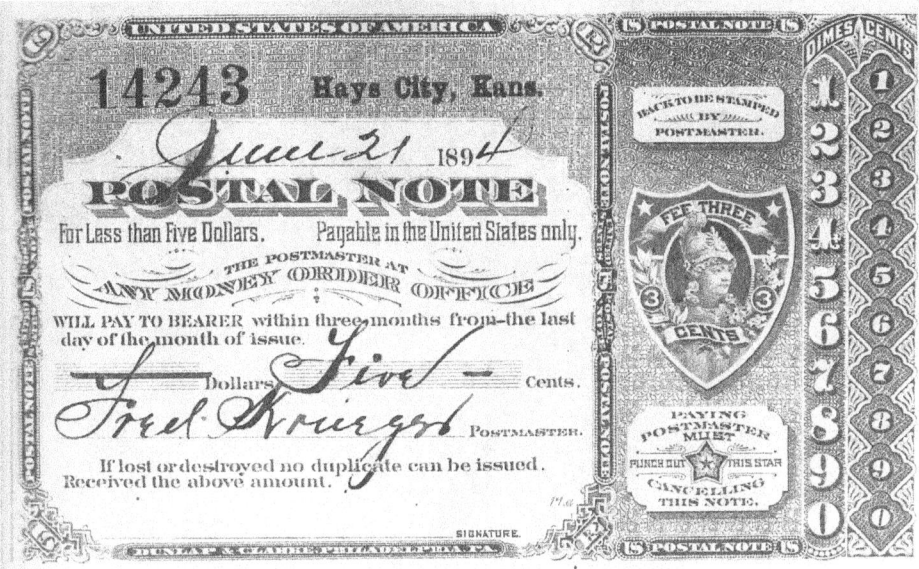

POW Scrip from World War II

Many German and Italian prisoners were brought to the United States during World War II and placed in camps, including several in Kansas. Cardboard, rectangular shaped scrip in small denominations was produced for prisoner use. Camp Phillips near Salina, and Fort Riley near Manhattan provide examples of this type of scrip.

Kansas "Coins"

A single issuer of substitute "One Cent" Civil War storecards is known from Kansas. This was A. Cohen, who was located on lower Delaware Street in Leavenworth. There are also several 25¢ and 50¢ U.S. coins dated in the 1850s known, that were counterstamped with the name: "Frazer, Jeweler, Lawrence, K.T." These items are extremely rare.

Tokens

And finally, another collecting field related to "State Money" is the pursuit of tokens. Tokens were made for many purposes from advertising to transportation and from taxes to good luck. They were usually round and made of metal, plastic, cardboard and other materials. Since many of them show a location they are popular state items for many hobbyists. This is really a separate collecting area from paper money and cataloging has only begun. There are literally thousands of these items that can make up a great "localized" collection.

Conclusion

Undoubtedly many more examples of "Kansas money" were produced throughout the state's history. However, it is strongly believed that most commonly collected Kansas material included in the category of "Obsolete Money," has been seen and cataloged. More "Lookalikes" and depression scrip will undoubtedly surface, but not many new bank notes nor Civil War merchant scrip pieces will appear from Kansas in the future.

VI

National Bank Note Period, 1864–1935

By 1860, there were more than 1,500 banks in the United States issuing thousands of banknotes with differing designs. Each $1 bill looked different from every other $1 and so on. Many notes were counterfeited or raised to higher denominations by crooks and confidence men Large quantities of notes in circulation were worthless because the issuing bank had either gone broke or never existed in the first place. The conduct of business was a nightmare for anyone who had to deal in currency. Merchants used a periodical, called a "counterfeit detector," to determine whether bills were legitimate, and a "prices current" to determine the latest discount on tendered banknotes. Clearly, some control and organization was necessary to further the economic development of the country and minimize losses to the public.

At the time, Congress was working on a national banking act, which would give control of the nation's banks and the issue of currency to the government. The sudden Civil War crisis demanded immediate action, so two laws were passed. One allowed the issue of greenbacks on the faith of the government, while the other allowed banks to receive national charters and issue currency with standard designs against deposited government bonds. This not only standardized the nation's money, but created a market for government bonds which provided funds for the prosecution of the war. However; the changeover was not immediate. It took further legislation, including a confiscatory tax on state bank notes that went into effect in 1866.

In order to receive a national charter a bank had to comply with certain restrictions and government oversight. The bank could deposit government bonds with the circulation privilege and receive currency from the treasury department to loan to its customers. The notes bore the name and location of the bank and were signed by officers of the local bank. The features of national currency give these notes a unique local character. Not only do they identify the bank and city or town, but they are often hand signed by the early bankers. Many of these men achieved prominence in other fields, too, so many of the notes are also desirable from an autograph collecting standpoint.

National bank notes were issued from 1864 until 1935. There were three distinct charter periods, of approximately 20 years each, resulting in different designs and seal colors.

Many excellent reference books are available for the interested collector. They not only provide historical information about legislation, note designs and features of these notes, but also list every bank that issued notes, the dollar amount of each type issued, and the reported surviving examples from each bank.

In 1929, the United States made a significant change to its paper currency when standard designs were adopted for each denomination and class of currency, and the physical size of the notes was reduced. From 1929 to 1935, national banks in Kansas issued these new smaller sized notes. While not as attractive as their large size predecessors, these notes are of great interest because they come from Kansas. With the passing of the era, local, or "Kansas Money," was no longer produced. Fortunately for the Kansas collector and historian there are plenty of these old notes available, and more turn up from safe deposit boxes and family collections every year. This section includes a listing of cities and towns in Kansas that issued national currency and illustrates examples from each of the charter periods.

Kansas National Bank Notes

National Bank Notes were issued between 1864 and 1935. There were three charter periods and a small size note period from 1929 to 1935. First Charter notes were produced and issued by national banks from 1864 to 1902. The type of notes issued depended on the year the bank received its charter. Denominations were decided by the banks. In order for a bank to have issued first charter period notes, it would have to have been chartered by 1882.

Banks chartered, or re-chartered, from 1882 until 1902 issued second charter period notes. These notes were produced in three different designs that vary by seal color and back design. First were the "brown backs" until 1908, followed by "datebacks" until around 1916 (with "1882–1908" displayed on their backs). The third type was the "value backs" with the denomination spelled out on the back, and issued until 1922.

Banks chartered, or re-chartered, between 1902 and 1928 issued third charter period notes. First issued with red seals, these were followed in 1908 by blue seal "date backs." From 1908 until 1916, new or renewed charter banks issued notes with "1902–1908" printed on their backs. From 1916 until 1928 new notes had blue seals with no dates on the back and are referred to as "plain backs."

In general, one can get an idea of the types of notes that may have been issued by a bank from its organization date. For details about actual amounts, types, denominations issued and rarity, refer to Don Kelly's book on nationals or the Hickman/Oakes reference work listed in the bibliography. These references also provide a more thorough explanation of the national banking system. Peter Huntoon has also published volumes of detailed information about national bank note dating practices.

Following is a listing of Kansas cities and counties that had note issuing national banks between 1864 and 1935. Below each city listing are the bank titles and charter numbers of the banks that issued notes. The date the bank was chartered and the date (if before 1935) when the bank wound up its affairs is also listed.

Abilene
    Abilene NB
    Farmers NB
    First NB

Dickinson County
#3377   1887
#8379   1906
#2427   1879–1890

Alma
    Alma NB
    Commercial NB
    Farmers NB
    First NB in Alma
    First NB of Alma

Wabaunsee County
#5104   1897–1932
#8357   1906–1912
#10195   1912–1932
#13601   1932
#3769   1887–1890

Almena
    First NB

Norton County
#8255   1906

Americus
    Farmers NB

Lyon County
#10902   1916–1924

Anthony
    Anthony NB
    Citizens NB
    First NB
    Harper County NB

Harper County
#3394   1885–1891
#6752   1903
#3385   1885
#3384   1885–1889

Arkansas City
    American NB
    Farmers NB
    First NB
    Home NB
    Security NB

Cowley County
#3992   1889–1890
#4640   1891–1897
#3360   1885–1897
#4487   1890
#10746   1915

Ashland
    First NB
    Stockgrowers NB

Clark County
#3710   1887–1891
#5386   1900–1933

Atchison
    Atchison NB
    City NB
    Exchange NB
    First NB
    United States NB

Atchison County
#2082   1873–1899
#11405   1919
#2758   1882
#1672   1867–1924
#3612   1886–1891

Attica
    First NB

Harper County
#10359   1913

Atwood
    Farmers NB

Rawlins County
#10644   1914

Augusta
    First NB

Butler County
#6643   1903–1933

Barnard
    First NB

Lincoln County
#8396   1906

Baxter Springs   Cherokee County
   American NB   #11056   1917
   Baxter NB   #5952   1901
   First NB   #1838   1871–1875
Beaver   Barton County
   Farmers NB   #11177   1918
Belleville   Republic County
   First NB   #3386   1885–1890
   Peoples NB   #9559   1909
Beloit   Mitchell County
   First NB   #323   11884
   German NB of Northern KS*   #6701   1903–1923
   Note: became Union NB of Beloit in 1917
Bonner Springs   Wyandotte County
   First NB   #9197   1908–1931
Burlingame   Osage County
   Burlingame NB   #9157   1908–1914
   First NB   #4040   1889
Burlington   Coffee County
   Burlington NB   #1979   1872–1907
   Farmers NB   #6955   1903–1924
   Peoples NB   #3170   1884
Burr Oak   Jewell County
   First NB   #3880   1888–1891
   Jewell County NB   #7302   1904–1933
Caldwell   Sumner County
   Caldwell NB   #6333   1902–1909
   First NB   #3658   1887–1893
Caney   Montgomery County
   Caney Valley NB   #5349   1900
   Home NB   #5516   1900–1931
Cawker City   Mitchell County
   Farmers & Merchants NB   #4618   1891–1896
   First NB   #2640   1882–1888
Cedar Vale   Chautauqua County
   Cedar Vale NB   #5608   1900
   Dosbaugh NB*   #6530   1902–1933
   Note: became Citizens NB in 1921
Centralia   Nemaha County
   First NB   #3824   1887
Chanute   Neosho County
   Chanute NB   #4036   1889–1897

VI. National Bank Note Period, 1864–1935

First NB	#3819	1887
National Bank of	#6072	1901–1903
Cherokee	Crawford County	
First NB	#5447	1900–1932
Cherryvale	Montgomery County	
Cherryvale NB	#4288	1890–1892
First NB	#3277	1884–1895
Montgomery County NB	#4749	1892–1931
Peoples NB	#7383	1904–1909
Chetopa	Labette County	
First NB	#1902	1871–1875
National Bank of	#11374	1919–1932
Cimarron	Gray County	
First NB in	#13329	1929
First NB of	#3751	1887–1889
Clay Center	Clay County	
First NB	#3072	1883–1933
Peoples NB	#3345	1885
Clifton	Washington County	
First NB	#7178	1904
Clyde	Cloud County	
Exchange NB	#11775	1920
First NB	#3115	1884–1892
Coffeyville	Montgomery County	
Condon NB	#6797	1903
First NB	#3324	1885
Colby	Thomas County	
Citizens NB	#11047	1917–1925
First NB	#3512	1886–1888
Thomas County NB	#13076	1927
Coldwater	Comanche County	
Coldwater NB	#6767	1903
First NB	#3703	1887–1891
Collyer	Trego County	
First NB	#11855	1920
Colony	Anderson County	
First NB	#11531	1919–1931
Columbus	Cherokee County	
First NB	#6103	1902
Concordia	Cloud County	
Citizens NB	#3748	1887–1898
Concordia NB	#3090	1883–1886
First NB	#3066	1883

Conway Springs
    First NB

Cottonwood Falls
    Chase County NB
    Exchange NB

Council Grove
    Council Grove NB
    First NB

Delphos
    First NB

Dexter
    First NB

Dighton
    First NB
    First NB

Dodge City
    First NB
    NB of Commerce*
    *Note: became First NB in
      Dodge City in 1921

Downs
    Downs NB
    Exchange NB
    First NB

Edmond
    First NB

Edna
    First NB

El Dorado
    El Dorado
    Exchange NB
    Farmers & Merchants NB
    First NB
    Merchants NB
    National Bank

Elk City
    First NB
    Peoples NB

Ellsworth
    Central NB
    First NB

Emporia
    Citizens NB

Sumner County
#8467   1906

Chase County
#2764   1882–1928
#2764   1903

Morris County
#5757   1901
#2001   1872–1876

Ottowa County
#7532   1904

Cowley County
#9225   1908–1914

Lane County
#3888   1888–1897
#9773   1910

Ford County
#3596   1886–1894
#7285   1904

Osborne County
#11318   1919
#3563   1886–1887
#3569   1886–1892

Norton County
#9160   1908–1925

Labette County
#7590   1905

Butler County
#6494   1902
#3213   1884–1896
#4981   1894
#1957   1872–1875
#3833   1888–1889
#3035   1883–1891

Montgomery County
#8145   1906
#8708   1907–1910

Ellsworth County
#3447   1886–1931
#3249   1884–1891

Lyon County
#5498   1900

Commercial NB & TC	#11781	1920
Emporia NB	#1983	1872–1920
First NB	#1915	1872–1898

Englewood
    First NB   Clark County
     #9097   1908–1933

Erie
    First NB   Neosho County
     #3963   1889–1892

Eureka   Greenwood County
    Citizens NB   #5655   1900–1935
    First NB   #3148   1884–1924
    Home NB   #7303   1904

Formoso
    First NB   Jewell County
     #8596   1907

Fort Leavenworth
    Army NB   Leavenworth County
     #8796   1907

Fort Scott   Bourbon County
    Citizens NB   #3175   1884
    First NB   #1763   1871–1908
    Merchants NB   #31927   1872–1878

Fowler
    First NB   Meade County
     #9595   1909–1933

Frankfort
    First NB   Marshall County
     #2809   1882–1891

Fredonia   Wilson County
    First NB   #3835   1888–1894
    Fredonia NB   #7218   1904–1904

Galena
    Galena NB   Cherokee County
     #4798   1892–1934

Garden City   Finney County
    Finney County NB   #3900   1888–1893
    First NB   #3448   1885–1933
    Garden City NB   #7646   1905–1934

Garnett   Anderson County
    Anderson County NB   #4032   1889–1897
    First NB   #2973   1883–1896
    NB of Commerce   #5292   1900–1932

Gaylord
    First NB   Smith County
     #6970   1903

Girard
    First NB   Crawford County
     #3216   1884

Glasco
    First NB   Cloud County
     #7683   1905

Goff — Nemaha County
- First N — #7416 — 1904

Goodland — Sherman County
- Farmers NB — #7882 — 1905–1927
- First NB in — #14163 — 1934
- First NB of — #6039 — 1901–1934

Great Bend — Barton County
- Citizens NB — #5705 — 1901–1932
- Farmers NB — #11707 — 1920
- First NB — #3363 — 1885–1933

Greenleaf — Washington County
- First NB — #3567 — 1886–1888

Greensburg — Kiowa County
- Farmers NB* — #10557 — 1914–1932
- First NB of — #3667 — 1887–1888

*Note: became First NB in Greensburg in 1930.

Gypsum — Saline County
- Gypsum Valley NB — #9695 — 1910

Halstead — Harvey County
- Halstead NB — #3443 — 1886–1889

Hamilton — Greenwood County
- First NB — #6932 — 1903

Harper — Harper County
- First NB — #3265 — 1884–1890
- Harper NB — #3431 — 1886–1890
- National Bank* — #8307 — 1906
- Security NB — #8308 — 1906–1911

*Note: became First NB in Harper in 1920.

Hartford — Lyon County
- Hartford NB — #8197 — 1906–1931

Havensville — Pottawatomie County
- First NB — #5506 — 1900–1933

Hays City — Ellis County
- First NB — #3885 — 1888

Herington — Dickinson County
- First NB — #4058 — 1889

Hiawatha — Brown County
- First NB — #2589 — 1881–1932

Highland — Doniphan County
- First NB — #9136 — 1908–1932

Hillsboro   Marion County
- First NB   #6120   1902

Hoisington   Barton County
- First NB   #9232   1908
- Hoisington NB   #12694   1925

Holton   Jackson County
- First NB   #3061   1883–1931
- National Bank   #5041   1896–1909

Horton   Brown County
- First NB   #3810   1887

Howard   Elk County
- First NB   #3242   1884
- Howard NB   #3794   1887

Hoxie   Sheridan County
- First NB   #5687   1901

Hugoton   Stevens County
- First NB   #11300   1919

Humboldt   Allen County
- Humboldt First NB   #3807   1887–1896
- Humboldt NB   #6963   1903

Hutchinson   Reno County
- Commercial NB   #8430   1906–1923
- Exchange NB   #13106   1927
- Farmers NB*   #10765   1915
- First NB   #3180   1884
- Hutchinson NB   #3199   1884–1893
- NB of Commerce   #3861   1888–1892
- *Note: became American NB in 1917.

Independence   Montgomery County
- Citizens NB*   #4592   1891–1934
- Commercial NB   #4499   1891–1930
- First NB   #3021   1883–1917
- Security NB   #13492   1930–1932
- *Note: became Citizens First NB in 1918. Became First NB in 1931.

Iola   Allen County
- Northrup NB*   #5287   1900–1930
- *Note: became First NB in 1923.

Jetmore   Hodgeman County
- First NB   #3805   1887–1892

Jewell City   Jewell County
- First NB   #3591   1886

Junction City   Geary County

Central National Bank, Junction City

Central NB	#4284	8890
First NB "in"	#1977	1872–1875
First NB "of"	#3543	1886

Kanorado   Sherman County
   First NB   #11860   1920–1934

Kansas City   Wyandotte County
   Bankers NB   #8602   1907–1909

Series 1929 small size $5 National Currency on The Commercial National Bank of Kansas City, Kansas

The Commercial National Bank, Kansas City, Kansas, ca. 1930

Commercial NB	#6311	1902
First NB	#3706	1887–1891
Inter-State NB*	#4381	1890
Peoples NB	#9309	1909–1934
Security NB	#13801	1933
Wyandott NB	#3726	1887–1897

*Note: became the Inter-State NB of Kansas City, Missouri in 1911.

Kensington — Smith County
- First NB — #7493 — 1904

Kingman — Kingman County
- Citizens NB — #3737 — 1887–1888
- Farmers NB — #7412 — 1904–1909
- First NB — #3509 — 1886
- Kingman NB — #3559 — 1886–1890

Kinsley — Edwards County
- First NB — #3759 — 1887–1894
- National Bank — #5810 — 1901–1928

Kiowa   Barber County
    First NB   #8220   1906
Kirwin   Phillips County
    First NB   #3454   1886–1895
LaCrosse   Rush County
    First NB   #3970   1889–1898
LaHarpe   Allen County
    First NB   #7226   1904–1933
Larned   Pawnee County
    First NB of   #2666   1882–1896
    Moffat Brothers NB*   #7125   1904
    *Note: became First NB in Larned, 1922
Lawrence   Douglas County
    The Douglas County NB*   #3849   1888
    *Note: became the Lawrence NB in 1889
    Merchants NB†   #3584   1886
    †Note: became the First NB of
        Lawrence in 1930

Lawrence, Kansas, street scene, 1866, NB of Lawrence at right

VI. National Bank Note Period, 1864–1935

Lawrence National Bank, Lawrence, Kansas

Third Charter $10 Red Seal National Currency on The Lawrence National Bank

First Charter $1 National Currency on The National Bank of Lawrence, Wm. Lykins signature

Kansas Paper Money

Watkins National Bank of Lawrence, Kansas

Second Charter $10 National Currency on The Watkins National Bank of Lawrence

National Bank of	#1590	1865–1889
Second NB	#1732	1870–1876
Watkins NB	#3881	1886–1928
LeRoy	**Coffey County**	
First NB	#6149	1902
Leavenworth	**Leavenworth County**	
First NB	#182	1864
Leavenworth NB	#3033	1883
Manufacturers NB	#3908	1888–1930

VI. National Bank Note Period, 1864–1935

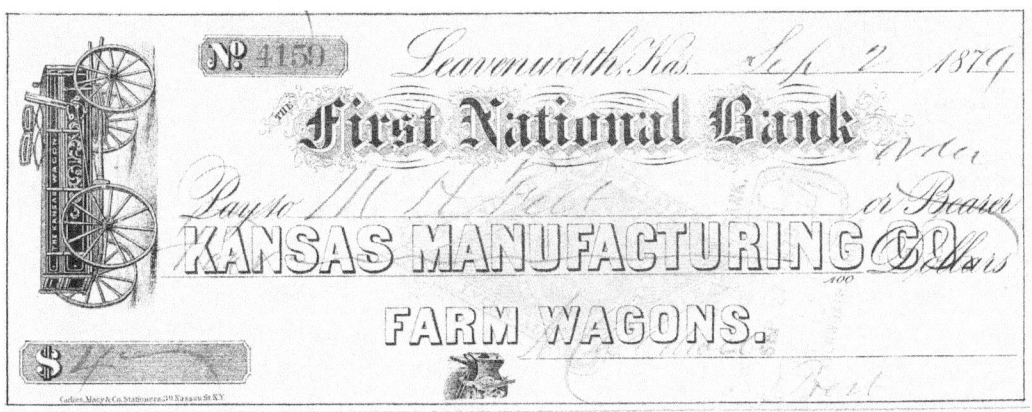

Check drawn on The First National Bank, Leavenworth, Kansas, 1879, with Alexander Caldwell signature

Leavenworth, Kansas, street scene, First National Bank at left

Third Charter $10 Blue Seal National Currency on The First National Bank of Leavenworth

Metropolitan NB	#3194	1884–1887
Second NB	#1448	1865–1874

Lebanon — Smith County
| First NB | #5799 | 1901 |

Leoti City — Wichita County
| First NB | #3844 | 1888–1892 |

Lewis — Edwards County
| First NB | #10863 | 1916 |

Liberal — Seward County
| First NB | #6720 | 1903 |
| Peoples NB | #13406 | 1929 |

Lincoln — Lincoln County
| Farmers NB | #6672 | 1903 |
| First NB | #3464 | 1886–1894 |

Lindsborg — McPherson County
| First NB | #3589 | 1886–1930 |

Logan — Phillips County
| First NB | #6841 | 1903 |

Longton — Elk County
| First NB | #8525 | 1907–1909 |
| Home NB | #9911 | 1910–1935 |

Louisbug — Miami County
| First NB | #11798 | 1920 |

Lucas — Russell County
| First NB | #7561 | 1904–1934 |

Luray — Russell County
| First NB | #10065 | 1911–1934 |

Lyndon — Osage County
| First NB | #7222 | 1904–1934 |

Lyons — Rice County
Chandler NB	#14048	1934
First NB	#3577	1886–1895
Lyons NB	#5353	1900–1934

Madison — Greenwood County
| First NB | #5529 | 1900 |

Manhattan — Riley County
First NB	#2094	1873–1877
First NB	#3782	1887
Union NB	#4008	1889

Mankato — Jewell County
| First NB | #3745 | 1887–1893 |
| Jewell County NB | #3812 | 1887–1890 |

VI. National Bank Note Period, 1864–1935

First National Bank, Manhattan, Kansas

Mankato NB* #6817 1903
*Note: became the First NB in Mankato in 1922

Marion Marion County
    Cottonwood Valley NB #3928 1888–1894
    Farmers & Drovers NB #10980 1917

Marysville Marshall County
    First NB #2791 1882–1924

Mayetta Jackson County
    First NB #9934 19111

McCune Crawford County
    First NB #12191 1922–1932

McPherson McPherson County
    First NB #3521 1886–1899
    McPherson NB #3803 1887–1895
    Second NB #3791 1887–1891

Meade Meade County
    First NB #7192 1904

Meade Center Meade County
    First NB #3695 1887–1890
    Meade County NB #3853 1888–1890

Medicine Lodge Barber County
    Citizens NB #3594 1886–1891
    First NB #3253 1884–1894

Millbrook Graham County
First NB #3758 1887–1890

Town / Bank	County	Charter #	Years
Minneapolis	Ottawa County		
Citizens NB		#4931	1893
First NB		#3353	1885–1893
Minneapolis NB		#3731	1887–929
Moline	Elk County		
First NB		#7318	1904–1934
Moline NB		#8107	1906–1926
Mound Valley	Elk County		
First NB		#8107	1906–1909
Mount Hope	Sedgewick County		
First NB		#8559	1900
Natoma	Osborne County		
First NB		#9384	'909
Neodesha	Wilson County		
First NB		#6914	1903
Neodesha NB		#6895	1903
Ness City	Ness County		
Citizens NB		#8081	1906–1924
First NB of		#3542	1886–1896
National Bank*		#8142	1906–1934
*Note: became First NB "in" in 1930			
Newton	Harvey County		
First NB		#2777	1882
German NB		#3473	1886–1889
Midland NB		#4860	1893
Newton NB		#3297	1885–1893
Norcator	Decatur County		
First NB*		#8290	1906
*Note: became Decatur County NB of Oberlin in 1934			
Norton	Norton County		
First NB		#3687	1887
National Bank		#8339	1906–1910
Nortonville	Jefferson County		
First NB		#5359	1900
Oakley	Logan County		
First NB		#10041	1911–1933
Oberlin	Decatur County		
Farmers NB		#7298	1904
First NB		#7298	1886–1897
Oberlin NB		#4642	1891–1934
Olathe	Johnson County		
First NB "of"		#1828	1871–1874
First NB		#3720	1887

VI. National Bank Note Period, 1864–1935

Oberlin National Bank, Kansas

Onaga	Pottawatomie County	
First NB	#12353	1923
Osage City	Osage County	
First NB	#3813	1887–1898
Osborne	Osborne County	
Exchange NB	#3472	1886–1934
Farmers NB	#5834	1901
First NB	#3319	1885–1928
Oswego	Labette County	
First NB	#3038	1883–1894
First NB	#11576	1920
Ottawa	Franklin County	
First NB	#1718	1870
Peoples NB	#1910	1871
Overbrook	Osage County	
First NB	#7195	1904
Paola	Miami County	
First NB	#1864	1871–1877
Miami County NB	#3350	1885
National Bank	#3795	1887–1898
Peoples NB	#3991	1889–1924

Peoples National Bank, Ottawa, Kansas

Parsons
    Farmers NB
    First NB

Labette County
#11537   1919–1924
#1951   1872

Peabody
    First NB

Marion County
#3134   1884–1931

Phillipsburg
    First NB

Phillips County
#3601   1886

Pittsburg
    First NB
    Manufacturers NB
    National Bank
    NB of Commerce*
    *Note: became American Exchange
        NB in 1926

Crawford County
#3463   1886–1932
#4136   1889–1897
#3475   1886
#8418   1906–1928

Plainville
    First NB

Rooks County
#7313   1904–1928

Pleasanton
    First NB

Linn County
#8803   1907

Prairie View
    First NB

Phillips County
#9373   1909

Pratt
    First NB "of"
    National Bank*

Pratt County
#3649   1887–1895
#6229   1902

Pratt County NB	#3787	1887–1891

*Note: became the First NB "in" in 1920

Randall
    Randall NB   Jewell County   #11887   1920

Richmond
    First NB*   Franklin County   #11728   1920

*Note: became Peoples NB in 1929

Russell
    First NB   Russell County   #3657   1887–1899

Russell Springs
    First NB   Logan County   #3775   1887–1888

Sabetha   Nemaha County
    Citizens NB   #2990   1883–1885
    First NB   #2954   1883–1885
    National Bank   #4626   1891–1932

Saint John   Stafford County
    First NB   #3467   1886
    Saint John NB   #7844   1905

Saint Marys   Pottawatomie County
    First NB   #3374   1885–1933
    National Bank   #4619   1891–1910

Salina   Saline County
    American NB   #4317   1890–1894
    Farmers NB   #4742   1892
    First NB   #2538   1881–1892
    NB of America   #4945   1894
    Salina NB   #3531   1886–1895

Scandia
    First NB*   Republic County   #3779   1887

*Note: became NB of Belleville in 1894 and First NB in Belleville in 1921

Scott City
    First NB   Scott County   #8808   1907

Sedan   Chautauqua County
    First NB   #3855   1888
    Peoples NB   #7535   1904–1909
    Sedan NB   #4150   1889–1892

Seneca   Nemaha County
    First NB   #2952   1883–1924
    National Bank   #5101   1897

Smith Center
    Smith County NB   Smith County   #3630   1887–1899

Smith Centre	Smith County	
First NB	#3546	1886
Solomon	Dickenson County	
Solomon NB	#9794	1910
Spearville	Ford County	
First NB	#10161	1912
Stafford	Stafford County	
Farmers NB	#8883	1907
First NB	#3852	1888–1892
Sterling	Rice County	
First NB	#3207	1884
Stockton	Rooks County	
First NB	#3440	1886–1890
National Bank	#8274	1906–1927
Stockton NB	#7815	1905
Strong City	Chase County	
Strong City NB	#3002	1883–1888
Syracuse	Hamilton County	
First NB	#8114	1906
Thayer	Neosho County	
First NB	#9465	1909
Topeka	Shawnee County	
Capital NB	#7907	1905–1910
Central NB	#3078	1883
Farmers NB	#10390	1913–1931
First NB "of	#2646	1882–1905
Kansas NB	#3790	1887–1894
Kansas Valley NB*	#1660	1866–1873

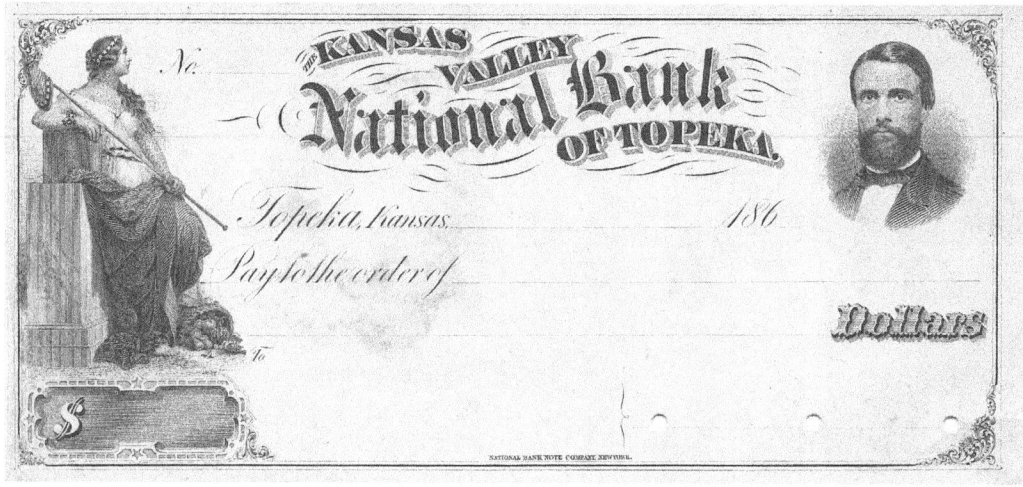

Kansas Valley National Bank of Topeka, Dan Adams portrait (at right)

Kaw Valley NB	#11398	1919–1931
Merchants NB	#3909	1888
National Bank	#12740	1925
State NB	#2192	1874–1875
Topeka NB	#1945	1872–1878

*Note: became First NB of Topeka in 1873

Toronto — Woodson County
First NB — 6819 — 1903

Towanda — Butler County
Towanda NB — #11154 — 1918–1926
Towanda NB — #12935 — 1926–1935

Troy — Doniphan County
First NB — #8162 — 1906

Union Stock Yards — Sedgewick County
Union Stockyards NB — #9758 — 1910

Valley Falls — Jefferson County
First NB — #11816 — 1920–1931

Wakeeny — Trego County
First NB — #3776 — 1887–1893

Wamego — Pottawatomie County
First NB — #3434 — 1886

Washington — Washington County
First NB — #2912 — 1884
Washington NB — #3167 — 1884

Waverly — Coffey County
First NB — #6101 — 1902

Wellington — Sumner County
First NB "of" — #2879 — 1883–1895
NB of Commerce — #8399 — 1906
State NB — #3564 — 1886–1890
Sumner NB — #3865 — 1888–1896
Wellington NB* — #3091 — 1883

*Note: became First NB "in" Wellington in 1921

Westmoreland — Pottawatomie County
First NB — #3304 — 1885–1897

Wetmore — Nemaha County
First NB — #8974 — 1907

White City — Morris County
First NB — #7970 — 1905

Wichita — Sedgewick County
First NB "of" — #1913 — 1872–1876

Fourth NB	#3683	1887
Kansas NB*	#2782	1882
National Bank	#6392	1902–1908
NB of Commerce	#5169	1899–1920
Southwest NB	#12346'	1923
State NB	#3524	1886–1894
Union NB	#11010	1917
West Side NB	#3756	1887–1891
Wichita NB	#2786	1882–1894

*Note: Became First NB "in" in 1920

Winfield — Cowley County
Cowley County NB	#4556	1891–1922
First NB	#3218	1884
Winfield NB	#3351	1885

Wyandotte — Wyandotte County
First NB	#1840	1871–1878

Yates Center — Woodson County
Woodson NB	#3108	1884–1892
Yates Center NB	#6326	1902–1913

Appendix A.
Modern Reproductions

Beginning in the 1970s, reproductions of bank notes from plates held in the archives of the American Bank Note Company began to be produced. These often were included as part of a souvenir card produced for some numismatic convention or promotion. The Time-Life Company produced a series of collectible engravings of the Old West beginning in 1978 that included two Kansas obsolete notes. Most of these items include a certificate on the back that explains their status as copies or reproductions.

It also appears that a number of modern reproductions were made by the ABNCo for internal purposes. When a note was selected for reproduction, apparently a modern proof of the entire plate was created. Many of these "modern proofs" surfaced in the sale by Christie's of the property of American Bank Note in 1990–1991. These are not marked as copies on their backs. They are detected by the type of paper on which they were printed, which is not 1860s bank note paper but rather heavier and whiter in color. They also have a red ABNCo stamp on the back. Four such notes of the Union Military scrip issue turned up in the sale and are catalogued herein. (Obsolete currency dealer Hugh Shull calls these "S-proofs.") A partial modern proof sheet of the $50, $100 Kansas Valley Bank sheet and at least two full sheets of the $5, $3, $5, $10 sheet of the Bank of the State of Kansas also surfaced

Also D.C. Wismer, the father of obsolete note collecting, in a 1924 letter to N.T. Thorsen, curator of the Boys Town Philamatic Center, warned that "counterfeit notes had been produced for collectors for the past 25 years from old plates." The only Kansas note that may fall into this category is a $1, incomplete note of the Simpson Brothers Bank of Lawrence. These notes have been a mystery to this collector since seeing the first one more than 30 years ago. The note is incomplete as to obligation and is printed on thick paper that feels like book paper. There are four copies known, all plate A, and the earliest documented evidence of their existence is a 1956 inventory of the Kansas State Historical Society. The other three copies were located in The Boys Town Museum at Omaha, the Western Reserve Historical Society Museum in Cleveland and a prominent private collection during the 1970s. Could the plate have been used to make a reproduction with the four notes then cut apart and donated or traded to the museums? Except for the Kansas State Historical Society, the other collections have since been dispersed and the notes are now scattered. There are other notes known from this bank with a similar design, but produced on genuine bank note paper of the 1860s. This adds further questions about the thick paper issues. Until some evidence surfaces about the origin of these notes, they are listed as possible reproductions. They also could be proofs.

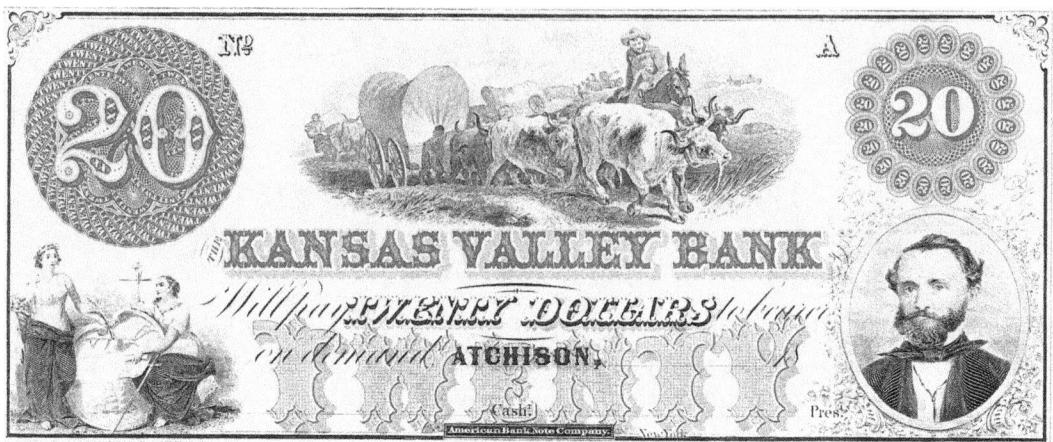

#44r. $20, Kansas Valley Bank, Atchison. Reproduced for the ABNCo State set in the 1990s. Copy certificate on back.

This certifies that the Banknote Intaglio printing on the face of this document was printed in 1980 by the American Bank Note Company.

Attested to by: *Robert P Charles*
Robert P. Charles
Sr. Vice President

#56r. $3, Bank of the State of Kansas. ABNCo for the Bank Note Reporter Souvenir card to promote subscriptions, 1980. Copy certificate on back. The tint plate used for the reproduction differed from the original note.

#57r., 56r., 57r., 58r. Sheet; Bank of the State of Kansas. ABNCo At least two full
($5, $3, $5, $10)   sheets were reproduced; probably at the time when the $3 note was selected for the Bank Note Reporter souvenir card.

#45r., 46r., Partial sheet reproduced probably at the time the $20; #44r, was
($50, 100) selected for inclusion in the state set.

#253r? $1, Simpson Brothers Bank, Lawrence. Tentatively listed as a possible reproduction because of the thick paper used. (four copies known)

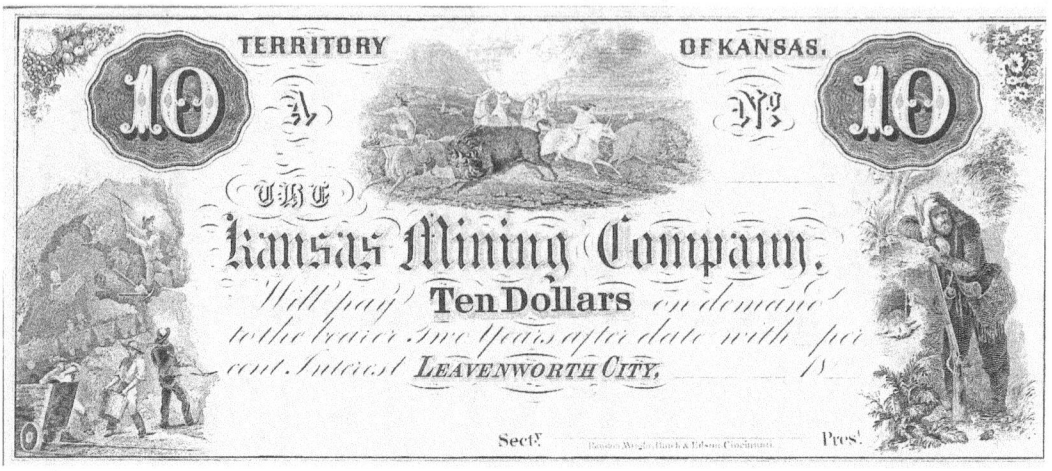

#307r. $10, The Kansas Mining Co., Leavenworth. ABNCo in 1978 for the Time Life Series on the Old West. Copy certificate on back.

#425r. $50, Union Military Scrip, Topeka. ABNCo in 1978 for the Time-Life Series on the Old West. Copy certificate on back.

#423r. $10, Union Military Scrip. Modern copy made by the ABNCo. Has ABNCo stamp on back in red. Turned up in Christie's sale of ABNCo property in 1990. Hugh Shull calls these "S Proofs"

#424r. $20, Union Military Scrip, same as #423r above, except for denomination.

#425r2. $50, Union Military Scrip, same as #423r above, except for denomination.

Appendix B.
Altered Notes

Altered Kansas notes are quite scarce. Perhaps a dozen have been examined over the last 30 years by this writer. Unfortunately copies were not made of most of them. Some notes attributed to Kansas are actually alterations of other "Kansas" notes. These are the notes of the so called "Bank of Easton," which apparently are all alterations of the fraudulent notes on the Delaware City Bank, Delaware City, Kansas, issue dated 1854. The Delaware City notes are frequently found altered to pass on a legitimate bank in the state of Delaware. In fact some of this issue of notes for a non-existent bank seemed designed for alteration.

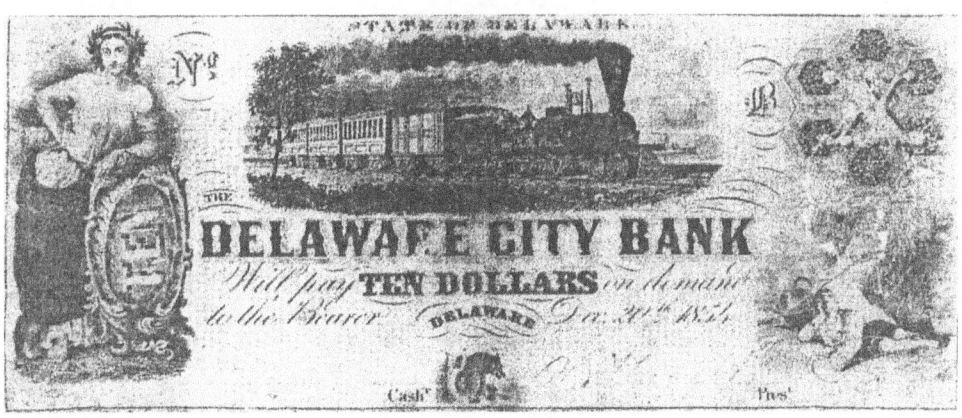

#81ALT. $1, Delaware City Bank, 1854. Raised to $10 denomination and altered to the state of Delaware. (Haxby lists a $10 denomination for this bank.)

Opposite: #426r. $100, Union Military Scrip, same as #423r above, except for denomination.

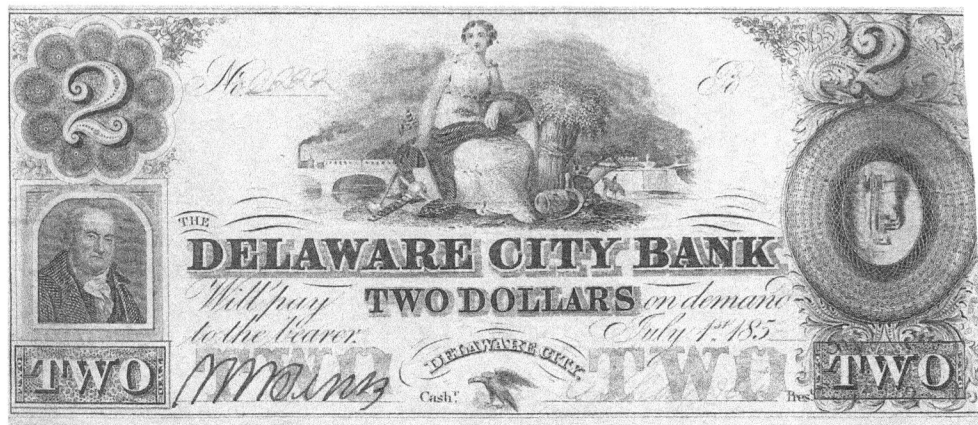

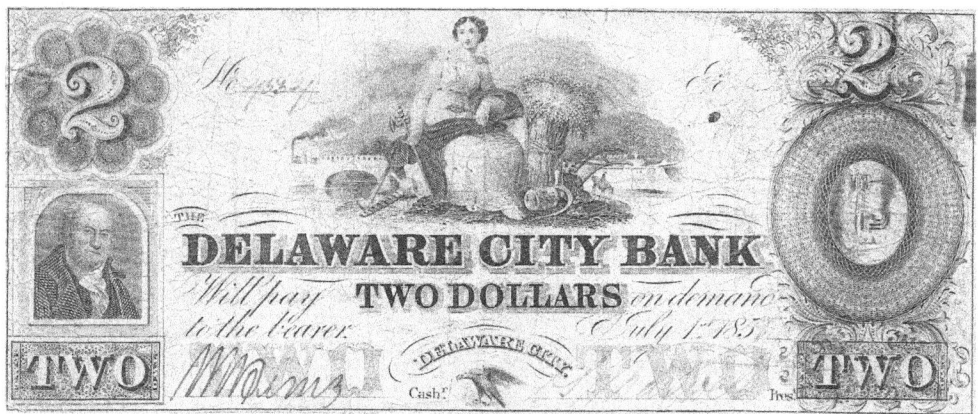

#84ALT. $2, Delaware City Bank, 1858. Often found with the designation "Kansas" trimmed from the right border or obliterated by pen and ink, thus becoming altered to the state of Delaware.

#84ALT. $2, Delaware City Bank, 1858. Altered to The Merchants Bank, New Bedford, Mass.

#93ALT. $1, Easton Bank, 1855. Altered from #81, $1 of the Delaware City Bank.

#94ALT. $2, Easton Bank, 1855. Altered from #82, $2 of the Delaware City Bank.

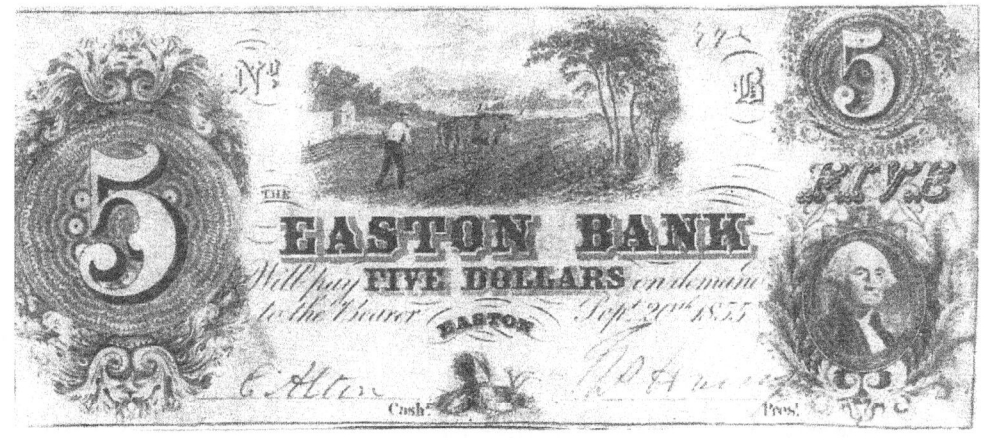

#95ALT. $5, Easton Bank, 1855. Altered from #83, $5 of the Delaware City Bank.
#122ALT. $10, Drovers Bank, 1856. Alterations seen, no details.

#134ALT. $5, Merchants Bank, Ft. Leavenworth. Altered to Merchants Bank, Lowell, Mass; Paterson, New Jersey; and Mousam River Bank, Sandiford, Maine (likely others also)

#135ALT. $10, Merchants Bank, Ft. Leavenworth. Altered to Merchants Bank, Albany, New York, and Newport, R.I. (Note, the $2.00 to Paterson, New Jersey and $3.00 have also been seen altered, no details.)

Appendix C.
Known Written Denomination Scrip

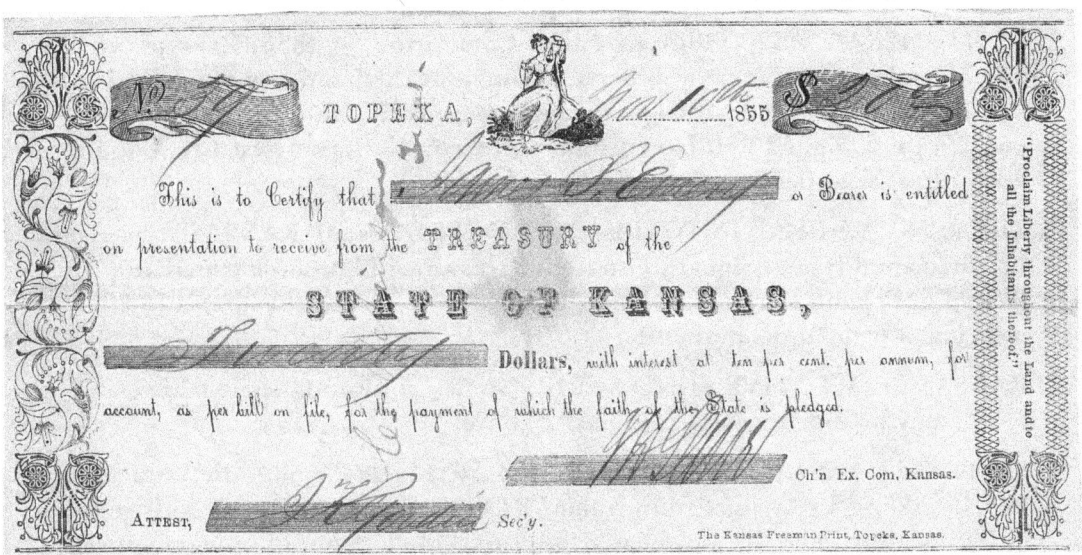

1. STATE OF KANSAS ____1855. (L) Floral design across end. (C) top, small seated female "JUSTICE" w/ sword and scales. (R) Vertical across end: "Proclaim Liberty throughout the land and to all the inhabitants thereof" Written "Topeka" and hand dated Jan. 17th, 1856, over printed 1855. 10 percent per annum. Signed J.K. Goodin Sec'y and J.H. Lane Chm'n Ex Com. Kansas. Imprint: The Kansas Freeman Print, Topeka, Kansas. The Western Reserve Historical Society also had one with TOPEKA printed.

Issued to pay expenses of the "Topeka Movement" (cf Connelley, pg 461). The Chicago Tribune said $50,000 of this paper was issued. The Topeka Legislature was dispersed by U.S. troops under Colonel Sumner on July 4th, 1856. (See *Collections*, Vol XIII, pp 148, 151, 152.)

2. **OFFICE OF PROTECTION COMMITTEE, Lawrence 1856:** (C) small cannon facing right. "For services rendered in the formation of a STATE GOVERNMENT and protection of the cities of Kansas with interest at ten per cent per annum." Dated Feb. 29, 1856; Signed C. Robinson, J.H. Lane, J.K. Goodin, G.W. Deitzler. Vertical across left end "Millions for Defence-not one cent for Tribute>" No Maker's imprint visible.

   This scrip was issued to liquidate losses during the invasion of the Missourians of Dec., 1855 (the Wakarusa War). The amount issued was stated at $23,858. Governor Robinson eventually secured donations in Massachusetts to redeem $10,000 of this issue. On white & blue paper? KSHS has a copy.

3. **LEAVENWORTH CONSTITUTION SCRIP.** Lindsay included in one of his lists "$2.50—1858." KSHS had one in their collection in 1956. Described as 185_ printed. (C) Eagle on flag; factories and ship in background. Simple floral border on all four sides. Uniface; no maker.

4. **STATE OF KANSAS___Office Executive Committee____1856** (L) across end in ornamental frame "Proclaim Liberty throughout the Land and to all the Inhabitants thereof." (R) Spread Eagle, facing left on rock. Hand written Topeka, Jan. 27, 1856. Signed J.H. Lane Chm'n Ex. Com; Kansas: Attest J.K. Goodin Sec'y. 10 percent per annum. No imprint visible.

5. **TREASURY WARRANTS TOPEKA $5.** 1856 "STATE OF KANSAS" across end in ornamental frame. Signature space for treasurer; Light blue paper. Imprint: Herald of Freedom Print, Lawrence, Kansas. Bore 10 percent interest. (This note had a printed denomination.)

6. **KANSAS PROTECTIVE FUND SCRIP;** No description. Questionable existence, may be the same as Lawrence #2 above.

7. **STATE OF KANSAS, AUDITORS OFFICE WARRANT**—non interest bearing, Topeka, 1856. (L) Across end in frame "STATE OF KANSAS" (C) Sailing ships in harbor, top. Pay _____ or bearer, bill for __ dollars out of moneys appropriated by act dated Mar. 15, 1856. Signed G.A. Cutler, Auditor of State. Hand dated July 10th, 1857, over 1856. No imprint visible. KSHS has a copy. These were listed in 1970 as "Free State Warrants."

8. **QUINDARO TOWN COMPANY.** Illustrated in Moore. 185_ (L) female in field holding sheaf of grain. Uniface; Imprint: Herald of Freedom Print, Lawrence, Kansas. "Denomination to be written in."

9. **MINNEOLA TOWN COMPANY.** 185_ (L) Female standing with sword and scales; small spread eagle above. Uniface; Imprint: Herald of Freedom Print. "Denomination to be written in."

10. **LECOMPTON AUDITORS WARRANT.** 18__. Printed (L) Standing female with sword and scales "JUSTICE," male bust on pedestal behind; Small spread eagle above. Imprint: Herald of Freedom Print.

Known Written Denomination Scrip 241

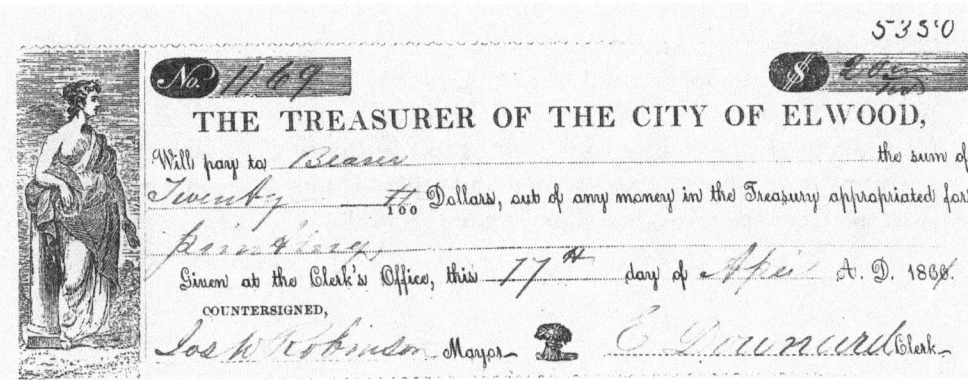

11. **UNION MILITARY SCRIP.** Write in denomination, 1867 and later. No vignettes, inscription identical to the printed denomination notes. Uniface; locally produced without imprint.

12. **THE CITY OF ELWOOD.** Write in denomination, 1860 and later. Locally produced without imprint.

There are numerous accounts of other cities and towns of Kansas having issued scrip. Most, if not all of these were undoubtedly of the "write in denomination" type. Junction City, Geary County, and Leavenworth are among those to have been reported.

Appendix D.
Pre-1863 Banks That
May Have Issued Scrip

Fort Scott — A. McDonald & Brother 1859–1871, became First National Bank
Highland — J.P. Johnson 1862–1880s
Leavenworth — D.R. Anthony 1857–1864
Leavenworth — Smoot, Russell & Co. 1857–1862
Wyandott — McHenry, Davis & Co. "during the war"

Note: If any private Kansas bank scrip is to turn up in the future, it will likely be from the firms listed above. There were many other "banks" that operated prior to the Civil War small change crisis, but all were gone by 1861.

Appendix E.
Printers and Engravers on Pre-1880 Notes

A
American Bank Note Co., New York
Ames, 205 Broadway, New York
W.H. Arthur & Co., New York

B
P. Barnes, Printer New York
Braden & Burford, Lith. Inds

C
Continental Bank Note Co., New York
Combe Litho. St Joseph, Mo.
B.F. Corlies & Macy, Stationers, New York

D
Danforth, Wright & Co., New York & Philada.
Doty & McFarlan, New York

F
Claude D. (?) Funk Printing Co., Wichita

G
Gardner Gazette Print
A. Gast & Co., Lith., St. Louis
T. Groom & Co., Stationers, Boston

H
Hall, Topeka
Hall Litho Co., Topeka
Hatch & Co. Trinity Building, 111 Broadway, N. York

Herald of Freedom Print, Lawrence, Kansas
T.R. Hiland, Lith., Boston

K
Kansan Printing Co.
K.C. Litho Co., Kansas City, Missouri

M
(?) McLean Lith., St Louis
Ferd Mayer & Co., 96 Fulton St., N. York
Edw Mendel, Chicago
Middleton, Strobridge & Co., Cincinnati

N
Novelty Adv Publ., New York
Novelty Ad Co., Peoria, IL

O
W.L. Ormsby, New York

P
J.M. Padgett, Phillipsburg, Kans.
J.M. Padgett Coupon Co., Topeka, Kans
Padgett Bros. Inventors, Topeka, Ks.

R
Rawdon, Wright, Hatch & Edson, Cincinnati

S
Sage Sons & Co., Buffalo, New York
C.J. Smith & Co., Lith. Leavenworth
Smoky Hill & Republican Union Print, Junction City, Kansas

State Journal Print
Chas. F. Strong Printer, unknown location
The R.P. Studley Co., St Louis, Missouri
W. Swaty, Dealer in Books and Stationery, Oberlin, Ohio

T
T.B. Eng Co., K.C.
M.H. Traubel Lith., Phila.

U
Union Bank Note Co. K.C., Missouri
Trade Mark Registered in U.S. Pat. Office

V
Vollmer Printers

W
Wellstood, Hay & Whiting, New York & Boston
Western Bank Note & Eng. Co., Chicago
Western Litho Co., Wichita
A. Whitcomb, Printer, Lawrence, Kansas

Appendix F.
Round Cardboard Tokens

Coal Company

The Larson Brothers, Weir City, Kansas. Circa 1904 or 1907; date and location are hand written on reverse.

10¢, Black on pale violet, 38mm R-7
50¢, Black on orange, 38mm R-7
$1, Black on white? (heavily soiled), 40 mm R-7

Trader

Tom Moses, Traders, Fort Wallace, Kansas. Circa 1870; Date is hand written on face of tokens. Fort Wallace was the last, and furthest western, Indian fort constructed in Kansas. Soldiers there saw much fighting with Indians who did not want to give up sacred lands threatened by the Smoky Hill Route to Denver and the West.

Appendix F

5¢, Black on salmon .... Unique
10¢, Black on canary yellow .... Unique
25¢, Black on violet .... Unique

Appendix G.
Reported Serial Numbers on Rare Notes

The determination of the numbers of genuine notes placed into circulation is important to an understanding of the role these notes played in the economic development, or even for understanding the everyday life of pioneer citizens. Unlike U.S. currency where meticulous records are kept of the serial numbers, dates of issue, and redemptions of notes, much of the information about obsoletes has to be painstakingly reconstructed. One of the ways to do this is to record every serial number that one sees over a lengthy period of time. Once sufficient data is available, if ever, some assumptions can be made.

We could do this statistically, depending on various population distributions, assumptions, and working the equations. But it probably makes as much sense to do it intuitively. For example, Fred Marckhoff, an early, dedicated collector and researcher of Kansas obsoletes, wrote years ago about the two varieties of Scott, Kerr & Co. $1.00 notes of Leavenworth. The first variety had the town name spelled incorrectly without an "A" and a number of circulated survivors had been seen. The later issue had the town name spelled correctly and several of them had also been reported. There was, however, a large gap between the recorded high number of the first issue and the low number of the second issue. Markhoff wrote that about 6,000 notes of the first issue were printed and circulated before the plate was corrected. But, over the last 30 years I have been able to document the serial numbers of thirteen of these notes, six of the type I and seven of the type II. And the gap has narrowed significantly. The high number on type I is now known to be 8771 and the low number on type II has been confirmed at 10841. So it is clear that more than 6000, in fact more than 8000, type I notes were issued. Because a competing bank in the city issued 25,000—$1 notes during the same period it appears reasonable that the Scott, Kerr Bank probably issued a total of $20,000. Therefore I am confident in stating authoritatively that 10,000 of each type were issued. I could be proven wrong if a new conflicting serial number turns up, or if the records of the American Bank Note Company are ever opened to researchers (possibly destroyed), and they provide better information. In the meanwhile, I'll stick with the 10,000 each theory.

Another good indicator is often found in contemporary newspaper articles. For example, the issue of small change scrip by the City Council of Atchison in 1862 was documented in the local paper, including the denominations and total amount to be issued. Another time a citizen complained to the editor of the Atchison paper about likely tax avoidance of the Exchange Bank there, and noted the reported circulation of the bank.

In a few cases, published statements still exist reporting on a bank's circulation. Some old bank ledgers have survived with notations on receipt of notes or serial number ranges signed by various officials. In states that required oversight of bank issues there may be registers around that recorded the number of notes countersigned, issued, and perhaps redeemed. So there are many possible sources to obtain more and better information about these issues. Often such information will allow a positive determination of the genuineness of a note through correct dating or signature comparison. In the early days of collecting obsolete notes apparently many dealers and collectors (still today?) added signatures to unissued remainders to make them more attractive to prospective purchasers.

A true collector will want to know if his notes are authentic; whether they are genuinely issued notes that actually circulated in the nineteenth century, and the true rarity of the pieces. To this collector the most valued notes are those that have the genuine signatures of the correct officials, are properly dated, have a serial number, and were actually used by the Kansas pioneers of the 1850s and 1860s. It is always better if the number is legible but often it will not be. If a note had serial numbers overprinted with a numbering machine, it should be easy to determine what it is. However, if the note was hand numbered, it often will be illegible, as also may be the date and signatures. Someday collectors will have access to sophisticated technology that will allow us to "read" these obliterated dates and numbers and then we will know whether the piece really comes from the past.

This section provides available information on the surviving notes of Kansas and their reported serial number ranges or serial numbers for genuinely issued notes that have survived. Where only one or two such notes are known, serial numbers are reported.

City of Atchison
   10¢ Note #11. Single survivor of the four denominations issued that totaled $2,000 to $3,000.

City of Chetopa
   $2 Note #71, genuine signatures, unique, no S.N.

The Exchange Bank, Atchison.
   $1 Note #23, genuine signatures, S.N. 112

The Exchange Bank of W. Hetherington.
   $1 Note #31 appears genuinely issued, S.N. illegible and S.N. 1004

The Kansas Valley Bank, Atchison
   $3 Note #41a genuine signatures, S.N. 186 (Smithsonian)
   $5 Note #42a genuine signatures, S.N. 98? (Smithsonian)
   Note: A $10. Note #43a has also been reported but not seen

The Bank of the State of Kansas
   $1 Note #55, 1862. Four genuine signed notes seen, S.N.s — 234, 520, 1160 and illegible.

The City of Independence
    $1 1875, genuine signatures, S.N. 3429

The Lawrence Bank (Ten genuinely signed and issued notes known)
    Issues dated 1859 and 1860 (SNs 1—1003 and 1004—1293, total $ 14,212) SENC
    Issue dated July 1, 1861 (Total $8,800 circulated, S.N.s 1— 800)
        $1 SENC
        $2 two known S.N. 6?4 and illegible
        $3 two known, both illegible
        $5 SENC
    Issue dated November 1, 1862 (Total $3,123 circulated as replacement for $3,123 of 1861 issue, redeemed and destroyed, apparently $1s and $2s only, SN 801—1841?)
        $1 three known S.N.s 864, 1009 and 1106
        $2 three known S.N.s 819, 1021 and 1100
        $3 and $5 probably not issued

The Bank of Wm. H.R. Lykins, Lawrence
    5¢ Note #225. Genuine signature, S.N. 1242
    $1. Note #227. Genuine signature, S.N. 833?

Simpson Brothers Bank, Lawrence
    $1 Note #256, S.N. # 217. Unique issued note, genuine signature

The City of Leavenworth
    $1 Note #274 High S.N. 2552
    $2 Note #275 High S.N. 2506
    $5 Note #276 High S.N. 2663

Clark, Gruber & Co., Leavenworth
    $1 Note #301 Two known S.N.s 3260 and 5642
    $1 Note #302 Three known, S.N.s 1407B, 2982A and 4515A
    Note: 12,500 two note sheets were printed for a total issue of $25,000

Banking House of J.W. Morris, Leavenworth
    5¢ Note #311 Unique issued note, genuine signature
    $1 Note #312 Reported, not seen

Scott, Kerr & Co.
    $1 Note #321 Unique, S.N. Illegible
    $1 Note #322 "LEVENWORTH" Seven known, S.N.s 1397, 1546, 1868, 2649, 4665, 8579 and 8771 and proof
    $1 Note #323 "LEAVENWORTH" Six known, S.N.s 10841, 11258, 11989, 12994, 13966 and 19204
    Note: Best guess is that 10,000, one-note sheets of each variety were printed and issued for a total of $20,000. All notes reported are plate letter A.

R.H. Farnham, Banker, Topeka
    10¢ Note #408 Two known with signature, S.N.s 953 and 960
    25¢ Note #411 Unique S.N. 188 over 187

Union Military Scrip, Topeka

$1 Note #421 High S.N. 25533
$5 Note #422 High S.N. 13014
$10 Note #423 High S.N. 14669
$20 Note #424 High S.N. 6953
$50 Note #425 High S.N. 1531
$100 Note #426 High S.N. 905

Note: There are sufficient printed records to determine the amount of this scrip issued totaled around $500,000. $1 notes were printed four to a sheet, plate letters A — D. $5 notes were printed two to a sheet, plate letters A and B. The $10 and $20 were printed on the same sheet of two notes as were the $50 and the $100 notes.

Kansas State Savings Bank, Wyandott
$1 Note # 447 High S.N. 9351 (S.N. 17 has genuine signatures)
$2 Note # 449 High S.N. 9992
$3 Note # 451 High S.N. 8964 (S.N.s 5 & 11 have genuine signatures)
Note: Probably 10,000 sheets of these notes, three to a sheet were printed.

The City of Wyandott
$1 Note #436 Eight unissued remainders are known, S.N.s 10773, 10866, 11292, 15622, 15652, 15666, 19776 and one with no S.N.
$2 Note #437 Six remainders known, S.N.s 2372, 5644, 5661, 5682, 6160 and 6835.
Note: Because the $1 note serial number ranges are between 10,000 and 20,000 and the $2 range is below 10,000, it is surmised that these were single note sheets and the $2s were printed first and numbered 1 to 10,000. (The sheets could have had the $2 at the top with the $1 beneath it.) Then the $1s were printed and numbered 10,001 to 20,000 for a total issue of 10,000 of each denomination. If a serial number surfaces that disputes this, I'll change my theory.

Appendix H.
Notices of Scrip Issues in Newspapers

Local Newspaper announcement that "Streeter & Strickler were issuing small notes because of the scarcity of small change."

Junction City Union, February, 1862

"Shinplasters, Colonel Wilson, Sutler at Fort Riley, has in circulation one dollar notes redeemable in current funds when presented in sums of five dollars. The scarcity of change makes them quite a convenience."

Smoky Hill and Republican Union, Junction City, March 20, 1862

"Everything is five dollar bills. You have to go up street on one side and down on the other, to get them 'broke,' and most of the time do not succeed. Change was never so scarce. To meet this emergency, some of our business men have issued shinplasters, in denominations of one dollar and of 50 cents," J.R. Swallow & Co. and Fisk & Eskridge have them out. The former redeems in quantities of $5, when presented. It will undoubtedly be used as a currency as long as change is so scarce."

Emporia News, June 28, 1862

"Small Change, Our city has issued $2000–$3000 in small denomination scrip for the convenience of the local merchants. Uncle Sam was too slow in getting out his own."

Freedom's Champion, Atchison, November 22, 1862

"Among the private banking offices operating in this town, we know of none better than that of J.S. Miller, of this city. His notes are only for the fractional part of a dollar and were issued only to overcome a public necessity. Mr. Miller's notes are as good as his word and every one is as safe as 'Uncle Sam's' Greenbacks."

Fort Scott Bulletin, November 8, 1862

"The issue of shinplasters is getting to be a nuisance in this section, as well as in other portions of the state. Nearly every peddler, banker and rum shop has his pasteboard in circulation, with the inscription, good for one shave, good for one drink, good for 10 cents, and then signed by Tom, Dick and Harry. If the advance in paper keeps up, as it has during the past month, the blanks will be worth the most in reality. Since the visit of the U.S. Tax Assessor, this currency has very much depreciated. The hundred dollar tax being an item for some of these institutions, they are fast fizzling out."

The Fort Scott Bulletin, January 16, 1863

"A Reliable Currency. Lewis Kurtz, who advertises regularly in Junction, has made his currency legitimate and accordingly extended its circulation. Mr. Kurtz has taken out a banker's license under the internal revenue law and made arrangements for the redemption of his bills at Leavenworth. Our settlers who do business at Leavenworth will thus be relieved of the inconvenience arising from the non circulation of these notes at a distance."

Smoky Hill and Republican Union, Junction City, March 21, 1863

"Shinplasters. Already there are three issues of shinplasters in Atchison, in addition to the city scrip. 'A' said he might as well issue it as 'B,' etc., until the whole area will be flooded with promises to pay, many of which never will be paid."

Freedom's Champion, Atchison, December 13, 1863

Bibliography

Primary Sources

Author's collection.
Bankers Magazine, 1857–1868.
City directories of Atchison, Junction City, Lawrence, Leavenworth, Manhattan, Topeka and Wichita.
Kansas State Historical Society. Newspaper Collections, various cities, 1854–1864.
_____. Paper Money Collections.
_____. Publications of the KSHS, *Collections*, Volumes I–XIV.
Memoirs of various early Kansas bankers and historical figures.
National Archives, National Bank Records, Washington, D.C.
Private collections.
Thompson's Commercial and Bank Note Reporter, 1855–1865.
University of Kansas. Research Manuscripts on the History of Banking in Kansas.

Secondary Sources

"Additional Kansas Obsolete Note Listings." *Numismatic Scrapbook*, Vol. 24 (May 1958): 933.
Anderson, George L. *Essays on the History of Banking*. Lawrence, KS: Coronado, 1972.
_____. *The Widening Stream: the Exchange National Bank of Atchison, 1858–1868*. Atchison, KS: Lockwood, 1968.
Andreas, A.T. *History of the State of Kansas*. Chicago: Culver, Page, Hoyne & Co.; R.R. Donnelley & Sons; The Lakeside Press; Ottaway Printing Co., 1883.
Baughman, Robert W. *Kansas in Maps*. Topeka: Kansas State Historical Society, 1961.
Burgett, Maurice M. "Obsolete Paper Currency and Scrip of Kansas, Corrections to Kansas Listing." *Paper Money*, Vol. 10 (First Quarter 1971): 15.
_____ and J.F. Lindsay. "Obsolete Paper Currency and Scrip of Kansas," *Paper Money*, Vol. 9 (Fourth Quarter 1970): 131ff.
_____ and Steven K. Whitfield. *Indian Territory/Oklahoma and Kansas Obsolete Notes and Scrip*. Society of Paper Money Collectors, Wismer Series, 1980.
Coin Collector's Journal, various issues, 1934–1954.
Cordley, Richard D.D. *A History of Lawrence, Kansas*. Lawrence: E.F. Caldwell, 1895.
Currency Auctions of America. Various auctions, 1989–present.
Giles, Fry W. *Thirty Years in Topeka*. Fry W. Giles, 1886. Reprint, Topeka, KS: Capper Special Services, 1960.
Hickman, John, and Dean Oakes. *Standard Catalog of National Bank Notes*. Iola, WI: Krause, 1982.
Huntoon, Peter. Articles on National Bank Notes. *Paper Money*, various issues.
_____. "Circus Posters from Heartland Kansas." *Numismatist*, Vol. 116 (May 2003): 44–46.
"Kansas Union Military Scrip." *Numismatist*, Vol. 92 (October 1979): 2129–2136.
Kelly, Don. C. *National Bank Notes, 3rd ed.* Oxford, OH: Paper Money Institute, 1997.
Knight, Lyn. *Coins & Currency*, various auctions, 1985–present.
Lindsay, James F. "Kansas Obsolete Notes, Observations on Issuers." *Paper Money*, Vol. 10 (First Quarter 1971): 17.
Majors, Alexander. *Seventy Years on the Frontier*. Minneapolis, MN: Ross & Haines, 1965.
Marckhoff, Fred. R. "Development of Currency and Banking in Kansas." *Coin Collector's Journal*, Vol. 14 (March-April 1947): 32ff.

_____. "Development of Currency and Banking in Kansas." *Coin Collectors Journal*, Vol. 14 (May-June 1947): 57ff.

Martin, Geo. W. "A Chapter from the Archives." *Kansas Historical Collections*, Vol. XII: 359–375.

Mitchell, Ralph A., and Neil Shafer. *Standard Catalog of Depression Scrip of the United States: The 1930s*. Iola, WI: Krause, 1984.

Moore, H. Miles. *History of Leavenworth, Kansas*. Leavenworth: Samuel Dodsworth, 1906.

Moore, Waldo, C. "Territorial Kansas." *Numismatist*, Vol. 41 (September 1928): 504.

Numismatic Scrapbook. Various issues, 1958–1962.

Numismatist. Various issues, 1915–present.

Paper Money. Various issues, 1962–present.

Schingoethe, Herb, and Martha Schingoethe. *College Currency: Money for Business Training*. Port Clinton, OH: BNR, 1993.

Settle, Raymond W., and Mary Lun Settle. *War Drums and Wagon Wheels*. Lincoln: University of Nebraska Press, 1966.

Smythe, R.M. (Numismatic Antiquarian Service Corporation of America). Various auctions, 1978–present.

A Standard History of Kansas and Kansans. New York & Chicago: Lewis, 1918.

"A Summary Listing of Known Kansas Obsolete Notes." *Numismatic Scrapbook*, Vol. 24 (February 1958): 251.

Whitfield, Steven K. "Army Bank Here Robbed This Evening, Three Civilians Dead, Two Wounded." *Paper Money*, Vol. 37 (March/April 1998): 56ff.

_____. "The Bank Robbery at Liberty." *Paper Money*, Vol. 37 (May/June 1998): 83ff.

_____. "G.B. DeBernardi and the Labor Exchange Movement." *Paper Money*, Vol. 37 (September/October 1998): 147ff.

_____. "Kansas Bogus and Questionable Bank Notes: The Delaware City Bank." *Paper Money*, Vol. 16 (January/February 1977): 32ff.

_____. "Kansas Cattletown National Banks." *Paper Money*, Vol. 14 (May/June 1975): 140ff.

_____. "Kansas Obsolete Currency and Scrip, Supplemental Data." *Paper Money*, Vol. 11 (Second Quarter 1972): 70ff.

_____. "Kansas Obsolete Merchant Scrip of Streeter and Strickler." *Paper Money*, Vol. 14 (March/April 1975): 81.

_____. "Kansas Obsolete Merchant Scrip of the Eldridge Brothers." *Paper Money*, Vol. 15 (May/June 1976): 130.

_____. "Kansas Obsolete Notes & Scrip." *Paper Money*, Vol. 29 (September/October 1990): 141ff.

_____. "Kansas Union Military Scrip." *Paper Money*, Vol. 15 (January/February 1976): 28ff.

_____. "Kansas Update–Errata and Addenda." *Paper Money*, Vol. 30 (July/August 1991): 124ff.

_____. "Labor Exchange Scrip." *Paper Money*, Vol. 46 (November-December 2007): 442–448.

_____. "Lawrence Bank of Kansas, Territory and State." *Paper Money*, Vol. 30 (September/October 1991): 144ff.

_____. "A New Scrip Issue Documented for the Sutlers of Ft. Riley, Kansas." *Paper Money*, Vol. 27 (November/December 1988): 179.

_____. "Obsolete Merchant Scrip of John Pipher & Co. Manhattan." *Paper Money*, Vol. 14 (September/October 1975): 260ff.

_____. "Obsolete Merchant Scrip of the Eldridge Brothers." *Paper Money*, Vol. 15 (May/June 1976): 130ff.

_____. "Some Notes on Early Kansas Banks." *Paper Money*, Vol. 11 (Second Quarter 1972): 70ff.

_____. "Tom Moses and the Cardboard Scrip of Fort Wallace, Kansas." *Paper Money*, Vol. 30 (May/June 1991): 85.

_____. "The Type or Variety Dilemma for Collectors and Catalogers." *Paper Money*, Vol. 34 (January/February 1995): 19ff.

Wilson, Don W. *Governor Charles Robinson of Kansas*. Lawrence: University Press of Kansas, 1975.

Wismer, D[avid] C[assel]. "Descriptive List of Obsolete Paper Money, Kansas." *Numismatist*, Vol. 37 (June 1924): 400, and September 1928.

Additional sources

The author also consulted early state, city and town histories of Kansas and Colorado and the Kansas Valley Bank ledgers.

Index

A. Hood & Sons Implement Company 200
A. McDonald & Bro. (Fort Scott) 242
A.C. Andrews & Co 204
Abel, Peter T. 22, 48
Abeles, Simon 119
Abernathy, J.L. 147
Adams, Dan 228
Adams, Henry J. 38
Alderson, L.A. 102
Allen, Eugene B. 51
American Bank Note Co. 22, 50, 66, 44, 128, 132
American State Bank (Oswego) 193
Ames, D.S. (Fort Scott) 154
Anderson, Martin 134
Andreas, A.T. 79
Anthony, D.R. 147, 242
Arthur, John 138
Associated Banks of Pittsburg 183
Associated Banks of Topeka 184, 194
Atchison, Kansas 9, 47, 50, 66, 71, 101, 127, 155, 179, 181, 187, 269
Atchison, David 14
Atchison Chamber of Commerce 187
Atchison Savings Bank 179
Auld, David 58, 104
Ayer, Lucien 34

Babcock, Carmi W. 107, 108
Babcock & Lykins 107
Bailey, James G. 44
Bank of the State of Kansas 66, 70, 103, 127
Bank of Wm H.R. Lykins 107
banker's license 87
banking crisis 8, 38, 154

Banking House of J.W. Morris (Leavenworth) 122; see also Morris, Jenkin W.
Barker, R.A. 133
Barnett, W.B. 80
Barnett National Bank 80
Battle of Mine Creek 76, 132
Battle of Westport 76, 83, 113, 132
Beechler & Lewis 156
Benton, Milton R. 71
Big Stranger Creek 29
Bird, Greenup 125
Blood, James 57
Borland 123
Boston, Massachusetts 36
Boudinot, Elias 29
Bowman, William 71
Boys Town Philamatic Center 70, 113, 231
Branson, Jacob 60
Broadwell, J.P. 138
Broadwell, Moses M. 138
Brown, George 90
Brown, Willis 96
Buffalo Bill Cody 84
Bulkley 123
Bunker Hill 187
Bunker Hill Community Center 187
Business College Bank 175

California 8
California Pikes Peak & Stage Co. 50
Canadian paper 75
Captain Jack 45
Captain Terry 19
Carney, Thomas 124
Caulkins, M.D. 156
Central Overland and Pikes Peak Express 52

Certificate of Deposit 11
Challacomb, W.B. 147
Chanute 188
Chanute Thrift Dollars 188
Chase, H.J. 204
Chase Manhattan Money Museum 47, 70, 118
Chester, H.W. 114
Chetopa 143
Choctaw Nation 101
Christies 48, 54, 231
Cincinnati and Kansas Land Co. 88
Citizens National Bank (Independence) 182
Citizens State Bank (Wichita) 185
City Bank (Leavenworth) 38
Civil War 7, 69, 75, 89, 95, 127; post-war 131
Clark, Austin M. 60, 118, 123
Clark, Milton E. 81, 118
Clark Gruber & Co. (Denver) 117, 118, 120
Clark Gruber & Co. (Leavenworth) 117–122
Clarke, W.B. 85, 117
Clay Center 188
Clay Center Chamber of Commerce 188
Clay County Savings Association 125
"Cleveland" (self-styled marshal) 102
Coffin, William G. 109
coins 206
"College Currency" 1, 3, 4, 153, 172
Commercial Institute Bank (Holton) 173
Commercial National Bank (Independence) 182
Confederate currency 3, 82

255

Index

Connelly, Peter 138
Constitution (state) 65
Continental Bank Note Co. 132, 139, 145
Cook & Hopkins 203
Council Grove, Kansas 188
Craig, J.B. 145
Crawford, George A. 78
Crawford, Gov. Samuel J. 133
Creighton, W.W. 147
Crew, James S. 115
Cribbs & Kennedy 204
Crippen, J.J. 114
Currier, C.F. 23
Curtis, General Samuel R. 133

D.S. Ames (Fort Scott) 154
Danforth, Wright & Co. 48
Dean, W.F. 167
Delaware City 27
Delaware City Bank 27
DeLong, James 145
Demand Notes 81, 143, 156
Denly, Tom 2
Denver Mint 118
Department of the Interior 76
Dobyns, H.R. 143
Dodge City 167
Doniphan 47, 10
Drovers Bank (Fort Leavenworth) 31
Drovers Bank (Leavenworth City) 31–34, 167
Durfee House (Lawrence) 155

Eastin, General L.T. 29
Easton, Kansas 29
Easton, Pennsylvania 29
Easton Bank 29, 237
Economy Clothing (Garden City) 158
Ehrnich, Henry 158
Eldridge, Edwin S. 15
Eldridge, James M. 15
Eldridge, Shalor W. 15
Eldridge, Thomas B. 15
Eldridge Brothers 14–22, 57
Eldridge Stage Line 17, 19
Elliot, Robert M. 90
Elwood 241
Emporia, Kansas 73, 161, 164
Emporia and Lawrence Express Line 73
Englehart, Jacob 79
Englehart & Fairchild (Hiawatha) 79
Eskridge, Charles Vernon 73
Exchange Bank (Atchison) 101, 102, 104, 126
Exchange Bank of William Hetherington 101–104
Exchange National Bank of Atchison 104, 180

Fairchild, George 49, 55, 66
Fairchild, R. Scott 79
Farmers Co-Op Grain & Supply Co. 193
Farnham, M.G. 98
Farnham, R.H. 97
Ferguson, G.F. 202
Findlay, George W. 169
First Kansas Colored Volunteer Infantry Regiment 75, 100
First National Bank (Denver) 118
First National Bank (Independence) 182
First National Bank (Leavenworth) 122
First National Bank (Oswego) 193
First National Bank (Parsons) 183
First National Bank of Atchison 53, 103, 181
First National Bank of Junction City 84, 85
First National Bank of Leavenworth 124
First National Bank of Macauley's Institute 174
First National Bank of National Business Colleges 178
First National Bank of Western Business 176, 177
Fisher, Don 2
Fisk & Eskridge Dry Goods 73
Florence 172
Florence Public Schools 172
Fort Leavenworth, Kansas 31, 34
Fort Riley, Kansas 74, 75, 83
Fort Scott, Kansas 10, 75–79, 154, 169, 172
Frankfort 166
Frazer, S.E. 22
Free State 9, 14, 26
Freedom, Kansas 196
Fremont 74
Frizell Hardware (Larned) 158

G.W. Findlay & Co. 169
Garden City 158, 181, 189
Gardner 189
Garnet 189
German Bank 119
German Savings Bank 119
ghost towns 13
Gilpin, Gov. William (Colorado) 121, 122
"good fors" 52, 69, 71
Goodwill Barter & Exchange Centers 191
Graham, F.M. 143
Graham, George 134
Grant, U.S. President 84
Graves, Henry 79
Great Bend 190

Greenbacks 69, 131
Gruber, Emanuel H. 117, 118, 124

Hadley, Washington 108
Halderman, John A. 1146
Hanks, Mr. 19
Harper's Weekly 19, 129
Harrison, William Henry 35
Harsh, Samuel 23
Haxby, James 29, 30
Hayes, Josiah 134
Hays City Post Office 205
Herman & Schlane 203
Hetherington, Clifford S. 104
Hetherington, William 101, 103, 180
Hiawatha, Kansas 79, 80
Hickok, "Wild Bill" 84
Higinbotham Brothers 90
Hillsboro 190
Hillsboro Bonus Day Certificates 190
Hilyer, George 60
Holton 173, 190
Hood, A. 200
Houston, Levi 146
Howard, W.E. (Hutchinson) 166
Hudson, William (Winfield) 158
Hulet, A. 204
Huntress, Orville 91
Hutchinson 165, 166

Independence, Kansas 144, 157, 182, 190
Independence Guaranteed Scrip 190
Indian Bureau 59
Indian Expedition 132
Ingalls, Senator John J. 23
Isett, Brewster & Co. 117, 124

J.R. Swallow & Co. (Emporia) 74
Jackson, Andrew 7
Jackson County Chamber of Commerce 190
Janes, Lorenzo 80
Jesse James gang 125, 138
John Pipher & Co. (Manhattan) 88–93
Johnson County 190
Johnson County Chamber of Commerce 190
Johnson, J.P. (Highland) 242
Jones, C.J. "Buffalo" 189
Jones, Sheriff Samuel 14
Junction City, Kansas 81

Kansas Branch Bridge 158
Kansas City, Kansas 11, 190, 191
Kansas City Clearing House 190
Kansas City Lithography Co. 516

Kansas Historical Society Museum 19, 23, 31, 32
Kansas Mining Co. 22
Kansas Normal College 172
Kansas Pacific Railway 163
Kansas State Agricultural College 200
Kansas State Historical Society 19, 23, 113, 132, 231
Kansas State Savings Bank (Wyandott) 138–142
Kansas Valley Bank (Atchison) 10, 47–57, 127
Kaup & Trumble 202
Kaw Valley Hotel (North Lawrence) 159
Kerr, John 125
Kidder, William 44
Knight, Lyn 2
Knowles, Edward 97
Kohn, Morris 162
Kuhn, Henry 104
Kurtz, Lewis (Manhattan) 82, 87, 124

Labor Exchange (Freedom) 196
Labor Exchange (Osage City) 196
Labor Exchange (Salina) 196
Landbloom & Roseberg 203
Lane, U.S. Senator James 60
Lappin, Samuel L. 95
Lappin & Scrafford (Seneca) 95
Larned 158
Larson Brothers (Weir City) 191
Lawrence, Kansas 14, 36, 57, 65, 67, 107, 112, 129, 174, 191, 218, 219, 220
Lawrence Bank 10, 57–64, 67, 129
Lawrence Business College 175
Lawrence Clearing House 191
Lawrence National Bank 96
Leamer, William 81
Leavenworth, Kansas 9, 22, 31, 38, 40, 47, 117, 122, 124, 145–151, 157, 167, 176, 197, 221
Leavenworth Pikes Peak Express Co. 118
Lecompton, Kansas 10, 44
legislation 9
Lender, R.D. 76
Lewis & Edwards (Emporia) 164
Lincoln, Abraham 60, 93
Lindsay, James 70, 240
Litchfield, Kansas 160
Long Branch Saloon 144
Losse, I.G. 23
Luray 192
Luray Chamber of Commerce 192
Lykins, Johnston 107
Lykins, William H.R. 107, 108; see also Bank of William H.R. Lykins

Manhattan, Kansas 89, 200
Manhattan Bank 90
Manufacturers National Bank (Leavenworth) 123
Marchkoff, Fred 92
McBratney, R. 85
McCracken, Nate 87
McHenry, Davis & Co. (Wyandott) 242
McMurtrie, D.C. (Emporia) 161
Medicine Lodge 160
merchant banker 9
Merchants Bank (Fort Leavenworth) 34
Merchants Exchange (Council Grove) 188
Methodist Church (Manhattan) 89
Miller, John S. (Fort Scott) 76, 77
Miller Brothers & Co. (Mulberry) 171
missionaries 13
Missouri money 9, 87
Missouri River 27
Missouri Valley Life Insurance Co. 197
Mitchell, R.B. 64
Moore, H. Miles 22
Mormon War 31
Morrill, Edmond N. 79
Morris, Jenkin W. 23, 38, 119, 123, 125
Morris Kohn & Co.'s New York Store 162
Morrow, Robert 57, 59, 79
Moses, Tom 245
Mulberry, Kansas 171

national bank notes 207–230
National Bank of Lawrence 108, 115
National Bank of Wichita 185
Neodesha 192
Neodesha Chamber of Commerce 192
Neosho Rapids 74
Ness City 193
New, John D. 53, 129
New Boston 88
New England Emigrant Aid Society 48
New Fifth Avenue Hotel (Arkansas City) 198
Newmark, Myer & Co. (Lawrence) 155
Newton, Kansas 182
Newton Clearing House 182
Nineteenth Kansas Volunteer Cavalry Regiment 76

North Lawrence, Kansas 159
Norton & Seley Bank 101, 102

Oak Hall Clothing House 159
Oildorado Dry Goods & Groceries 158
Olathe, Kansas 161, 196
Oregon Trail 44, 75
Ormsby, Waterman Lily 34, 38, 41, 43, 45
Osage City, Kansas 196
Osage Indians 143
Osage River Bank (Osawatomie) 57
Oswego, Kansas 193
Oswego Coal Co. (Weir City) 170
Overland Stage Line 95

Palace Drug Store (Olathe) 161
Paola, Kansas 94
Parker & Giles (Topeka) 158
Parsons, Kansas 157, 183, 194
Parsons Commercial Bank 182, 194
Pease, Robert Levi 51
Pikes Peak 10
Pinneo, William H. (Paola) 94
Pipher, John 88; see also John Pipher & Co.
Pittsburg, Kansas 169, 170, 183
Plum Hunters (militia) 133
Pomeroy, Samuel 48, 57
Pony Express 50, 95
Postage Stamp currency 73, 83, 98
postal notes 205
Pottawatomie County Scrip 91
POW scrip 205
Prentiss, Doctor Samuel 113
Price, General Sterling (CSA) 76, 79, 83, 113, 132, 133
printers and engravers 243
Purcell, E.B. 90

Quantrill, William Clark 19, 62, 82, 87, 108, 113

R.D. Lender & Co. (Fort Scott) 76
R.P. Studley & Co. 139, 143
Ralstine, C.M. 145
Rawdon, Wright, Hatch & Edson 22
Redwing Bank (Lawrence) 36
Reeder, Governor Andrew 29
Richardson, Kansas 72
Riley, Kansas 202
Riley County Bank 92
Robinson, Governor Charles 57, 58
Robinson, John 60
Rochat, Louis 155

Rock Castle 95
Rogers Coal Co. 169
Russell, Kansas 194
Russell, Majors and Waddell 49, 50
Russell, William H. 38, 49, 56

Saint George, Kansas 87
St. Joseph, Missouri 31, 178
Salt Lake City, Utah 31, 43, 118
Santa Fe Railroad 48
Santa Fe Trail 72, 75
Savings Bank Act 131
savings banks 11, 131
Schingoethes, Herb 71
Schingoethes, Martha 71
Schuler, Albert H. 201
Scott, Kerr & Co. 87, 117, 124–126
Scott, Lucien 124
Scott, Lyman 124
Scott, Winfield 125
Scott & Co. 125, 126
Scrafford, Charles G. 95
Seburn, Harvey 79
Second National Bank of Leavenworth 119
Sedan 194
Sedan Chamber of Commerce 194
Seley, C.M. 101, 102
Seneca, Kansas 95
Shackleford, W.H., Sr. 138
Shawnee, Kansas 10, 47
Shawnee County 26
Shawnee County scrip 99
Sheheen, Austin 2
Shull, Hugh 2, 231
Siam 146
Simpson, Henry M. 112
Simpson, Samuel N. 112
Simpson, William 112
Simpson Brothers Bank (Lawrence) 112–117
Sipple Brothers (Parsons) 157
slavery 8, 14, 145
Smith, Ethan Allen 58, 59, 108
Smith, Samuel C. 60
Smith, Ulmer 157
Smoot, Luther 49, 57
Smoot, Russell & Co. (Leavenworth) 50, 242

Southwestern Business Colleges 177
Spalding, A.J. 165
Spaulding, Sutler Harvey (1st K.C.V.) 100
Standiford, Youmans & Eldred 160
Star Clothiers (Hutchinson) 165
State Bank (Lecompton) 44
The State Bank of Kansas 96
Stebbins & Porter 53, 103
Stevens, Robert 58
Stingley, Ashford 91
Stone, James C. 60, 123
Streeter, James 81
Streeter & Strickler (Junction City) 81
Strickland, J.B. 203
Strickler, Samuel M. 81
Studebaker 92
Sturtridge, Gary 70
Sumner 23
Sumner, George 23
Sumner Company 23
Swallow, J.R. 74
Swift, A.C. 48

Taylor, Zachary 35
Taylor & Taylor 166
Tecumseh, Kansas 26
Thompson, Woodruff & Co. 87
Thorsen, A.T. 231
Time-Life Company 231
tokens 206, 245, 246; cardboard 245
Tom. Moses & Co. (Fort Wallace) 245
Topeka 11, 98, 158, 163, 178, 184, 194, 195
Topeka Clearing House Association 195
Torre, George W. 36

Ulmer Smith & Co. (Independence) 157
"Uncle Wilson" (former African slave) 146
Union Bank (Manhattan) 90
Union military scrip 132–138
U.S. currency 81, 82, 85
U.S. demand notes 81

U.S. Department of the Interior 58, 76
U.S. government postal currency 73
U.S. Land Office 97, 98
U.S. Secret Service 153
U.S. Sugar & Land Co. 181
U.S. Tax Assessor 75
Utley, J.N. 101

Voigt, William A. 203

Waddell, William 49, 56
Wakarusa War 60
Walker, James C. 48
Watkins, W.H. 164
Waverly 195
Wear Coal Co. (Pittsburg) 170
Webb, Jonathon W. 92
Weir City 168, 170, 171
Wertenberger, A.D. 204
Western Business College 176, 177
Western Reserve Historical Society 70, 113, 231
Wheatly, W.T. 138
Wheeler, John P. 23
White, John P. 78
White & Bridgens (Fort Scott) 76, 78
White Cloud 95
Whitridge, M.D. 114
Wichita 11, 162, 177, 178, 185 187, 195, 202
Wichita Clearing House Association 185, 186
Wichita Unemployed Trading Post 195
wildcat banks 34, 58
Williams, Col. James M. 100
Willmore, Kansas 153
Wilson, Col. Robert (sutler) 74, 81
Winchip, J.K. 92
Winfield 158, 168
Wismer, David C. 113, 231
Woodward, A.G. 22
Wright, Robert W. 144
Wyandot Indians 151
Wyandott, Kansas 55, 65, 131, 126, 151
Wynkoop, Edward W. 44, 45

www.ingramcontent.com/pod-product-compliance
Lightning Source LLC
Chambersburg PA
CBHW081547300426
44116CB00015B/2785